SHARING LINKED DATA FOR HEALTH RESEARCH

Health research around the world relies on access to data, and much of the most valuable, reliable, and comprehensive data collections are held by governments. These collections, which contain data on whole populations, are a powerful tool in the hands of researchers, especially when they are linked and analysed, and can help to address 'wicked problems' in health and emerging global threats such as COVID-19. At the same time, these data collections contain sensitive information that must only be used in ways that respect the values, interests, and rights of individuals and their communities. *Sharing Linked Data for Health Research* provides a template for allowing research access to government data collections in a regulatory environment designed to build social license while supporting the research enterprise.

Carolyn Adams is a Senior Lecturer in the Law School at Macquarie University. She has three decades of experience working in the fields of administrative law, human rights and privacy in senior policy positions at federal, state, and territory levels in Australia, at the Australian Law Reform Commission, and in academia. She has been a member of the Macquarie University Human Research Ethics Committee (Humanities and Social Sciences) since 2015. She was a member of the Population Health Research Network (PHRN) Ethics, Privacy, and Consumer Engagement Advisory Group.

Judy Allen is an Honorary Fellow of the Law School at the University of Western Australia with expertise in in torts, health law, and research ethics. She has provided policy advice to the Western Australian (WA) data linkage unit, government data custodians, and the PHRN on ethics, privacy, and data sharing processes. She has extensive experience in human research ethics and has chaired the WA Department of Health Human Research Ethics Committee, a specialist committee providing ethical review of data-based research projects, and the WA Country Health Service Human Research Ethics Committee.

Felicity Flack is the Manager, Policy and Client Services for Australia's national data linkage infrastructure, the PHRN. She has extensive experience in the development, coordination, and operation of national data linkage systems particularly the navigation of cross-jurisdictional legislative, policy, and ethical issues. She also has many years of experience in research ethics including working as a research ethics manager as well as being a member and Chair of the Sir Charles Gairdner and Osborne Park Health Care Group Human Research Ethics Committee. Felicity is a Churchill Fellow.

CAMBRIDGE BIOETHICS AND LAW

This series of books – formerly called Cambridge Law, Medicine and Ethics – was founded by Cambridge University Press with Alexander McCall Smith as its first editor in 2003. It focuses on the law's complex and troubled relationship with medicine across both the developed and the developing world. In the past twenty years, we have seen in many countries increasing resort to the courts by dissatisfied patients and a growing use of the courts to attempt to resolve intractable ethical dilemmas. At the same time, legislatures across the world have struggled to address the questions posed by both the successes and the failures of modern medicine, while international organisations such as the WHO and UNESCO now regularly address issues of medical law. It follows that we would expect ethical and policy questions to be integral to the analysis of the legal issues discussed in this series. The series responds to the high profile of medical law in universities, in legal and medical practice, as well as in public and political affairs. We seek to reflect the evidence that many major health-related policy and bioethics debates in the UK, Europe and the international community over the past two decades have involved a strong medical law dimension. With that in mind, we seek to address how legal analysis might have a trans-jurisdictional and international relevance. Organ retention, embryonic stem cell research, physician-assisted suicide and the allocation of resources to fund health care are but a few examples among many. The emphasis of this series is thus on matters of public concern and/or practical significance. We look for books that could make a difference to the development of medical law and enhance the role of medico-legal debate in policy circles. That is not to say that we lack interest in the important theoretical dimensions of the subject, but we aim to ensure that theoretical debate is grounded in the realities of how the law does and should interact with medicine and health care.

Series Editors

Sharing Linked Data for Health Research

TOWARD BETTER DECISION MAKING

CAROLYN ADAMS
Macquarie University Law School

JUDY ALLEN
University of Western Australia

FELICITY FLACK
University of Western Australia

CAMBRIDGE
UNIVERSITY PRESS

CAMBRIDGE
UNIVERSITY PRESS

University Printing House, Cambridge CB2 8BS, United Kingdom

One Liberty Plaza, 20th Floor, New York, NY 10006, USA

477 Williamstown Road, Port Melbourne, VIC 3207, Australia

314–321, 3rd Floor, Plot 3, Splendor Forum, Jasola District Centre, New Delhi – 110025, India

103 Penang Road, #05–06/07, Visioncrest Commercial, Singapore 238467

Cambridge University Press is part of the University of Cambridge.

It furthers the University's mission by disseminating knowledge in the pursuit of education, learning, and research at the highest international levels of excellence.

www.cambridge.org
Information on this title: www.cambridge.org/9781108426640
DOI: 10.1017/9781108675789

First published 2022

A catalogue record for this publication is available from the British Library.

ISBN 978-1-108-42664-0 Hardback

'Would you tell me, please, which way I ought to go from here?'
'That depends a good deal on where you want to get to,' said the Cat.
'I don't much care where —' said Alice.
'Then it doesn't matter which way you go,' said the Cat.
'— so long as I get somewhere,*' Alice added as an explanation.*
'Oh, you're sure to do that,' said the Cat, 'if you only walk long enough'

Lewis Carroll, *Alice's Adventures in Wonderland*

Contents

Figures

Tables

Foreword

I have dedicated my working life as a doctor and an epidemiologist to improving the lives of children and their families. As an epidemiologist, I believe that the best way to identify the causal pathways to health and disease, to prevent disease, or to enhance health is through rigorous research. As we are unable to conduct randomised controlled trials (accepted as the gold standard for the evidence of care) on many of the most important things affecting children and their environments (including social and emotional as well as physical), we need to use the best alternative methods. This is why I have championed the use of population-level linked data. Linked data can tell us much about the social and environmental determinants of health and other outcomes, which guide our service agendas for prevention and improvement. They can evaluate whether and for whom the expensive services, policies and practices are working, are useless or are even causing harm, and, if we are clever, we can provide cost-effective evidence to guide decision making across governments.

Over the decades of establishing databases, such as registers of health data, and accessing agency data and linking them, we have many examples of research that has delivered huge benefits to the community. For example, my work with Professor Carol Bower on the link between folate deficiency and neural tube defects in babies required linked data to demonstrate that folate supplementation and fortification prevent neural tube defects. Our linked data clearly demonstrated the impact of this intervention, but it showed that poor and Indigenous women were not responding. This led to major mandatory folate fortification of flour nationally, and our data sets showed the dramatic falls in neural tube defects in babies of these disadvantaged women. Many countries have now implemented folate fortification and supplementation programmes. I have been privileged to witness the impact this knowledge can make in people's lives.

I have also experienced the challenges, frustrations, and complexities of navigating access to government administrative data and have spent many years advocating for better access to these data for research. I was delighted when the authors, whose careers I have supported and encouraged, asked me to write the Foreword to this book.

It is critical, in my view, that government data collections of personal health information are seen as a public good, as a resource to be used for societal benefit. Although the information in these data collections relates to individuals, the collections themselves relate to communities and populations and can provide invaluable information about their health and well-being. Using and sharing these data collections for research has unlimited potential to improve the quality of healthcare and to save lives. And early interventions for families and children have been shown, using these data, to enhance their whole of life chances, not just in relation to health, but to education, disability, employment, and avoiding interactions with the justice system.

This book considers the ethical, human rights, and legal issues that arise when making decisions about how such data collections are used and shared. Decision-makers in this realm – law and policy makers, ethics committees, and data custodians – hold the keys to realising the benefits of the rich research resources held by governments at all levels in Australia and around the world. It is imperative that this decision-making power is exercised in a way that recognises the full range of stakeholders and the full range of interests at stake in the research enterprise. The authors' analysis of these issues is both thoughtful and thought-provoking. The book provides a detailed critique of the current decision-making processes in Australia, Canada, and the United Kingdom, including where they give rise to unjustified barriers to meritorious and ethically sound research.

This is not just an issue of national concern. The interdependence of people everywhere has been demonstrated in a stark fashion by the COVID-19 pandemic. Protecting and improving public health cannot be achieved within national borders. Cooperation between nations in understanding health challenges is vital. The rapid movement of people around the world makes sharing and linking reliable data across international borders crucial to this endeavour. Many countries are now engaged in linking data for health research in different ways. The cultural and historical contexts vary greatly, and the differences in process and principles for researcher access reflect this variation.

A common understanding of the appropriate ethical and legal parameters consistent with international human rights is essential to global cooperation in linking and sharing data. This book makes an important contribution to this endeavour. It examines the international research ethics guidelines and international human rights instruments and compares the ways in which these are applied in the domestic law and approval processes in Australia, Canada, and the United Kingdom. It illustrates the similarities between these jurisdictions and draws out the essential ingredients for good decision making by governments in using and linking data for health research. By comparing the experience gained in other countries, we can move towards shared principles and facilitate future international collaboration.

One of the most important achievements of this book is to draw attention to the importance of including the community in decision making about the use of government data for linkage and research. When I began my career, research was carried out in a paternalistic way. Research into the health of Aboriginal children in Australia, for example, was typically initiated by city-based researchers who determined the research questions and then went out into communities and gathered their data. There has now been a radical change, and research today is initiated by Aboriginal communities and Aboriginal health services and is conducted in collaboration with communities by Aboriginal researchers. This has had a profound effect on the quality and application of Indigenous research. Giving power to Aboriginal health professionals during the Australian COVID-19 pandemic resulted in them having the best outcomes in the world. This should now be the model of how research is conducted and how services are developed for the diverse community groups in our society. The vital need to give information to such groups about vaccination is another example, as is the need to collect and access data to evaluate that success (or not!).

At the Telethon Kids Institute, Perth, Western Australia, we have had a focus on community involvement for many years and fostered the establishment of the Consumer and Community Health Research Network which works with universities, health and medical research institutes, health service providers, and non-governmental organisations to bring together consumers and people with lived experience and connect them with health and medical researchers. This transformation is reflected in the expansion of community participation in the design and conduct of research in many areas of health research. It is equally important that the community is involved in making decisions about the use of health data collections for research. Increasingly, governments (federal, state and local) are requesting our input into their decision making for service provision and policies. This book argues that this is essential, both morally and pragmatically.

The three authors of this book are uniquely placed to traverse this multidisciplinary landscape, bringing to their research and writing decades of experience in the legal and ethical regulation of research using linked data. They are all scholars as well as practitioners and, as such, bring both theoretical and practical perspectives to bear on the complex issues under consideration. They provide a detailed and evidence-based analysis of existing decision-making processes and make many profound and practical suggestions for reform. It is a book for our time and essential reading for all those who do research and develop and implement policy, and for those professionals who need to know that what they are doing will be good and not harmful.

Professor Fiona Stanley AC

Acknowledgements

This book was conceived on the shores of Lake Geneva with the generous support of the Brocher Foundation. It could not have been completed without the ongoing support of our families, colleagues, and friends. We would also like to thank Lisa Billington for her tireless and efficient work on our manuscript. Special thanks to the Population Health Research Network for its support and for bringing us together and inspiring us to write this book.

Abbreviations

ACT	Australian Capital Territory
AIDS	acquired immune deficiency syndrome
AIHW	Australian Institute of Health and Welfare
ALRC	Australian Law Reform Commission
APPs	Australian Privacy Principles
CAG	Confidentiality Advisory Group (UK)
CEO	chief executive officer
CHI	Community Health Index
CIHI	Canadian Institute for Health Information
CIHR	Canadian Institutes of Health Research
CIOMS	Council for International Organizations of Medical Sciences
COE	Council of Europe
CT	computed tomography
Cth	Commonwealth of Australia
DASH	Data Access Support Hub (Canada)
DHHS	Department of Health and Human Services (Tasmania)
DHSC	Department of Health and Social Care (UK and Scotland)
DNA	deoxyribonucleic acid
DPA	Data Protection Act
ECHR	European Convention on Human Rights
eDRIS	Electronic Data Research and Innovation Service (Scotland)
ERB	Ethics Review Board
ESC	Economic, Social and Cultural Rights
EU	European Union
EU	GDPR European Union General Data Protection Regulation
FAQs	frequently asked questions
GAfREC	Governance Arrangements for Research Ethics Committees (UK)
GDPR	General Data Protection Regulation (EU)
HDRN	Health Data Research Network Canada

HIV	human immunodeficiency virus
HPV	human papillomavirus
HRA	Health Research Authority (UK)
HREC	Human Research Ethics Committee
HUGO	Human Genome Organisation
ICD	International Classification of Diseases
IC/ES	Institute for Clinical Evaluative Sciences (Ontario, Canada)
ID	identifier
IDI	Integrated Data Infrastructure (New Zealand)
IRB	Institutional Review Board
IT	information technology
LGBTIQA	lesbian, gay, bisexual, transgender, intersex, queer/questioning, asexual
MCHP	Manitoba Centre for Health Policy
NHMRC	National Health and Medical Research Council (Australia)
NHS	National Health Service (UK)
NHSCR	National Health Service Central Register (UK)
NSS	National Services Scotland
NSW	New South Wales
NZ	New Zealand
OAIC	Office of the Australian Information Commissioner
OAS	Organization of American States
OECD	Organisation for Economic Co-operation and Development
OPCC	Office of the Privacy Commissioner of Canada
PBPP	Public Benefit and Privacy Panel for Health and Social Care (Scotland)
PHRN	Population Health Research Network (Australia)
PIPEDA	Personal Information Protection and Electronic Documents Act (Canada)
REB	Research Ethics Board
REC	Research Ethics Committee
SAIL	Secure Anonymised Information Linkage (Wales)
SeRP	Secure eResearch Platform
SPIRE	Scottish Primary Care Information Resource
SURE	Secure Unified Research Environment (Australia)
TDLU	Tasmanian Data Linkage Unit
UDHR	Universal Declaration of Human Rights
UK	United Kingdom
UK	GDPR United Kingdom General Data Protection Regulation
UN	United Nations
UN	ICCPR International Covenant on Civil and Political Rights

UN	ICESCR International Covenant on Economic, Social and Cultural Rights
UNESCO	United Nations Educational, Scientific and Cultural Organization
USA	United States of America
Vic	Victoria
WA	Western Australia
WHO	World Health Organization
WMA	World Medical Association
WWII	World War II

Introduction

Water, water everywhere,
Nor any drop to drink.[1]

THE PROBLEM AND THE POTENTIAL

The genesis of this project was the experience of the authors working with researchers, data custodians, ethics committees, and linkage units over the past decade or more managing access to government administrative data for research. Our individual backgrounds, experience, and expertise meant that we brought a diverse, interdisciplinary approach to the table. We started to identify the problems: we heard from researchers that there were concerns with unjustified delay and lack of access to data for research that was in the public interest; we heard from data custodians that they found the decision-making process difficult because they did not have sufficient resources or guidance; we heard from ethics committees that they found data linkage projects complex and difficult to assess; and we heard from consumer representatives that there were concerns about privacy, transparency, community awareness, and consultation.

We all understood the potential of this field of data research. We had experience working with passionate researchers who underlined for us the importance of using government administrative data for the greater good. We also understood the risks, having decades of expertise in privacy law and ethical review. Was it possible, we wondered, to achieve these great benefits while minimising the risks? What were the roadblocks, and could we help to clear the way? We all understood, to a greater or lesser degree, the mechanics of data linkage, having worked with and for the Australian Population Health Research Network (PHRN) in different capacities over the years as staff members, consultants, and members of advisory groups. We have watched at close hand this field of endeavour develop with ever increasing speed. The need for a better, more consistent approach to the regulatory frameworks

[1] S Coleridge, *The Rime of the Ancient Mariner* (Chatto & Windus, 1971).

and decision-making processes became clearer and more urgent as the problems of cross-jurisdictional linkage at the national level looked to become insurmountable at the international level unless a more consistent and sustainable model was developed.

While this book has strong theoretical foundations, we have focused on developing and presenting practical solutions to the problems faced by researchers, data custodians, ethics committees, the community, and other stakeholders in this complex and evolving environment. We have aimed to ensure that the discussion of specialist areas such as human rights, ethics, and law is accessible to everyone, rather than just experts in these fields. The future of public health research, and a great deal of other research essential to the well-being of the community, will rely on the use and linkage of data collections in the hands of government and beyond. This book aims to ensure that the field of research using linked data develops on sound ethical, rights-based, and lawful foundations. This will help to attract and sustain the social licence needed to support the use of this valuable community resource for the benefit of the community, locally, nationally, and globally.

Modern advances in information technology mean that we now live in a world awash with data collected from personal devices, public buildings and facilities, service providers, and other sources. In the last two decades, there has been a revolution in computational and statistical techniques so that it is now possible to analyse and make sense of these large volumes of data. The amount of data collected and the power to analyse and make use of it are set to increase exponentially. As a result, there are legitimate concerns about Big Data and the widespread collection and use of personal information by governments and the private sector.

A great deal of information about people is collected by governments, with and without their consent, while administering health programmes and providing public health services. While the data discussed is primarily health data, health research can be enhanced by linking health data to other personal information – such as education, justice, housing, and social welfare data – also held by government. All this information is sensitive and, while it is used in legitimate ways to administer and improve the public health system, it can also be used in illegitimate ways to profile and unjustly discriminate against individuals and groups. For this reason, the collection, use, and release of the information – including release for research – is highly regulated.

Despite this, there remains a danger that concerns about Big Data are having a detrimental impact on the beneficial use of government data collections for health and other research, conducted in highly regulated and privacy-protective environments. Access to population-wide collections of individual-level data is essential to support health research and to promote evidence-based health policy development. Use of existing data resources provides a time and cost-effective way to understand, monitor, and improve health and welfare. The challenge is to realise the potential benefits to health and health systems across the world offered by the use of this data, while respecting and responding to community concerns and minimising the risks to individuals and groups.

The focus of this book is on decision making. Access to government administrative data for research is based on a series of decisions by data custodians, ethics committees, and others that seek to balance the risks and benefits associated with the use of this data for research. These decisions operate as keys that unlock access for researchers to a well-guarded and extremely valuable community resource. It is critical that each key works well and is fit for purpose.

DATA LINKAGE

While many of the issues discussed in this book are relevant to all research using individual-level data we have chosen to focus on linked data. This is because linking data from different sources is the future of population health research. Linkage of population-wide data collections provides research resources that are inclusive, representative, accurate, and cost-effective as well as being an effective and efficient use of existing data.[2] It provides researchers with access to larger volumes of detailed data on individuals and groups, allowing for increasingly varied and comprehensive population-wide research.

Linkage of health data from different sources is occurring in a number of countries around the world, including across jurisdictional boundaries in federal and devolved systems such as Australia, Canada, and the United Kingdom (UK). This adds a layer of complexity to the ethical, legal, and policy arrangements. Working through this complexity is necessary to achieve nationally significant research results. Cross-jurisdictional linkage at the international level provides an even greater challenge. In a world of increasing population mobility, global epidemics of infectious diseases, and the shared responsibility for providing health care for everyone, it is essential to confront this challenge.

The COVID-19 pandemic provides the perfect example of our shared vulnerabilities and responsibilities and the need for a coordinated global response, including the linking of data across national boundaries. Linked data can be used to track the movement of the virus around the world, to learn about the progression of the disease and its symptoms, to evaluate the safety and efficacy of vaccines, to evaluate the efficacy of treatment, and to identify those who are most vulnerable for medical, socio-demographic, or geographical reasons.[3] An international understanding and approach to the ethical, legal, and policy issues will be required to support

2 F Stanley, 'Record Linkage: Public Good or Invasion of Privacy' (Conference Paper, International Conference of Data Protection and Privacy Commissioners, 10 September 2003)

3 PHRN, 'Linked Data in the Fight against COVID-19', *Impact Stories* (Web Page) <www.phrn.org.au/media/82041/impact-story-linked-data-in-the-fight-against-covid-19.pdf>.

linkage across international borders so that the benefits of data linkage research at the national level can be translated to the global context. We hope that the principles and practice discussed in this book will provide a foundation for successful national and international linkage initiatives.

With the increased benefits of linked data, however, come increased risks to privacy, confidentiality, and security of the data. As the data collections to be linked increase in number, the legal requirements become more complex, as different legislation may apply to each data source linked. To address these increased risks and legal complexity, many countries have established specialist data linkage infrastructure and processes. These regional and national infrastructures take varied approaches to the range of ethical, legal, and policy issues inherent in data linkage research but there has been limited consideration of the strengths and weaknesses of the different approaches. One of the aims of this book is to examine these different approaches and consider what can be learned from them.

THE ETHICAL, LEGAL, AND PROCEDURAL ISSUES

The ethical, legal, and procedural concerns inherent in research using linked data include the impact of such research on individual autonomy and privacy and on relationships of confidentiality; the impact of research outcomes on individuals and collectives; the importance of data security; the difficulties with inconsistent and complex regulation across jurisdictions; requirements for approval from multiple ethics committees and data custodians; and the timeliness and transparency of decision making by data custodians and other stakeholders.

Some of these concerns stem from the fact that research using linked data involves whole populations and, because of this, individuals are not usually given the opportunity to consent to participation in the research. Instead, decisions are typically made on behalf of the community at the political level to establish data linkage infrastructure. The decision to permit access to linked data about individuals is then delegated to a variety of decision makers, including data custodians, ethics committees, and privacy committees. These regulatory systems have been developed over time to protect individual and organisational interests, but they are often complex and time-consuming. This has led to frustration among researchers and the decision makers themselves.

The aim of this book is to propose a framework for decision making about the linkage of individual-level data for research that will unlock critical public health benefits in a timely way while acknowledging and protecting the fundamental individual rights and community interests involved. The suggested framework of principles and practice is also intended to help maintain community support, or 'social licence', for the relevant decision making as well as for the resulting research.

SOCIAL LICENCE

The continued use of individual-level data without consent for research relies to a large extent on ongoing approval and broad social acceptance by the community and other stakeholders. The existing regulatory frameworks are sophisticated and complex; however, compliance with formal regulatory frameworks is not sufficient to establish a social licence for research unless the frameworks themselves adequately support social licence by ensuring trust and legitimacy.

The collection, use, and disclosure of individual information without individual consent – and generally without the knowledge of the individual – go beyond general norms of confidentiality and privacy. This is why community acceptance and support are critical for research using linked data. It needs to underpin the decisions made on behalf of the community that allow each step in the process, both in the public sector and in academic institutions. The role of private commercial interests either directly or as funders of research further complicates the picture.

Although social licence is intangible, without it research 'may experience ongoing challenge and contestation'.[4] This book examines the current regulatory systems in light of this claim and considers whether they effectively support social licence and how they might be improved in order to better build and maintain social licence.

DECISION-MAKING PRACTICE AND PROCESS

The book focuses on three regulatory frameworks for decision making in the context of data linkage: human rights, research ethics, and law. It then goes on to consider the practice and process of decision making within these frameworks. The focus on decision making in this book is necessary and appropriate because decision making is at the heart of administration,[5] and good decision making lies at the heart of good administration.[6] In addition, decision makers in the context of data linkage research are gatekeepers and guardians. They are the gatekeepers that regulate researcher access to the rich and valuable resources of government data collections. They are the guardians of the individual, community, and public interests involved in the endeavour. They make decisions about which data collections are linked, the way they are linked, and the way they are stored and accessed.

Research using linked data is the end result of a number of steps:

- the original collection of data;
- the establishment of linkage infrastructure; and
- the linkage, extraction, and use of data for particular research projects.

4 P Carter, G Laurie, and M Dixon-Woods, 'The Social Licence for Research: Why care.data Ran into Trouble' (2015) 41(5) *Journal of Medical Ethics* 404, 404.

5 H Simon, *Administrative Behavior: A Study of Decision-Making Processes in Administrative Organizations* (Macmillan, 1947).

6 Queensland Ombudsman, 'Good Decision-Making' (Web Page, 3 June 2019) <www.ombudsman.qld.gov.au>.

Each of these steps involves different stakeholders and different decision makers. The original collection of data is often for administrative – rather than research – purposes, for example the administration of public health insurance schemes and public hospitals. Such data collections generally include large numbers of people, often whole populations. The stakeholder community therefore includes the whole population. Governments must have legal authority to collect such data, and the decision makers involved in authorising that collection therefore sit in government and the legislature. In representative democracies, these decisions makers are tasked with making decisions on behalf of citizens.

In Australia, Canada, and the UK – the jurisdictions under consideration in this book – data linkage infrastructure has been established either by government or by public universities, so the stakeholder community is once again very broad. It includes the whole population as potential data donors and taxpayers, the research community, and data custodians.

The linkage and extraction of data for specific projects engage a smaller pool of data donors. Some projects may involve specific communities such as a particular disease group, a particular ethnic group, or a particular geographic or socio-demographic group. However, the impact of the project may reach beyond those whose data is included in a particular project. Other projects may include very large numbers of people spread across the whole population. The decision to share data for individual research projects is entrusted to data custodians and privacy and ethics committees.

The book considers the governance arrangements and the decisions that lead to the release of linked data for research and seeks to describe 'good decision making' in the context of linking and releasing data for research. In developing an approach to good decision making, we have drawn on the principles of public administration, which have been developed over hundreds of years to regulate government decision making about individual matters. These principles include having a sound legal basis for decisions; appointing appropriate decision makers; making decisions that are in the public interest based on explicit and publicly available criteria; and providing reasons for decisions linked to those criteria. These governance arrangements are intended to drive greater trustworthiness, transparency, accountability, and community engagement in the decision-making process. These in turn support social licence for the process and the resulting decisions.

TERMINOLOGY

There are several terms that appear throughout the book that require some clarification. The focus of the book is the use of data for research, a term that can be difficult to define. We have taken 'research' to mean the creation of new knowledge and/or the use of existing knowledge in a new and creative way so as to generate new concepts, methodologies, inventions, and understandings.

The term 'linked data' is used throughout the book to mean data derived from different sources but relating to the same individual or event in a single file. The method of creating linked data is called data linkage rather than other terms used in the literature, including record linkage and data integration.

The term 'individual-level data' is used in the book to refer to data about an individual person, whether or not the person is identified. It is contrasted with aggregated data which combines data about different people. The arguments in the book apply to all individual-level data and are not confined to personal information. The terms 'personal information' and 'personal data' are used in international human rights law and data protection legislation around the world and are defined as information about individuals that is identified or reasonably identifiable. 'Reasonably identifiable' is context-dependent so that information in one context may be 'personal information', that is, information about an individual who is reasonably identifiable, but may not be 'personal information' in another. Advances in the ability to link and analyse data mean that it is becoming increasingly difficult to ensure that data has been de-identified and that individuals cannot be re-identified. The terms 'personal information' and 'personal data' are only used in the book where they are descriptive of existing law, ethical principles, or procedures.

We use the term 'data protection legislation' to describe legislation that governs the collection, use, and disclosure of personal information by both private and government entities. Data protection legislation is also known, in different jurisdictions, as privacy legislation or personal information protection legislation.

We have chosen to use the generic term 'ethics committee' throughout the book for a committee that reviews research proposals involving human participants to ensure that they are ethically acceptable. We acknowledge that these committees are known by a range of terms in different countries, including Human Research Ethics Committee (HREC), Institutional Review Board (IRB), Ethics Review Board (ERB), Research Ethics Committee (REC), and Research Ethics Board (REB).

STRUCTURE OF THE BOOK

The book is divided into three parts. In Part I, the concept of data linkage is explained, the potential benefits of using linked individual-level data described, and an overview of approaches to managing and minimising privacy and other risks in different countries is included. The individual, community, and public interests in the use of linked data for research are introduced and the concept of social licence is discussed. In Part II, the three regulatory frameworks for making decisions about whether linked data can be used for research – human rights, research ethics, and law – are explored. In Part III, case studies and examples are used to investigate how these decision-making frameworks are implemented in different countries and how this might impact access to data for researchers and the social licence for research using linked data. The challenges that emerge in the implementation of decision-making processes are considered and recommendations made to enhance the regulatory and governance structures as well as support social licence.

SCOPE OF THE BOOK

While this book focuses primarily on health-related research, the concepts and arguments discussed in the book are generally applicable to other kinds of research using linked data. The challenges of regulating data use and making good decisions about the collection and use of data for research are apparent everywhere and are being addressed in different ways in different countries. The description of the legal and ethical frameworks, in Chapters 5 and 6, and the examples and case studies in Parts II and III, are drawn from common law countries that have advanced data linkage programmes: mostly Australia, Canada, and the UK. They illustrate the way in which these challenges are currently being addressed in these jurisdictions. The comparative and critical approach taken to this material will, we trust, ensure that the general concepts discussed in this book are internationally applicable and will be relevant to addressing those challenges in all jurisdictions. The law and other content in the book are up to date as of 30 June 2021.

PART I

Context for Decision Making

In this book, we are interested in assessing and improving the decision-making process that grants or denies access to government data collections for research. Sound decision making is foundational to good administration, including managing public resources efficiently and effectively. The Australian, Canadian, and United Kingdom (UK) governments have all made clear that the data they hold is a resource that must be managed for the benefit of the community.[1]

Governments make a great deal of administrative data publicly available for easy access and reuse. However, this is clearly not appropriate in relation to individual-level data about intimate aspects of people's lives, such as their health information. When open access to data is not an acceptable option, then decisions must be made about each individual use and release of the data.

This book is concerned with one use of that information – linking data for research – and the way decisions are made about this use of data. These decisions are challenging because of the multiplicity of interrelated interests and the impact they have on individuals and the wider community. They engage deeply held moral values and convictions.

In Part I, the context for decision making in relation to the use of data for research is established. The current landscape of data linkage for research is described, the interests of the stakeholders are discussed, and the concepts used to analyse and evaluate the decision-making frameworks and procedures are examined.

1 Australian Government, 'Public Data Policy Statement' (Policy Statement, 7 December 2015) <https://pmc.gov.au/sites/default/files/publications/aust_govt_public_data_policy_statement_1.pdf>.

In Chapter 1, the concept of data linkage is explained and the potential benefits of using linked individual-level data are described. The types of data that are the focus of the book are introduced, and an overview of the approaches to managing and minimising privacy risks adopted in different countries is included.

Chapter 2 considers the perspectives of different stakeholders in research using linked data and examines the interests of those who conduct the research, the interests of individuals whose information is used, collective interests, and public interests in the use of linked data for research. The complexity and interrelationship of these interests reveal how challenging it is to make decisions that take all of them into account. The chapter goes on to consider some concepts that shed light on the way those interests should be evaluated when decisions are made.

Chapter 3 introduces the concept of social licence and considers its application to research using linked data. Social licence is essential for the ongoing viability of research using linked data. The concerns about data linkage and the conditions that support a social licence for research using linked data are discussed. The necessary attributes of governance mechanisms and the implications for the regulation of research using linked data are examined.

1

Research Using Linked Data

1.1 WHAT IS LINKED DATA USED FOR?

Throughout a person's life, data is collected about them as they interact with different people and organisations. Data is collected about major life events such as birth and death as well as medical events such as doctors' visits, hospitalisation, and pharmaceutical prescriptions. Detailed data about diagnosis and treatment as well as the results of medical tests – including pathology results, computed tomography (CT) scans, genetic test results, and genomic sequencing – are also collected. Social data – such as education level, socio-economic status, interactions with the

TABLE 1.1 *Examples of linked data uses for researchers*

Assess the outcomes of clinical or therapeutic interventions	Human papillomavirus (HPV) causes cervical cancer. In Scotland, researchers used linked cervical smear data and HPV vaccination records to show a massive reduction in infections in girls vaccinated at the age of 12–13 years. Based on this data, a 90% reduction in cervical cancer in Scotland is predicted.	Kavanagh et al (2017)
Assess the safety, quality, and costs of healthcare and other government services	The primary treatment for breast cancer is surgery. In addition, a number of adjuvant therapies (radiotherapy, chemotherapy, and hormonal therapy) are now available that improve symptoms and outcomes. Australian researchers used linked breast cancer screening and cancer registry data to show that patients living close to cancer treatment facilities were more likely to use adjuvant therapies than those who lived further away.	Hsieh et al (2015)
Investigate the influence of personal, economic, and lifestyle factors on health and well-being	A study in Ontario, Canada, investigated the relationship between living near major roads and neurodegenerative diseases. A range of data collections were linked, including Ontario's Registered Persons Database, hospital, physician, and prescription medication data. Postcodes were used to calculate proximity to major roads. The study showed an association between living near a major road and dementia. There was no association with Parkinson's disease or multiple sclerosis.	Chen et al (2017)
Investigate social and community influences on individual and community health and well-being	Researchers in Australia were able to show that people living in supportive housing – a combination of affordable housing with onsite services – used fewer government services and had significantly improved outcomes compared with those who were homeless. A range of data was linked, including emergency department presentations, hospital, mental health contact, ambulance use, court appearances, prison, probation, parole time, police arrests, victims of crime and police custody, and use of homeless accommodation services. The results showed that people living in supportive housing showed a 52% reduction in criminal offending, a 54% reduction in being a victim of crime, and a 40% reduction in time spent in police custody. Their use of short-term crisis accommodation reduced by 99% and mental health service used declined by 65%.	Parsell et al (2017)

Assess the effectiveness of preventative programmes	A number of studies have compared health outcomes before and after the introduction of smoke-free legislation in Scotland by linking hospital data to birth and death data. They have shown a 10% drop in hospital admissions for strokes and reductions in pregnancy complications.	Mackay et al (2012, 2013)
Obtain valuable follow-up information on participants in research studies and surveys	The '45 and Up Study' is a longitudinal cohort of people aged ≥45 years in New South Wales (NSW), Australia. The dietary information collected in the cohort baseline questionnaire was linked to the NSW registry of deaths to show that there was no difference between the all-cause mortality for vegetarians and non-vegetarians.	Mihrshahi et al (2017)
Understand the risks and causes of diseases and ill health	Some women suffer from depression during their pregnancies and need to take serotonin reuptake inhibitors (SSRIs). By linking births, hospital, prescription, and physician billing records, researchers in Canada were able to show that babies born to mothers who take SSRIs during pregnancy are more likely to suffer from respiratory distress and low birth weight.	Oberlander et al (2006)

justice system, housing quality, and location – are also collected by governments and other service providers. By linking this data together, researchers can understand not only the stories of individual lives but also the stories of whole populations. Table 1.1 outlines some of the ways in which linked data has been used by researchers.

1.2 WHAT ARE THE ADVANTAGES OF USING LINKED DATA FOR RESEARCH?

There are a number of advantages to using linked, routinely collected data for health and health-related research over other methods.

1.2.1 *Cost-Effectiveness*

Public funds are used to collect large quantities of health and related data every day in the course of providing health services. The reuse of this routinely collected data for research increases the value for money for the community. These government data collections are built up on a continuous basis and hold data collected over many years. The cost of collecting such data from the whole population across decades for a specific research project would be prohibitive. The reuse of existing data is a cost-effective solution. Linkage of these publicly funded data collections increases the types of research that can be conducted using the data, resulting in additional value for money.[1]

1.2.2 *Whole Population Coverage*

The inclusion of all eligible people in routinely collected data collections and the longitudinal nature of the collections means that, particularly when multiple data sources are linked, a more complete picture of the community is possible than when using other methods. The large numbers of people included in these collections mean that they can be used to study rare events and outcomes as well as minority groups, for example indigenous communities. In addition, linkage within and between population data collections enables the study of familial and generational impacts on health and well-being.[2]

1.2.3 *Avoidance of Bias*

The inclusion of all eligible people in routinely collected data collections means that the data is often less biased than prospectively collected research data. As this data is collected in the course of providing a service, reporting and recall biases are also minimised. The linkage of multiple data collections exposes duplication errors and other technical issues with the data, which can result in improvements to the quality of the data.[3]

1.2.4 *Timeliness*

The linkage of existing data collections is much quicker than collecting data from scratch which, for some studies, could take decades. It also provides the ability to react quickly to changing health trends, identify and monitor epidemics, detect health service problems, and improve clinical practice.

1.2.5 *Real-World Data*

The evaluation of new treatments in clinical trials requires trial participants to meet specific and sometimes narrow criteria. Once registered and implemented into usual

[1] B Sibthorpe, E Kliewer, and L Smith, 'Record Linkage in Australian Epidemiological Research: Health Benefits, Privacy Safeguards and Future Potential' (1995) 19(3) *Australian Journal of Public Health* 250; C Holman et al, 'A Decade of Data Linkage in Western Australia: Strategic Design, Applications and Benefits of the WA Data Linkage System' (2008) 32(4) *Australian Health Review* 766; L Jorm, 'Routinely Collected Data as a Strategic Resource for Research: Priorities for Methods and Workforce' (2015) 25(4) *Public Health Research and Practice* 30.

[2] Jorm (n 1).

[3] Ibid; Holman et al (n 1); J Price, C Estrada, and D Thompson, 'Administrative Data versus Corrected Administrative Data' (2003) 18(1) *American Journal of Medical Quality* 38.

practice, treatments are often used on a wider range of people who have additional co-morbidities, take prescription and non-prescription medications not permitted in the trials, and are exposed to a variety of environmental and psychological factors. Once in general use, treatments may also be used 'off-label' in circumstances unforeseen during the clinical trials. The use of linked, routinely collected data enables the evaluation of treatments in the real-world setting as well as the evaluation of treatments and services that were not evaluated in a randomised trial setting.[4]

1.3 WHAT DATA IS LINKED FOR RESEARCH?

Any data collected about individuals can potentially be linked with other data collected about those individuals and be used for research. The types of data collections most commonly linked and used for health research are administrative data, clinical data, project-specific data, and health and well-being data.

1.3.1 *Administrative Data*

'Administrative data' is the term given to those data collections that are made up of information that is routinely collected during the delivery of a service, such as the provision of healthcare.[5] This data is collected from service providers by government departments and agencies and used for policy, planning, management, monitoring, evaluation, and research purposes.

The collection of administrative data is generally required or authorised by law. Typically, mandatory reporting requirements allow this data to be collected from service providers without individual consent.[6] It is important to note that the content information recorded in administrative data collections is often only summary information, for example hospital admission data collections contain coded diagnosis, date of admission, and treatment records. Individual service providers may collect and maintain more detailed service records.[7]

The typical features of administrative data are that:

- it is originally collected during service delivery;
- it is subsequently collected into an administrative data collection without express consent;
- collection is mandated by statute; and
- the data is used by government agencies for planning, monitoring, and funding.

4 Jorm (n 1).

5 J Davies, H Barnes, and C Dibben, *Education Administrative Data: Exploring the Potential for Academic Research* (Report, 2010) 2.

6 J Allen et al, 'Privacy Protectionism and Health Information: Is There Any Redress for Harms to Health?' (2013) 21(2) *Journal of Law & Medicine* 473, 476.

7 Ibid.

The information is stored in secure data collections within each agency, and access to the data is controlled by a data custodian (an authorised nominee of the agency who holds the data).

1.3.2 *Clinical Data*

Clinical data is the detailed patient records collected and used by health professionals in the provision of patient care. This includes medical notes, pathology results, imaging – for example, X-ray and CT scans – and other health test results. Clinical data is generally collected directly from the patient or with the knowledge and consent of the patient.

The key features of clinical data are that it is:

- collected during service delivery;
- collected with consent; and
- used by health professionals for the provision of clinical care.

1.3.3 *Project-Specific Data*

Governments and other organisations – for example, research institutions – collect information from time to time for a particular purpose, such as a survey or a specific research project. The key features of project-specific data collections are that they are:

- collected for research or a specific purpose which is not administrative or clinical;
- collected with consent; and
- sometimes include consent for access to other information.

1.3.4 *Individual Health and Well-Being Data*

Individuals are increasingly collecting health and well-being data about themselves. This data may be collected using wearable technology, for example activity trackers that track movement, food, weight, and sleep and provide motivation to meet health and fitness goals. The companies that sell these devices, in addition to providing the purchased service, may use or sell the data they collect for marketing, data analysis, research, and surveys. This is usually articulated in the terms and conditions of use and/or the company privacy policy.

Other companies offer genomic sequencing and genealogy services. These companies may also use the individual-level data they collect for a range of other purposes, as articulated in their terms and conditions and/or privacy policy.

The key features of individual health and well-being data are that it is:

- collected for individual use;
- collected with consent; and
- potentially used by the provider for other purposes.

1.4 HOW IS DATA LINKED?

Data linkage, in simple terms, is a method of bringing together information derived from different sources, but relating to the same individual or event, into a single file.[8] For example, bringing together the records of individuals who appear in both the hospital admissions data collection and the death register can be used to determine how many people die within thirty days of a hospital admission. There are two main methods reported in the research literature used to link data: deterministic and probabilistic.

Deterministic linking is the matching of two records based on exact agreement of selected unique identifiers. This method relies on each data collection including at least one characteristic (variable) of each individual which ideally:

- is available for all records;
- is unique for each individual;
- does not change over time; and
- is simple to record and verify.[9]

It is almost impossible to find a perfect deterministic linkage variable as few individual characteristics meet all of these requirements. The closest example is the personal identification numbers issued by some countries, such as the Swedish personal identification number.[10] Deterministic linkage can also be conducted using exact matching of more than one variable, for example name and date of birth. Deterministic linking is a simple and quick method which works well for small data sets with few errors or missing data in the linkage variable fields.

High-quality deterministic linkage variables are often not available across all the data collections to be linked. In these cases, linkage is conducted using the available identifying and demographic variables – most commonly name, address,

8 M Hobbs and M McCall, 'Health Statistics and Record Linkage in Australia' (1970) 23(5) *Journal of Chronic Diseases* 375.

9 L Gill, *Methods for Automatic Record Matching and Linking and Their Use in National Statistics*, National Statistics (Methodological Series No 25, 2001); P Christen and K Goiser, 'Quality and Complexity Measures for Data Linkage and Deduplication' in F Guillet and H Hamilton (eds), *Quality Measures in Data Mining* (Springer, 2007) 127.

10 J Ludvigsson et al, 'The Swedish Personal Identity Number: Possibilities and Pitfalls in Healthcare and Medical Research' (2009) 24(11) *European Journal of Epidemiology* 659.

and date of birth. However, addresses and names can change over time and are also often recorded differently or inaccurately, for example Katherine, Kathryn, or Catherine. Instead of exact matching (deterministic linking), probabilistic linking is the linkage of records from two (or more) files based on whether their common linkage variables (such as name, address, date of birth) mostly agree or mostly disagree.[11] The decision that two records are a match is based on determining the probability of a match rather than an exact match. The algorithms used in probabilistic linkage can be designed to take into account that some variables are more discriminating or reliable than others. For example, the chance of two records with the same date of birth belonging to the same person is greater than two records with the same sex.[12]

1.4.1 *Methods to Minimise and Manage Privacy Risks in Data Linkage*

Historically, researchers were given fully identifiable data from different sources so that they were then able to link the data themselves. The major reason for the release of personal identifiers to researchers in the past was to enable them to find and manually link records.[13] There is now a range of methods to link data that avoids the provision of identifiers to researchers and improves the protection of individual privacy.

1.4.1.1 The Separation Principle

The separation principle was developed in 2000–1 and involves the separation of personal identifiers from content information and the separation of the roles of data custodian, data linker, and researcher.[14] This principle was described at the time as the best-practice approach to addressing privacy issues for research projects involving linked data. The main elements of this approach are still used by data linkage units around the world today.

The main strength of this method is that it enables population-level research to be conducted without researchers having access to personal identifiers such as names and addresses. This minimises the risks to individual privacy while enabling the conduct of health and medical research. This balance between individual privacy and scientific advancement is accomplished in two ways as described in this section (Figure 1.1).

11 Christen and Goiser (n 9).

12 Gill (n 9).

13 Holman et al (n 1).

14 C Kelman, A Bass, and C Holman, 'Research Use of Linked Health Data: A Best Practice Protocol' (2002) 26(3) *Australian and New Zealand Journal of Public Health* 251.

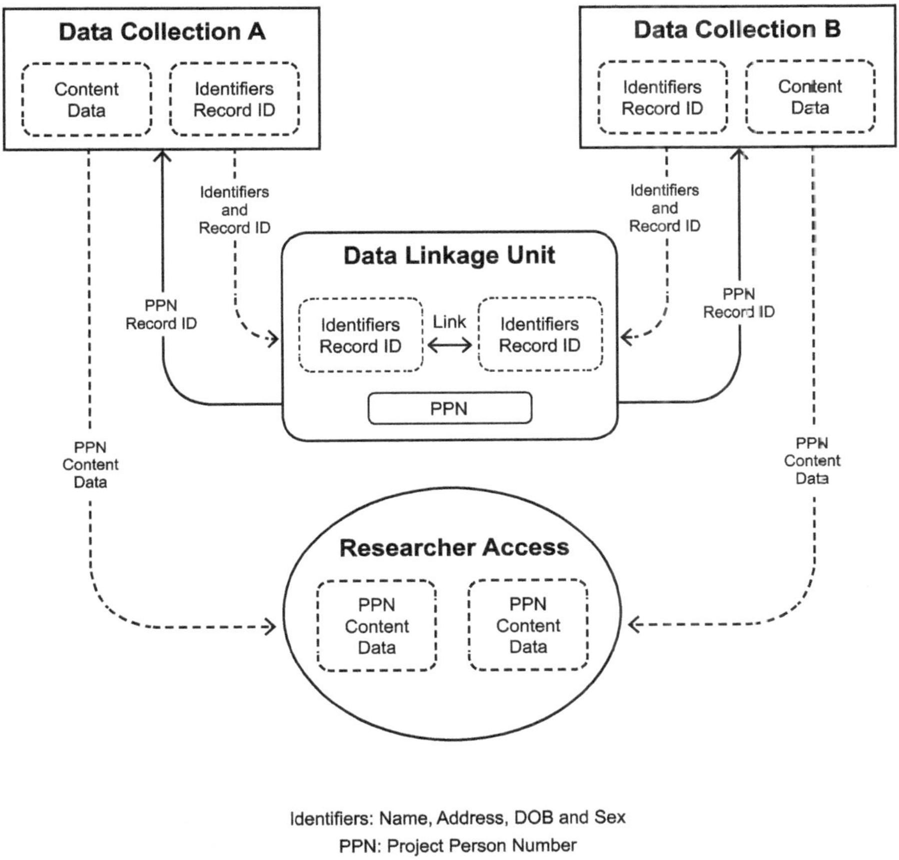

FIGURE 1.1 Example of the separation of personal identifiers from content data
* PPN: Project Person Number

THE SEPARATION OF PERSONAL IDENTIFIERS FROM CONTENT DATA. The data used for linkage (linkage variables) is restricted and includes only the specific data items that are needed to ensure accurate data matching (such as full names, date of birth, sex, address, and unique record identifier). Authorised specialist data linkage units use the linkage variables to determine which records belong to the same person and to allocate a unique identifier to each person. The unique identifier is sometimes called a linkage key or linkage ID. Data linkage units create and maintain master linkage maps or files. These are tables containing the association between the linkage keys and record identifiers. The master linkage maps or files are stored separately from the original source data and do not contain any of the content data such as diagnosis or treatment information.

In the ideal version of the separation principle method, the content information, for example diagnosis and/or procedure, remains with the original data collection and the data custodians of each collection remain the only people who have access to the complete data collection. The complete content data from each collection is not copied and stored in multiple locations. In this model, data linkers do not have access to content information about individuals and researchers do not have access to the linkage variables (personal identifiers) about individuals. This significantly reduces the possibility that a researcher is able to identify an individual from any clinical or healthcare-related information.[15]

In practice, this model can be inefficient as it requires multiple data custodians to extract content data for each new research project. Understandably, variations of this model have arisen and are used in several places across the world. The most common variation used, for example by Secure Anonymised Information Linkage (SAIL) Databank in Wales, involves the data custodians periodically copying the content data and sending it to a single content data repository.[16] In this variation, the data linkers still do not have access to the content data; however, instead of multiple data custodians extracting content data for one research project, the content data can be extracted by a single officer of the content repository. This enables more efficient access to the content data for researchers.

THE SEPARATION OF FUNCTIONS AND RESPONSIBILITIES. This second part of the separation principle involves the separation of the data linkage process from the custodianship of data and the analysis of linked data by researchers. The individuals undertaking data linkage (and having access to personal identifiers) are different from the data custodians of the data collections being linked and from the researchers who are involved in the analysis of linked content information. The data linkers who are responsible for creating linkage keys are not involved in the analysis of the linked content data or discussion of the data at the individual unit record level with the researchers.[17]

The separation of the identifying information from the content data and the separation of roles in the process serve as the basis for a robust privacy-preserving 'best-practice' protocol. Data linkage following this approach facilitates the use of data for research and the monitoring and evaluation of health services and minimises the intrusions on individuals' privacy.

The separation of functions and responsibilities requires each role in the data linkage process to be clearly described and defined. The terminology for these roles used by linkage systems across the world varies, but there are generally three roles:

15 Ibid.

16 D Ford et al, 'The SAIL Databank: Building a National Architecture for E-Health Research and Evaluation' (2009) 9 *BMC Health Services Research* 157.

17 Kelman, Bass, and Holman (n 14).

- Data custodians (sometimes called data stewards) are responsible for managing the collection, use, and disclosure of data.[18] They collect and hold data on behalf of data providers, including individuals and public or private sector organisations. Data custodians collect and store identifying information (such as name, sex, date of birth) and also the related content information (eg, health information such as diagnosis and treatment details).
- Data linkers are the people who create linkage keys from identifying information and maintain the master linkage maps that allow data to be linked within and between data collections. Data linkers usually work in specialist data linkage units.
- Researchers are the people who use the data for the purpose of analysis and research.

1.4.1.2 Blindfolded Linkage Techniques

A range of methods have emerged that render linkage variables non-identifiable by hashing, encryption, or bloom filters.[19] Linkage is then conducted using the blindfolded linkage variables instead of the actual variables. These methods aim to protect individual identities from the data linkers. These methods may be useful when personal identifiers cannot be provided to the data linkers, for example, if legislation prevents the transfer of personal identifiers between organisations or jurisdictions.

These techniques have a range of limitations. First, they only minimise the risk that the data linkers will have access to identifiable information. They do not have any impact on the identifiability of the content data provided to researchers as this data is not blindfolded. Using these techniques also limits the type of linkage and the quality of the linkage that can be conducted. For many of these techniques, only deterministic (exact matching) linkage can be conducted, which results in inaccurate matching, particularly for large, complex data sets. Some techniques have been described that allow for probabilistic linking using blindfolded linkage variables, but the quality of linkage may still not be as good as linkage using identifiable variables because it is not possible to conduct a manual review of the matches.[20]

1.4.2 *Systematic Approaches to Data Linkage*

Data collections can be linked for a specific research project on a one-off or ad hoc basis. This can be done by the researchers themselves or by a specialised data

[18] National Statistical Service, 'Rights, Responsibilities and Roles of Data Custodians' (Web Page) <www.nss.gov.au/nss/home.nsf/pages/Data+Integration+-+Roles+and+responsibilities+of+data+custodians?opendocument>; ibid.

[19] D Vatsalan, P Christen, and V Verykios, 'A Taxonomy of Privacy-Preserving Record Linkage Techniques' (2012) 38(6) *Information Systems* 946.

[20] A Brown et al, 'Estimating Parameters for Probabilistic Linkage of Privacy-Preserved Datasets' (2017) 17(1) *BMC Medical Research Methodology* 95.

linkage unit. However, for large population-level data collections, it is more efficient and minimises privacy risks if the collections are linked in a routine and systematic fashion. There are a number of countries and jurisdictions that have a systematic approach to the linkage and use of linked data in research. Each of these data linkage systems applies a version of the separation principle and includes some or all of the following elements: linkage; content data management; data discovery; application and approval process; and researcher access.

1.4.2.1 Linkage

How the separation is achieved and exactly how the linkage is done varies from system to system. In some data linkage systems, the linkage variables are only shared with a trusted third party who conducts the linkage. For example, in Tasmania, the Department of Health and Human Services (DHHS) holds a range of administrative data collections, such as admitted hospital patients. The DHHS copies the linkage variables from these collections and sends them to the Tasmanian Data Linkage Unit (TDLU) at the Menzies Institute for Medical Research which conduct the linkage. For approved research studies, the TDLU generates project-specific person numbers and sends them to the data custodian who extracts the data necessary for the project and provides this to the researcher, with the names and addresses replaced with the project-specific person number.[21]

In other data linkage systems, the data custodians send all their data to the data linkage unit, which both conducts the linkage and manages the content data. The separation is maintained internally using technical IT approaches and separation of roles for the staff. For example, the Institute for Clinical Evaluative Sciences (IC/ES) receives identifiable data from Ontario's publicly funded health system. The data linkage and content data management are all conducted within IC/ES.[22]

Most linkage systems only link data from within a single jurisdiction. However, the data linkage infrastructure in Australia enables the linkage of data collections within each jurisdiction and between states, territories, and the Commonwealth. It consists of a network of data linkage units servicing each jurisdiction. Linkage variables are transferred between data linkage units to enable cross-jurisdictional linkage. This enables researchers to study people who receive health services in different jurisdictions and to have access to larger data sets than is possible from a single jurisdiction.[23]

21 B Stokes et al, 'Tasmanian Data Linkage Unit: Supporting Innovative Research, Planning and Policy Formulation in Australia through the Provision of High-Quality Linked-Data Services' (2020) 4(2) *International Journal of Population Data Science* 09, 1–7.

22 ICES, 'Frequently Asked Questions' (Web Page) <www.ices.on.ca/About-ICES/FAQs>.

23 F Flack and M Smith, 'The Population Health Research Network: Population Data Centre Profile' (2019) 4(2) *International Journal of Population Data Science* 01, 1–7.

1.4.2.2 Content Data Management

In the strictest version of the separation principle, content data is managed by the original data custodian, who is also responsible for providing access to the content data approved for each specific research project. This is sometimes described as a distributed model. TDLU is an example of a distributed model.[24] A more efficient model is for the content data to be managed in one central data repository or warehouse. Examples of large linked or linkable content data repositories include the Manitoba Centre for Health Policy and the SAIL Databank.[25] Other systems have hybrid models where some content data is managed in an in-house repository and other content data remain with the data custodian, for example the Western Australia (WA) Data Linkage Branch.[26]

1.4.2.3 Data Discovery

Data linkage systems usually include some kind of information (metadata) that describes the linked data collections that are available for researchers to access through the system. At a minimum, there is a list of the names of each data collection, but more detail is required to enable researchers to design their research projects. The types of information that data linkage systems might provide include: the available dates of the data collection; lists of individual data items; information on data quality; and concept dictionaries that describe analytical techniques, statistical approaches, and code for use on specific data collections. A good example of a data discovery portal is the Manitoba Centre for Health Policy. This portal includes extensive details about the data collections and data items as well as a comprehensive concept dictionary.[27] The Population Health Research Network (PHRN) website in Australia provides information about routinely linked data collections across Australia.[28]

1.4.2.4 Application and Approval Processes

All data linkage systems require researchers to submit an application for approval before they are granted access to the linked data. A detailed discussion of approval processes can be found in Chapter 7. The information captured in the application

[24] Stokes et al (n 21).

[25] A Katz et al, 'Population Data Centre Profile: The Manitoba Centre for Health Policy' (2019) 4(2) *International Journal of Population Data Science* 10, 1–10; K Jones et al, 'A Profile of the SAIL Databank on the UK Secure Research Platform' (2019) 4(2) *International Journal of Population Data Science* 03, 1–12.

[26] Data Linkage Western Australia, 'Custodian Administered Extract Server', *Western Australia Department of Health* (Web Page) <www.datalinkage-wa.org.au/dlb-services/cares/>.

[27] Rady Faculty of Health Sciences, 'Manitoba Population Research Data Repository Data List', *University of Manitoba* (Web Page) <http://umanitoba.ca/faculties/health_sciences/medicine/units/chs/departmental_units/mchp/resources/repository/datalist.html>.

[28] PHRN, 'Data Collections Available' (Web Page) <www.phrn.org.au/for-researchers/data-collections-available/>.

form is determined by the specific regulatory requirements of the jurisdiction/s in which the data linkage system operates. The application forms can be a simple word document, for example eDRIS Scotland.[29] Some data linkage systems operate across multiple jurisdictions and have more sophisticated online applications, such as the PHRN online application system or the Canadian Data Access Support Hub (DASH).[30]

1.4.2.5 Researcher Access

Different data linkage systems have different approaches to data access. The most highly controlled option is for researchers only to be allowed access to linked data in a secure, physical data laboratory where only approved researchers are given access and the researchers are under constant video surveillance, as, for example, in New Zealand IDI and Scottish Safe Havens.[31]

Virtual data laboratories are used by a number of data linkage systems. These virtual laboratories can be accessed online by the researcher wherever they are, but all the data transferred into the laboratory is checked for compliance with approvals and only aggregate data is permitted to be removed from the laboratory, for example SURE and SeRP. There are some data linkage systems which transfer linked data by managed file transfer services directly to an approved researcher's institution where it must be managed according to the terms and conditions of a data transfer agreement, for example the WA Data Linkage Branch.

1.5 THE POTENTIAL AND CHALLENGES OF INTERNATIONAL DATA LINKAGE

1.5.1 *Potential*

The world's population is more mobile than it has ever been through migration – both managed and refugee – travel, and open borders such as those in the European Union (EU).[32] This means that people are increasingly using health services in multiple jurisdictions and the potential for the spread of disease is greater.

[29] Public Health Scotland, 'Your Research Proposal – What's Next?' (Web Page) <www.isdscotland.org/Products-and-Services/eDRIS/Research-Proposal/>.

[30] PHRN, 'PHRN Online Application System Log In' (Web Page) <https://oas.phrn.org.au/Account/Login?ReturnUrl=%2F>; Data Access Support Hub, 'How DASH Works', *Health Data Research Network Canada* (Web Page) <https://dash.hdrn.ca/en/how-it-works>.

[31] Department of Statistics, 'Accessing the Stats NZ Database', *University of Auckland* (Web Page) <www.auckland.ac.nz/en/science/about-the-faculty/department-of-statistics/stats-nz-data-lab.html>; Public Health Scotland, 'Use of the National Safe Haven' (Web Page) <www.isdscotland.org/Products-and-Services/EDRIS/Use-of-the-National-Safe-Haven/>.

[32] J Belluz, '4 Reasons Disease Outbreaks Are Erupting Around the World', *Vox* (Web Page, 31 May 2016) <www.vox.com/2016/5/31/11638796/why-there-are-more-infectious-disease-outbreaks>; ibid.

Linkage of data across international borders has the potential to contribute to a better understanding of disease transmission and the use of healthcare services across borders and will allow for better planning, cooperation, and delivery of these services.

The EU is an example of a regime of open borders that generally enables the free movement of people, goods, and services across national borders. The EU Directive 2011/24/EU establishes 'rules for facilitating access to safe and high-quality cross-border healthcare in the Union and to ensure patient mobility'.[33] The Directive applies both to patients wishing to access services across borders and healthcare practitioners providing services across borders. It is important to understand how this Directive is impacting on healthcare service usage, costs, and outcomes. The EU currently uses a system of questionnaires to evaluate demand for cross-border health service use.[34] The use of linked data would provide more accurate data on usage, costs, and outcomes.

Infectious diseases remain a significant global public health issue, which was highlighted by the emergence of COVID-19 in December 2019 and its subsequent global spread.[35] The Ebola epidemic in West Africa in 2014–15 affected five countries and resulted in more than 10,000 deaths.[36] The Zika virus epidemic in 2016 affected sixty-one countries.[37] Tuberculosis continues to be a major global problem, particularly drug-resistant strains. There were 600,000 new cases with resistance to rifampicin in 2016.[38]

The preparation for, and response to, infectious disease epidemics requires accurate predictions about:

- the risk that a new infection will appear in a given host population;
- the likelihood of an infectious disease outbreak;
- how the disease will spread; and
- how to control it.[39]

33 *Directive 2011/24/EU of the European Parliament and of the Council of 9 March 2011 on the Application of Patients' Rights in Cross-Border Healthcare* [2011] OJ L 88/45, 45 [10].

34 Health Connect Partners, *European Member State Data: Cross-Border Patient Flows Based on Directive 2011/24/EU Year 2016* (Report, 2016) <https://ec.europa.eu/health/sites/health/files/cross_border_care/docs/ev_20171019_co01_en.pdf>.

35 World Health Organization, *Coronavirus Disease 2019 (COVID-19)* (Situation Report No 45, 5 March 2020) <www.who.int/docs/default-source/coronaviruse/situation-reports/20200305-sitrep-45-covid-19.pdf?sfvrsn=ed2ba78b_2>.

36 World Health Organization, 'Ebola Data and Statistics' (Web Page, 31 March 2015) <http://apps.who.int/gho/data/view.ebola-sitrep.ebola-summary-20150331?lang=en>; B Aylward et al, 'Ebola Virus Disease in West Africa – The First 9 Months of the Epidemic and Forward Projections' (2014) 371(16) *New England Journal of Medicine* 1481.

37 World Health Organization, *Zika Situation Report* (Report, 23 June 2016) <www.who.int/emergencies/zika-virus/situation-report/23-june-2016/en/>.

38 World Health Organization, *Global Tuberculosis Report 2019* (Report, 17 October 2019) <www.who.int/tb/publications/global_report/en/>; ibid.

39 S Wilson, 'Data Protection: Big Data Held to Privacy Laws, Too' (2015) 519(7544) *Nature* 414.

The risk of the emergence of new infectious diseases and/or new outbreaks of disease depends on a range of factors outside the genetic and physical traits of the hosts.[40] These factors include ecological (weather, climate change), political (migration, trade), and socio-economic factors. The linkage of data covering these different sectors across countries would provide much more accurate information to better understand infectious diseases, how they spread, and how to combat them.

Increasingly, patients are travelling overseas to access cheaper treatment or treatments not available in their home countries. In countries such as Australia and Canada, patients travel for a range of services such as dentistry, cosmetic and obesity surgery, and reproductive treatments. There is little information about the short- and long-term follow-up of these patients or the outcomes of these treatments. There is also little information about the impact of medical tourism on the health systems involved. Linkage of data across borders would shed light on these issues.[41]

1.5.2 *Challenges*

Efforts to achieve data linkage within federations such as Australia have demonstrated the likely challenges for international data linkage. The challenges include:

- data quality and standards – for meaningful and accurate analysis, researchers need to know that they are comparing like with like when analysing linked data. This may not be the case when data is collected by different people in different jurisdictions. Approaches to addressing this challenge include using international standards for coding such as ICD 10; entering into agreements about data definitions and standards, for example, the Australian Health Information Agreement; or negotiating definitions for specific projects.
- the number of governments, agencies, and private sector organisations involved – all parties will need to agree on a range of issues, including the value of linkage and how to minimise any risks.
- data custodians' lack of trust in agencies and organisations outside their own jurisdiction.
- differences in legal and privacy regimes.
- questions about whether community support for research using linked data extends beyond national borders.

40 J Suk et al, 'The Interconnected and Cross-Border Nature of Risks Posed by Infectious Diseases' (2014) 7(1) *Global Health Action* 25287.

41 N Lunt, D Horsfall, and J Hanefeld, 'Medical Tourism: A Snapshot of Evidence on Treatment Abroad' (2016) 88 *Maturitas* 37.

1.6 WHY IS A NEW APPROACH TO DATA LINKAGE FOR RESEARCH NEEDED?

Existing approaches to data linkage for research were conceived in the 1970s to 1990s. Since then, there have been radical changes, including the emergence of Big Data (defined by volume, velocity and variety), advances in information technology and data science, and changes in public attitudes to personal information. The potential benefits of using linked data have increased but so have the risks to individual privacy. So much information about individuals is now publicly available to anyone with a smartphone or tablet (eg, from Facebook, Instagram, Twitter, LinkedIn, work websites, and online news) that the assumption that removing names and addresses renders data non-identifiable, which provides the foundation for the governance and structure of most data linkage systems, no longer applies. If linked data is to continue to be used for health and medical research without consent, the terms and conditions under which this occurs need renegotiation.

BIBLIOGRAPHY

Chen H et al, 'Living Near Major Roads and the Incidence of Dementia, Parkinson's Disease, and Multiple Sclerosis: A Population-Based Cohort Study' (2017) 389(10070) *Lancet* 718.

Hsieh J et al, 'Geographic Variation in the Intended Choice of Adjuvant Treatments for Women Diagnosed with Screen-Detected Breast Cancer in Queensland' (2015) 15 *BMC Public Health* 1204.

Kavanagh K et al, 'Changes in the Prevalence of Human Papillomavirus Following a National Bivalent Human Papillomavirus Vaccination Programme in Scotland: A 7-Year Cross-Sectional Study' (2017) 17(12) *Lancet Infectious Diseases* 1293.

Mackay D et al, 'Impact of Scotland's Smoke-Free Legislation on Pregnancy Complications: Retrospective Cohort Study' (2012) 9(3) *PLoS Med* e1001175.

Mackay D et al, 'Impact of Scotland's Comprehensive, Smoke-Free Legislation on Stroke' (2013) 8(5) *PLoS ONE* e62597.

Mihrshahi S et al, 'Vegetarian Diet and All-Cause Mortality: Evidence from a Large Population-Based Australian Cohort the 45 and Up Study' (2017) 97 *Preventive Medicine* 1.

Oberlander T et al, 'Neonatal Outcomes after Prenatal Exposure to Selective Serotonin Reuptake Inhibitor Antidepressants and Maternal Depression Using Population-Based Linked Health Data' (2006) 63(8) *Archives of General Psychiatry* 898.

Parsell C, Petersen M, and Culhane D, 'Cost Offsets of Supportive Housing: Evidence for Social Work' (2017) 47(5) *British Journal of Social Work* 1534.

2

Individual, Collective, and Public Interests

2.1 INTRODUCTION

Decision makers in the data linkage sphere – including data custodians and members of ethics and privacy committees – are asked to make decisions within existing legal and research ethics frameworks. These frameworks attempt to reflect the relevant interests of the individuals and groups involved in research using linked data and to balance these interests with the broader public interest. Within these frameworks, decision makers exercise a degree of discretion, for example when asked to approve the use of the linked data for a particular research project.

Research using linked data raises challenging questions for society on how the relevant interests of individuals, groups, and the broader public should be taken into consideration. These normative questions are at the core of decision making about the use of linked individual-level data for research. In our view, the existing legal and research ethics frameworks – developed originally in relation to research involving direct contact with participants – do not adequately reflect the range of rights and interests at play in the context of research using linked data. This chapter provides a survey of the range of individual, collective, and public interests at stake in this context and considers how these interests could be better taken into consideration. This discussion is important because it provides the foundations necessary for the moral legitimacy of research using linked data. In order to be morally legitimate, the decisions that underpin such research should be justifiable on substantive moral grounds. Chapter 3 will go on to discuss how such legitimacy can support the social licence for research.

Chapter 4 will consider how the human rights framework can assist to protect and promote many of the interests discussed here. We suggest in that chapter that the existing legal and ethical frameworks currently guiding decision makers do not reflect the full range of relevant rights. A better balance of rights in the decision-making frameworks would also contribute to the moral legitimacy of decision making and to the social licence needed to support research using linked data.

This chapter considers the interests of individual participants and relevant collectives – such as disease groups – as well as the wider public interests in research using linked data. First, the chapter considers the interests of individual research participants including dignity, autonomy, and privacy. We discuss the nature of these interests, the risks that arise in the context of research using linked data, and the ways in which such interests should be respected and protected. In particular, the chapter examines the traditional approaches to protecting individual interests in the research context – that is, consent and anonymisation – and concludes that these do not operate to effectively protect individual interests in the context of research using linked data. Second, the chapter considers the collective interests of groups recognised or created by the research. The outcomes of research using linked data can have significant impacts – both beneficial and detrimental – on particular groups in society as well as on the individuals making up those groups whether or not their data is included in the research. Third, the chapter considers the wider public interests in research using linked data. Research using linked data has the potential to provide significant benefits in improving public health and welfare, but it also comes with broad risks to the community.

Finally, there has been long-standing criticism that the current legal and ethical regulation of research using linked data does not appropriately take all these interests into consideration; that it is too individualistic in its approach; and that it unreasonably impedes such research at the expense of the public interest in improved community health and health care. How, then, should these regulatory frameworks be amended to allow decision makers to better balance the range of interests at stake? This chapter addresses this question by considering the approach taken in public health ethics and goes on to consider the place of solidarity and reciprocity in this context. Chapter 4 will take up the question from a rights perspective, which shares many foundational concerns and principles with research and public health ethics.

2.2 INDIVIDUAL INTERESTS

The linked data used in research is individual-level data and can include information about sensitive matters such as health, education, family and social welfare indicators, and criminal history. Much of the linked data available for research is data collected during the provision of services, such as health care and related services, and is not provided by the individual with the intention that it be used for research. While there is also increasing interest in linking data collected by the private sector through, for example, private sector health apps and social media platforms, the focus in this book is on the collection of individual-level data by government.

The context, then, is the provision of information to enable the provision of services. The terms of this exchange are rarely scrutinised and any secondary use of the data for research is unlikely to be a prominent consideration at the time the services are provided. Although some data is collected and linked with consent specifically for research, the bulk of research using linked data is conducted without the consent, and even without the knowledge, of the individuals concerned.

Such research carries risks to individuals with the possibility of significant harm if the protection of the data is compromised. The risks of individual harm from participation in this kind of research include risks to moral interests such as dignity and autonomy as well as more concrete harms. If information about the participant is negligently or deliberately disclosed, and the participant is identified, the potential harms include loss of reputation, stigmatisation, discrimination, and identity fraud. These harms can have serious impacts on employment, insurance, and the provision of services as well as cause stress and impact on individuals' health.[1]

Harm to individual dignity and autonomy can arise even if there is no negligent or intentional misuse of the information. People may be distressed if they discover that their information has been used without their knowledge or consent. Some people regard their sensitive information as part of themselves and using it without permission as demeaning and disrespectful. Loss of control of their information can trigger a sense of helplessness and disempowerment. There can also be a fear of the potential for future harm if the information is lost or misused.

The risk to individual privacy increases when data is linked because the degree of identifiability increases with the number of data items brought together. There is also increased risk attached to expanding the number of people who access the data to include researchers. These risks can be managed by minimising the identifiability of the data as soon and as much as possible and by minimising the number of people with access to individual-level data. Physical and technological barriers can

[1] G Laurie et al, 'A Review of Evidence Relating to Harm Resulting from Uses of Health and Biomedical Data' (Report, Nuffield Council on Bioethics and Wellcome Trust, 30 June 2014); M Otlowski, S Taylor, and Y Bombard, 'Genetic Discrimination: International Perspectives' (2012) 13(1) *Annual Review of Genomics and Human Genetics* 433.

provide protection against unauthorised access and contractual undertakings can reduce the risk of misuse. However, while best practice in securing and protecting the data is essential, complete security cannot be guaranteed, and the presence of risk should be acknowledged.

Voluntary and informed consent to participate has been foundational to managing risks to participants in the research environment but, for the reasons discussed in sections 2.2.1, 2.2.2, and 2.2.3, consent is problematic in relation to data linkage projects. As an alternative, reliance is often placed on anonymising data to protect individuals from harm. The practicability and effectiveness of both consent and anonymisation are challenged by the contemporary practice of Big Data analytics and research. How, then, do we practically and effectively respect and protect individual interests in this new and evolving environment?

2.2.1 *Dignity, Autonomy, and Respect*

Our dignity rests in being able to be the masters of our own journeys, and keep our identities and our choices open.[2]

Dignity, autonomy, and respect are core values in the Western philosophical tradition and the moral and political cultures of the countries considered in this book. These values also underpin the international human rights regime and are foundational principles in international and national research ethics guidelines.[3]

In moral philosophy, the term 'dignity' is used to refer to the intrinsic moral worth or value that is inherent in every human being. It is the basis for the Kantian argument that people are ends in themselves and should never be used simply as a means.[4] This approach dictates that humans must not be used in research simply as a means to an end, whether or not the end is in the broader public interest. The dignity inherent in every human being is the basis on which they should be offered moral recognition or respect.

The dignity of human beings, or their moral worth, can be founded on the argument that human beings are agents with autonomy. An agent is one who acts. To be an autonomous agent – or a self-determining agent – is to act on the basis of judgements and decisions that reflect one's own values and preferences, not those imposed by external forces. Free and informed consent to participate is one expression of our autonomy.[5] The concept of autonomy operates as a moral check on the exercise of paternalistic authority, including the exercise of authority by the state.

2 L Floridi, 'On Human Dignity As a Foundation for the Right to Privacy' (2016) 29(4) *Philosophy & Technology* 307, 310.

3 See also Chapter 4 'Human Rights' and Chapter 5 'Research Ethics'.

4 C Korsgaard, M Gregor, and J Timmermann, *Kant: Groundwork of the Metaphysics of Morals* (Cambridge University Press, 2012).

5 G Dworkin, *The Theory and Practice of Autonomy* (Cambridge University Press, 1988).

The centrality of autonomy to moral and political thought is reflected in both the common law and various statutory regimes that protect people from interference with their bodies without their consent and limit the use of their personal information without consent.[6] Respect for autonomy requires that people should have the right to choose for themselves whether they wish to participate in research and that their values and preferences should be respected. Voluntary participation enables people to participate in research that is consistent with their moral values and preferences and protects them from participation in research that is inconsistent with those values.

Voluntary and informed participation allows people to choose what risks they are prepared to accept and to weigh those risks against the value they see in participation. One qualitative study examining the meaning of consent for participants in a longitudinal cancer study found that participants valued consent as a way of expressing and reinforcing their identity as morally responsible people who contribute to society.[7] One participant explained that 'if I wasn't prepared to give for the right reasons, then I wouldn't give at all … I became involved with the thing because I thought good could come out of it'.[8]

Where individual-level data is linked and used for research without individual knowledge or consent, the individual's ability to act according to their values and preferences is constrained. The use of administrative data collections for research relies on statutory authority, rather than on the consent of the participants, so it involves the use of the coercive authority of the state. While it is the role of the state in a representative democracy to consider and balance the various interests in play when making decisions, the use of coercive authority to limit the autonomy of individuals calls for moral, as well as political, justification in order to support the legitimacy of the decision to impose such limits.

2.2.2 *Privacy*

'Privacy' is an umbrella term that encompasses a very broad range of related areas and concerns in law and moral philosophy.[9] It is closely linked to dignity and autonomy and includes control over access to ourselves and information about ourselves. There have been many and ongoing attempts to create typologies and taxonomies to describe and classify these areas and concerns.[10] Anita Allen described

6 See also Chapter 6 'Law'.

7 J Allen and B McNamara, 'Reconsidering the Value of Consent in Biobank Research' (2011) 25(3) *Bioethics* 155.

8 Ibid 163.

9 Privacy is discussed here as a moral interest held by individuals. The right to privacy, which protects the individual's moral interest in privacy, is discussed in Chapter 4 'Human Rights'.

10 See, eg, Prosser, who identified four harms protected by tort law – intrusion, private facts, false light, and appropriation: W Prosser, 'Privacy' (1960) 48 *California Law Review* 383, 389. Westin classified four states of privacy – solitude, intimacy, anonymity, and reserve: A Westin, *Privacy and Freedom* (Atheneum, 1967). See also B Koops et al, 'A Typology of Privacy' (2017) 38(2) *University of Pennsylvania Journal of International Law* 483.

four dimensions of privacy in the field of bioethics and public policy: informational privacy (access to personal information); physical privacy (access to persons and personal spaces); decisional privacy (government and other third-party interference with personal choices); and proprietary privacy (appropriation and ownership of interests in human personality).[11]

Daniel Solove's taxonomy of privacy took a different and more empirical approach. Rather than try to describe the complexities of privacy as a concept, he described the activities that can impinge on privacy. He identified four of these: (1) information collection; (2) information processing; (3) information dissemination; and (4) intrusion into spaces, relationships, and decision making.[12] The privacy concerns raised by research using linked data are principally in the area of informational privacy and are generated by information collection, processing, and dissemination. There is also an impact on decision making in terms of individual decisions to participate, or not to participate, in research. This is because individual consent is often not practicable in relation to research using linked data. Instead, decisions are made on behalf of the community by government data custodians and other third parties such as members of ethics and privacy committees.

Respect for privacy is a cultural universal, although norms vary between cultures.[13] Control of information about ourselves is an essential aspect of creating relationships and defining their boundaries. Choosing to share information about ourselves allows us to create intimacy and trust.[14] Privacy enables us to define our own identity by giving us 'breathing room' free of judgements, within which we can develop our self-conceptions, our values, and our goals.[15] It allows us to determine for ourselves who we are and it also allows us to set boundaries and to present different aspects of ourselves in different contexts. We do this in our face-to-face relationships in choosing what we share in different contexts. This curating of our identity is perhaps more explicit in digital mediums such as social and professional networking sites.

Individuals provide personal information to different recipients for particular purposes at different times. Data linkage brings this information together for a new purpose that may not be envisaged or expected. Where it is initially shared in the context of a confidential relationship – for example, with a healthcare practitioner – then

11 A Allen, 'Genetic Privacy: Emerging Concepts and Values' in M Rothstein (ed), *Genetic Secrets: Protecting Privacy and Confidentiality in the Genetic Era* (Yale University Press, 1997) 31. See also G Laurie et al, 'Managing Access to Biobanks: How Can We Reconcile Individual Privacy and Public Interests in Genetic Research?' (2010) 10(4) *Medical Law International* 315.

12 A variety of taxonomies have been developed to describe privacy: D Solove, 'A Taxonomy of Privacy' (2006) 154(3) *University of Pennsylvania Law Review* 477.

13 A Moore, 'Toward Informational Privacy Rights' (2007) 44(4) *San Diego Law Review* 809.

14 H Nissenbaum, 'Privacy As Contextual Integrity' (2004) 79(1) *Washington Law Review* 119; C Fried, 'Privacy' (1968) 77(3) *Yale Law Journal* 475.

15 Nissenbaum (n 14); J Cohen, 'What Is Privacy For?' (2013) 126(7) *Harvard Law Review* 1904; N Richards and J King, 'Big Data and the Future for Privacy' in F Olleros and M Zhegu (eds), *Research Handbook on Digital Transformations* (Elgar, 2016) 272.

the secondary use of the information for research may impact on the relationship of trust with that practitioner. The information is shared with others who are unknown and have a different purpose. The individual does not know who has access to the information, how the information will be linked, how it will be used, or how it might affect them. Personal information goes into a black box and the individual loses control over it. Fear is generated when you do not know what you do not know.[16]

The increasing collection and automated analysis of data have created the power to bring together large amounts of information about different aspects of a person's life that reveal a detailed picture of that person. Data linkage processes identify the records in various data collections that relate to the same person or event so that data can be aggregated into one record. Aggregation raises privacy concerns because the record that is created is much more revealing than the sum of its parts. The data is more potent for beneficial purposes but is also more potent for detrimental purposes. While shards of individual-level data may be relatively unimportant, together they create an intimate portrait. This new landscape is changing our understanding and expectations of privacy. The dominant approach in existing legal and ethical frameworks to protecting the individual interest in privacy has been to focus on individual control and management of access to personal information. However, data linkage for research has moved away from individual control and instead relies on minimising identification to protect individual privacy.

Because we are social beings, and sharing personal information is fundamental to social life and the functioning of community, privacy norms do not generally denote absolute exclusion or control. They are better understood as the accepted norms for access to and the movement of information. These norms are context-specific and will vary according to the type of information, the parties involved, and the way the information is transmitted.[17] They are not fixed. They can evolve gradually or they can be disrupted by sudden changes including technological developments such as the explosion of social media and the development of Big Data analytics. The contemporary norms about information flows are in a state of flux with concerns about the collection and use of data growing at the same time as people are readily sharing intimate details of their lives on social media and trading their data for services. The social and legal rules about how information is shared are being disrupted and challenged.[18] The social legitimacy of data linkage for research depends on whether the use of administrative data for research without individual consent is accepted under current norms.

16 Former United States Secretary of Defense Donald H. Rumsfeld referred to these as 'unknown unknowns': 'News Transcript', *Department of Defense News Briefing* (12 February 2002) <https://archive.defense.gov/Transcripts/Transcript.aspx?TranscriptID=2636>.

17 S Barocas and H Nissenbaum, 'Big Data's End Run around Anonymity and Consent' in J Lane (ed), *Privacy, Big Data, and the Public Good: Frameworks for Engagement* (Cambridge University Press, 2014) 44.

18 N Richards and J King, 'Big Data Ethics' (2014) 49(2) *Wake Forest Law Review* 393.

2.2.3 *Consent*

Consent has traditionally played a central role in human rights, research ethics, and law as a mechanism to acknowledge and respect the dignity and autonomy of research participants and to provide them with an opportunity to balance risks and benefits and protect themselves from exploitation. Research using linked data challenges this paradigm. There are practical problems in achieving voluntary informed consent in this context as well as issues with the impact on research outcomes.[19]

The strength of research using linked data is that it can include the data of whole populations. This gives it statistical strength and ensures inclusivity in the outcomes. Population-based research can include the data of millions of individuals, collected over many decades, many of whom will have changed address or died. Seeking consent in these circumstances is often impracticable.

It has also been suggested that requiring voluntary and informed consent may bias research samples and results, although the extent of the problem is unclear.[20] There are certainly examples where the requirement for consent has resulted in biased research samples and results. A clinical breast cancer registry in New Zealand was able to analyse data from patients who provided consent for inclusion in the registry and those that did not. The analysis demonstrated that the non-consenting patients were sicker and had lower survival than consenting patients. Thus, the exclusion of non-consenting patients resulted in an over-estimation of survival rates.[21] This study demonstrates that the informed consent process can be too burdensome for some people. This leads to the under-representation of certain groups, which does not only impact the scientific validity of research. It is also a potential problem in light of the ethical requirement to ensure that groups 'that are underrepresented in medical research should be provided appropriate access to participation in research'.[22]

Informed consent places the responsibility on individuals to make their own decisions about what they value and what risks they are prepared to take. This is problematic in the context of research using linked data because of both the difficulty of the task and the frequency of the task. If the growing use of linked administrative data for research required consent for every use, then individuals would find themselves having to consider many requests every year. Individuals

[19] M Mostert et al, 'Big Data in Medical Research and EU Data Protection Law: Challenges to the Consent or Anonymise Approach' (2016) 24(7) *European Journal of Human Genetics* 1096 (*'Big Data in Medical Research and EU Data Protection Law'*).

[20] M Kho et al, 'Written Informed Consent and Selection Bias in Observational Studies Using Medical Records: Systematic Review' (2009) 338(7698) *BMJ* 1–8; M Rothstein and A Shoben, 'Does Consent Bias Research?' (2013) 13(4) *American Journal of Bioethics* 27; S Hoffman and A Podgurski, 'Balancing Privacy, Autonomy, and Scientific Needs in Electronic Health Records Research' (2012) 65(1) *SMU Law Review* 85.

[21] J Elwood et al, 'Bias in Survival Estimates Created by a Requirement for Consent to Enter a Clinical Breast Cancer Registry' (2019) 58 *Cancer Epidemiology* 178.

[22] *World Medical Association Declaration of Helsinki – Ethical Principles for Medical Research Involving Human Subjects*, 64th WMA General Assembly (October 2013) art 13.

are already faced with constant requests to agree to the commercial use of their data collected online underpinned by complex privacy policies. Few people have the time, skill, or patience to read these policies and give any real consideration to their consent.[23] With so many entities collecting, sharing, and linking information about them it is no longer realistic for people to effectively manage their privacy by themselves.

A valid consent in human rights, ethics, and law must be voluntary and informed. The person seeking consent must ensure that potential participants have been adequately informed about the aims, methods, risks, and benefits of the research and have understood the information before seeking consent. In addition, the person seeking consent must consider issues such as whether the potential participant is competent to give consent, is in a dependent relationship with any of the relevant parties, or may otherwise be under duress to consent.

The usual practice for seeking consent to collect and use information for research is to ask for it at the point of collection. However, the use of linked data for research is often a secondary use that is removed in time and space from the original collection of the data. In health research, much of the linked data is collected when the individual receives health care or related services. There are a number of significant challenges to seeking consent at that time to use the information for subsequent linkage and research.

First, individuals seeking a health service may be ill and understandably focused on their treatment. There is a risk, in this context, that they will not adequately consider the necessary information about the future use of their information or that the stress of the situation may impact on their competence to consent. Second, if patients are very ill, distressed, and anxious it may be unreasonably burdensome to ask them to consider the complex issues relating to participation in research using linked data and seeking consent at that time. Third, if consent is requested as part of the routine paperwork to obtain treatment – for example, at hospital admission – the informed and voluntary nature of consent can be undermined. If consent is 'bundled' in this way, the information may not be read at all or it may not be clear that there is a real option to refuse to participate in the research.

Problems remain even if consent is sought at a later time or if the data is collected for the primary purpose of research. The research value of the data will extend for decades into the future and it may be impossible to anticipate how it will be used. The detailed information needed for a properly informed consent includes information about the purpose, risks, and benefits of the research, as well as the way in which the participants' interests will be protected. None of this will be known at the time the consent is requested. In order to be fully informed, consent would need to be sought for a particular use at the time it is proposed. This presents enormous

[23] Richards and King (n 18); F Cate and V Mayer-Schönberger, 'Notice and Consent in a World of Big Data' (2013) 3(2) *International Data Privacy Law* 67.

logistical and cost problems for research involving large cohorts that include millions of people and where data is collected over decades. If consent were required for each research use, then much current research would not be possible.

Various alternative models of consent have been proposed to address these problems, including unspecified consent, which covers any research use; extended consent, for research in a particular field; and advance research directives that specify preferences in relation to the use of data and whether specific consent is required.[24] Another alternative is dynamic consent, which uses IT to facilitate ongoing contact and communication between researchers and participants. Using this technology, participants can be asked to consent to new uses of their information, and they can provide input into the development of new research.[25]

These alternative forms of consent may be ethically acceptable in some circumstances.[26] They have their place, for example, where information is collected primarily for research and where there is direct contact between researchers and participants. However, they are more difficult to implement where information is collected during the provision of health and related services. In addition, they do not address more fundamental problems with consent in this context.

One of these problems is the adequacy of information. A great deal of effort has gone into improving the communication of necessary information to research participants. On the one hand, there have been efforts to ensure that the information is provided in a clear and accessible fashion. On the other hand, there have also been efforts to ensure that participants are fully informed with all the relevant information. This creates a dilemma that Barocas and Nissenbaum have described as the Transparency Paradox.[27] Where the subject matter is complex, it is impossible to provide both simplicity and sufficiently detailed information at the same time. Seeking consent for linking and analysis of data can give rise to this paradox.

As well as the problems of complexity, unknown future uses, and future technological developments there is an additional problem with data linkage. The nature of research using linked data is that the linkage reveals previously unknown patterns

[24] H Greely, 'Breaking the Stalemate: A Prospective Regulatory Framework for Unforeseen Research Uses of Human Tissue Samples and Health Information' (1999) 34(3) *Wake Forest Law Review* 737; M Rothstein, 'Expanding the Ethical Analysis of Biobanks' (2005) 33(1) *Journal of Law, Medicine & Ethics* 89; T Caulfield, R Upshur, and A Daar, 'DNA Databanks and Consent: A Suggested Policy Option Involving an Authorization Model' (2003) 4(1) *BMC Medical Ethics* 1; R Upshur and V Goel, 'The Health Care Information Directive' (2001) 1 *BMC Medical Informatics & Decision Making* 1.

[25] I Budin-Ljøsne et al, 'Dynamic Consent: A Potential Solution to Some of the Challenges of Modern Biomedical Research' (2017) 18(4) *BMC Medical Ethics* 1–10; H Teare et al, 'Reflections on Dynamic Consent in Biomedical Research: The Story So Far' (2021) 29(4) *European Journal of Human Genetics* 649.

[26] National Health and Medical Research Council, Australian Research Council and Universities Australia, *National Statement on Ethical Conduct in Human Research* (National Health and Medical Research Council, 2018 ed, 2017) 2.2.14.

[27] S Barocas and H Nissenbaum, 'Computing Ethics: Big Data's End Run around Procedural Privacy Protections' (2014) 57(11) *Communications of the ACM* 31 ('*Computing Ethics*').

and connections, and these outcomes can potentially create risks for participants and others. The impact of linking data in any particular case is not known and understanding and assessing the risks is therefore difficult. In this context, it is questionable whether fully informed consent is possible as people are unable to balance the risks and benefits involved.

A further difficulty with consent in this context is that the pre-eminence of individual consent ignores the wider impacts of research using linked data. These impacts are not confined to the participants in the research.[28] While the participants may agree to the use of information about them, risks such as discrimination and stigmatisation can affect all those who share certain traits, that is, there is a collective or group interest that requires consideration. Similarly, the intended benefits of the research are widespread and can extend to the whole community. In this context, it can be argued that a different approach is necessary to appropriately balance the full range of moral interests involved.[29] These issues are discussed in more detail in this chapter.

Consent remains important in demonstrating respect for people whose information is used in research using linked data. It continues to be essential where information is collected directly from participants for research purposes, but it may no longer be practical and sustainable in other contexts. There are good arguments that it is no longer effective in protecting autonomy and choice about risks and preferences. Privacy cannot be managed alone and is dependent on cooperation in establishing the norms of information sharing.[30] Reliance on consent as the moral justification for using linked data is misplaced and it is no longer able to bear the moral weight it is given.

2.2.4 *Anonymisation*

The protection of participants in data-based research has rested on two cornerstones – consent and anonymisation. The second of these, anonymisation – or de-identification – has been understood to be both possible and effective in providing protection for individual interests such as dignity, autonomy, and privacy.

Some research – for example, population health research involving the data of very large numbers of people – would be impracticable or impossible if each participant was required to give informed consent. In this context, the individual interests of each participant in maintaining their autonomy and privacy come into tension with the collective and/or community interests in the benefits of the research. For many years, the most common approach to dealing with this conflict has been to use

[28] A Ballantyne, 'Adjusting the Focus: A Public Health Ethics Approach to Data Research' (2019) 33(3) *Bioethics* 357; J Herrington and T Scott, 'The Social Risks of Science' (2020) 50(6) *The Hastings Center Report* 27.

[29] Ibid; Barocas and Nissenbaum, 'Computing Ethics' (n 27); O O'Neill, 'Informed Consent and Public Health' (2004) 359(1447) *Philosophical Transactions of the Royal Society B: Biological Sciences* 1133.

[30] J Fairfield and C Engel, 'Privacy As a Public Good' (2015) 65(3) *Duke Law Journal* 385.

anonymised or de-identified data. The assumption has been that this eliminates any risks of re-identification so that there are no longer any individual interests that must be protected.[31]

Generally, anonymisation or de-identification is the removal or suppression of personally identifying information from a data set to reduce the risk of re-identification of individuals. There are many definitions of anonymisation and de-identification. The definitions range from a process that substantially reduces the risk of re-identification to rendering data impossible to re-identify. Often the terms are used interchangeably, but sometimes they are used to describe distinctly different processes. Where a distinction is drawn between the two terms, then anonymisation is often used as a stronger term to indicate a complete inability to connect the data to an individual.[32] The possibility of ever meeting this strong standard is now questioned. It is also important to recognise that the degree of identifiability is dependent on context and on the knowledge and ability of the holder of the information.

Data protection legislation in all jurisdictions is based on the assumption that anonymisation or de-identification protects individuals from harm. This is reflected in the fact that the scope of such legislation is limited to information that is identified or reasonably identifiable. For example, the European Union General Data Protection Regulation (EU GDPR) states that the 'principles of data protection should therefore not apply to anonymous information, namely information which does not relate to an identified or identifiable natural person or to personal data rendered anonymous in such a manner that the data subject is not or no longer identifiable'.[33] An example at the national level is the 'Australian Privacy Principles' in the federal *Privacy Act 1988* (Cth), which reflect the general model and only apply to 'information or an opinion about an identified individual, or an individual who is reasonably identifiable'.[34] Thus, data that is not regarded as reasonably identifiable is excluded from the protection offered by the legislation.

In the health research sector, anonymisation is commonly used to enable healthcare organisations to release medical records to third-party researchers on the assumption that there will be little or no risk to the privacy of the individuals in the data set. The approach of 'consent or anonymise' allows data custodians simply to apply a rule and does not require a case-by-case evaluation of risk or ongoing monitoring of how the data is used and whether it is disclosed to a fourth party.[35]

31 Barocas and Nissenbaum, 'Computing Ethics' (n 27).

32 R Chevrier et al, 'Use and Understanding of Anonymization and De-Identification in the Biomedical Literature: Scoping Review' (2019) 21(5) *Journal of Medical Internet Research* e13484:1–15.

33 *Regulation (EU) 2016/679 of the European Parliament and of the Council of 27 April 2016 on the Protection of Natural Persons with Regard to the Processing of Personal Data and on the Free Movement of Such Data, and Repealing Directive 95/46/EC* (General Data Protection Regulation) [2016] OJ L 119/1, art 26.

34 Privacy Act 1988 (Cth) s 6, sch 1.

35 P Ohm, 'Broken Promises of Privacy: Responding to the Surprising Failure of Anonymization' (2010) 57(6) *UCLA Law Review* 1701; M Phillips, E Dove, and B Knoppers, 'Criminal Prohibition of Wrongful Reidentification: Legal Solution or Minefield for Big Data?' (2017) 14(4) *Journal of Bioethical Inquiry* 52; Mostert et al, 'Big Data in Medical Research and EU Data Protection Law' (n 19).

Some jurisdictions have embedded the use of anonymisation or de-identification as the alternative to informed consent in data protection legislation and research guidelines. For example, the 'Privacy Rule' made under the *Health Insurance Portability and Accountability Act 1996* (USA) defines a de-identification standard by listing the variables that must be removed. Once data has been de-identified according to this standard it is no longer considered personal health information and there are no longer any restrictions on its use or disclosure.[36] The data can be used for research without consent.

In the last decade, the effectiveness of this straightforward approach to protecting individual interests has been questioned. The concerns with anonymisation fall into three main areas:

1. re-identification may be easier than previously assumed;
2. de-identification has an adverse impact on the utility of the data; and
3. there are potential harms unrelated to re-identification.

2.2.4.1 Re-identification

There have been a number of highly publicised examples around the world where supposedly anonymised data sets have been re-identified. The re-identification in these cases has usually been done by academic researchers or journalists whose motives are to improve data privacy and security. People who are seeking to re-identify data for malicious purposes are unlikely to publish their results. These cases demonstrate that re-identification is technically possible, sometimes with little effort or technical skill.

In 2019, a group of researchers reported that they had developed methods that could re-identify 99.98 per cent of Americans in any available 'anonymised' data set by using just fifteen characteristics, including age, gender, and marital status.[37] In 2016, the Australian Government Department of Health published an anonymised 10 per cent sample of the Medicare Benefits Scheme and Pharmaceutical Benefits Scheme data on a public website. Shortly after publication, a group of researchers notified the government that they had been able to decrypt the identifiers for the healthcare providers in the data set and also re-identify a number of patients.[38]

Some experts in this area maintain that anonymisation is the best approach to privacy protection and that when appropriate anonymisation methods are used the risks to individuals are very low.[39] On the other hand, people who are concerned

[36] *Standards for Privacy of Individually Identifiable Health* 45 CFR §§ 164.510, 164.154 (2013).

[37] L Rocher, J Hendrickx, and Y de Montjoye, 'Estimating the Success of Re-identifications in Incomplete Datasets Using Generative Models' (2019) 10(1) *Nature Communications* 3069.

[38] C Culnane, B Rubinstein, and V Teague, *Health Data in an Open World* (Report No arXiv:1712.05627 [cs.CY], 18 December 2017).

[39] K El Emam, S Rodgers, and B Malin, 'Anonymising and Sharing Individual Patient Data' (2015) 350 *BMJ* 1–6; K El Emam and L Arbuckle, 'De-Identification: A Critical Debate', *Future of Privacy Forum* (Web Page, 24 July 2014) <https://fpf.org/2014/07/24/de-identification-a-critical-debate/>.

about the ease of re-identification suggest that as increasing volumes of data become available – both in the public arena and in collections held by a large number of private and public sector organisations – in conjunction with improving technology and skills available to those who seek to re-identify the data, this risk will only increase. In addition, sole reliance on anonymisation assumes all data custodians have the skills and resources to apply best-practice anonymisation techniques at all times. It is also likely to result in a never-ending re-identification arms race with those who seek to re-identify for malicious purposes.

2.2.4.2 Impact on the Utility of Data

Paul Ohm has claimed that '[d]ata can be either useful or perfectly anonymous but never both'.[40] The more you delete, supress, generalise, or otherwise perturb a data set in order to reduce the risk of re-identification the less useful it is to answer important research questions. Some types of data are particularly difficult to anonymise, for example images and free text.[41] Skilled data scientists continue to develop and improve anonymisation techniques while maximising the utility of the data. However, it is almost always necessary to trade off utility against privacy.[42] If anonymisation is required, then some research will not be possible or the quality and validity of the results may be questioned.

2.2.4.3 Other Harms

Anonymisation can only reduce or remove risks related to re-identification. There are other potential harms from the analysis of linked data even if the data is successfully anonymised. These include profiling, discrimination, and stigmatisation.[43] Such harms can extend beyond research participants to impact on anyone who shares relevant characteristics with research participants, for example increased insurance premiums for individuals that share a particular characteristic. As Barocas and Nissenbaum point out, anonymisation provides no protection from these kinds of risks:

> But rather than going to the trouble of attempting to re-associate 'anonymized' medical files with specific individuals, companies might instead discover patterns that allow them to estimate the likelihood someone has a particular medical condition. That certain institutions could meaningfully affect a person's experiences and prospects in the absence of identifying information or without violating

[40] Ohm (n 35) 1704.

[41] M Mostert et al, 'Privacy in Big Data Psychiatric and Behavioural Research: A Multiple-Case Study' (2018) 60 *International Journal of Law and Psychiatry* 40.

[42] J Rumbold and B Pierscionek, 'Contextual Anonymization for Secondary Use of Big Data in Biomedical Research: Proposal for an Anonymization Matrix' (2018) 6(4) *Journal of Medical Internet Research Medical Informatics* e47.

[43] Mostert et al, 'Big Data in Medical Research and EU Data Protection Law' (n 19).

> record-keepers' promises of anonymity defies the most basic intuitions about the value of anonymity.[44]

In addition, anonymisation does not protect against other potential harms, such as the infringement of individual dignity and autonomy caused by using personal information for research without consent. For the reasons discussed in this section, the traditional safeguards of voluntary and informed consent and anonymisation are not sufficient to adequately protect the moral interests of individuals in the context of research using linked data. A new paradigm is required to both protect individual interests and appropriately balance those collective and public interests that are also at play in this context.

2.3 COLLECTIVE INTERESTS

While individuals are recognised as moral agents with moral interests that demand respect and protection, there are other interests at play in the context of research using linked data, that is, the interests of particular groups and the broader public interest. It is possible to argue that groups or collectives have moral status and moral interests; but even without making this argument it is clear that groups, or the individuals who make up a particular group, have interests that might come into tension with the interests of a particular individual. This requires consideration of where a legitimate balance lies between the interests and rights of the individual and the interests of the collective or the public.

The whole community, for example, shares an interest in improved public health outcomes, that is, equitable access to improvements in health and well-being. Members of particular disease groups have an interest in advances related to their specific disease that may not be an interest shared by the whole community. Here, the whole community is one collective and the disease group is another collective. Groups can be harmed by, for example, poor public health outcomes but also by discrimination and stigmatisation based on public health research results. Because of this, and the nature of research using linked data, we would argue that the interests of individuals and of groups, including the whole community, need to be given serious consideration in decision making in this sphere.

The risks and benefits of sharing information are not necessarily confined to the individual who contributes data, since information about one person can reveal things about another. This is particularly acute with familial genetic information, but with Big Data analytics it now extends to all individual characteristics.

Linked data is used to examine the characteristics of a chosen cohort. The linked data sets extracted for health research are based on agreed characteristics or variables and then analysed for patterns and concurrence with other characteristics,

[44] Barocas and Nissenbaum, 'Computing Ethics' (n 27).

including diagnostic and treatment information, genetic information, behavioural patterns, and socio-demographic indicators. Participants are grouped according to their characteristics and those characteristics are given new significance by the research findings. Mittelstadt describes these as 'identity tokens based on shared characteristics'.[45] Current analytical techniques are used to make predictions and decisions about individuals based on shared characteristics. Everyone who shares those characteristics is affected, not just those whose data is included in the analysis, so the group has an interest in the conduct of the research and the application of the outcomes including any negative applications such as stigmatisation and discrimination.

Different types of groups who could potentially have interests in their data include:

- Groups that pre-exist the research project: the members are aware of their membership of the group either through active participation, for example a labour union, or through a collective identity, such as race, sex, religion, national origin, age, disability, or sexual orientation. The group may be the selected cohort for a research project or the identity marker may be a variable for analysis.
- Groups that are created by researchers using linked data: the identity of the group is defined by the classification system used in the research and the characteristics the researcher selects. The group characteristics then adhere to the individual, for example predictions about the future behaviour and preferences of group members are based on the group classification. The members are usually unaware they are part of a group.

In health research, the benefits of analysing large, linked data sets include a better understanding of the origins of disease and the efficacy of treatment. Population information is analysed to identify the concurrence of population characteristics with risk, protective factors, prognosis, and treatment efficacy. Linked data brings together real-world data from different sources and facilitates the longitudinal study of particular cohorts. Pre-existing collectives such as disease and disability groups or ethnic groups with a particular genetic or social risk can benefit from research focusing on the particular collective interest. These groups often initiate or sponsor research to address the area of collective interest.[46] Similarly, groups created by researchers can benefit from targeted improvements in diagnosis, treatment, and the delivery of health care.

45 B Mittelstadt, 'From Individual to Group Privacy in Big Data Analytics' (2017) 30(4) *Philosophy & Technology* 475.

46 See, eg, 'NTSAD', *National Tay-Sachs and Allied Diseases Association* (Web Page) <www.ntsad.org>; J Fitzpatrick et al, 'The Lililwan Project: Study Protocol for a Population-Based Active Case Ascertainment Study of the Prevalence of Foetal Alcohol Spectrum Disorders (FASD) in Remote Australian Aboriginal Communities' (2012) 2 *BMJ Open* e000968:1–11.

However, there are also collective risks in over-generalisation. Group characteristics can be used to entrench discrimination against recognised minority or marginalised groups and lead to stigmatisation.

> Racism, sexism, and other forms of bigotry and prejudice are still pervasive in contemporary society, but new technologies have a tendency to obscure the ways in which societal biases are baked into algorithmic decision-making.[47]

There are similar risks for groups created by researchers. The publication of results can lead to the stigmatisation of such groups. Discrimination may be evident in unequal treatment based on group predictions rather than on individual predictions based on individual health information.[48] Individuals may be unaware of the group characteristics with which they are being labelled and the way in which these characteristics are being used to make decisions. Some individual members of groups – for example, those based on race, sex, age, disability, and religion – have rights under anti-discrimination laws that can be pursued by individual members of the group, but the individual complaint mechanism does not address systemic problems. In any event, it may be difficult to seek redress for such harms in the context of algorithmic analysis. The implementation of automated decision making by computer systems could be seen as more objective than human beings making decisions on a case-by-case basis. It may, as a consequence, be more difficult to prove discrimination against a computer system that has denied a particular health care or social benefit when it was just running an algorithm.[49]

There can be a significant power imbalance between the data holders and each of these types of groups. This is because the data holders have large amounts of data on all groups, the skills and the technology to analyse the data, and often the power to act in ways that impact the groups and group members. Research using linked data will usually be opaque to the subjects of the research since they may have no knowledge that the research is being conducted or of the variables being analysed or the classifications and predictions being made and so are unable to exert any rights they may have to protect their interests. This power imbalance is magnified in the case of groups created by researchers as the members are likely to be unaware that they are members of a relevant group.

In the commercial field, for example, retailers regularly analyse purchase data to identify types of shoppers and target their advertising and pricing accordingly. In

47 D Boyd, K Levy, and A Marwick, 'Networked Nature of Algorithmic Discrimination' in S Gangadharan, V Eubank, and S Barocas (eds), *Data and Discrimination: Collected Essays* (New America Open Technology Institute, 2014) 53, 56.

48 M Favaretto, E de Clercq, and B Elger, 'Big Data and Discrimination: Perils, Promises and Solutions: A Systematic Review' (2019) 6(1) *Journal of Big Data* 1; I Cohen et al, 'The Legal and Ethical Concerns That Arise from Using Complex Predictive Analytics in Health Care' (2014) 33(7) *Health Affairs* 1139.

49 V Eubanks, 'Big Data and Human Rights' in Gangadharan, Eubank and Barocas (n 47) 48.

one case, the Target retail corporation used a combination of consent and anonymisation to conduct an analysis of purchase data to identify customers who were pregnant. The subsequent targeted advertising campaign resulted in the disclosure of sensitive health information about their pregnant customers. Individual female customers may have understood that they shared purchase information on unscented lotion, vitamins, and hand sanitiser with Target. It is unlikely that they were aware that conclusions were being drawn about their pregnancy status.[50]

Identity and the control of identity have a value apart from any resulting decisions or consequences. Members of a group may have an interest in the group's identity and hence in research that alters that identity. Loss of control of group identity is more likely to be felt by recognised groups who have a well-defined sense of collective identity. The dangers are illustrated by the case of the Havasupai Indian Tribe in Arizona. A genetic study commenced in the 1990s used blood samples collected from members of the tribe who understood that they would be used to study the high prevalence of diabetes in their community. The samples were shared with other researchers for various projects, including a study of schizophrenia and another on evolutionary genetics. These two studies were particularly problematic because of the risk of stigmatisation from the first and the damage to the tribe's origin beliefs from the second. Legal claims against the Arizona State University for misuse of the blood samples were ultimately settled out of court.[51] While these studies were not data linkage studies, they illustrate the risks to group identity.[52] Mittelstadt argues that a group's claim for protection from changes to identity without consent should be recognised.[53] Rather than focusing on consent by each individual in the group this suggests that negotiation, or at least consultation, with the group is required.

There may be other intangible harms that are felt at the group level. The complex and sometimes black-box approach of Big Data analytics, combined with the reality that some organisations have vast quantities of data and other groups have little access to data, may engender a sense of powerlessness in certain groups and communities. This may lead to disengagement at a community level. The constant profiling and surveillance of the whole population and subgroups within a population may also lead to the community feeling like it is constantly under surveillance. This can lead to a 'chilling effect'. In the health context, this could result in people from some groups being less likely to seek health care and, if they do, to try and conceal information from healthcare providers.

50 C Duhigg, 'How Companies Learn Your Secrets', *New York Times* (online, 16 February 2012) <www.nytimes.com/2012/02/19/magazine/shopping-habits.html>.

51 M Mello and L Wolf, 'The Havasupai Indian Tribe Case: Lessons for Research Involving Stored Biologic Samples' (2010) 363(3) *New England Journal of Medicine* 204.

52 Concerns over the appropriation of data have led to a movement for data sovereignty for indigenous people: see, eg, T Kukutai and J Taylor (eds), *Indigenous Data Sovereignty: Towards an Agenda* (Australian National University Press, 2016).

53 Mittelstadt (n 45).

These collective interests will not be protected by data protection legislation that focuses explicitly and exclusively on individual privacy interests or by requiring consent or anonymisation. Floridi emphasises the importance of this in the context of Big Data analytics, including anonymised data collections:

> Open Data is more likely to treat types (of customers, users, citizens, demographic population etc) rather than tokens (you, Alice, me ...), and hence groups rather than individuals. But re-identifiable groups are ipso facto targetable groups. It is therefore a very dangerous fallacy to think that if we protect personal data that identify individuals, the protection of groups will take care of itself.[54]

Current data protection legislation assumes that if we protect the data of each individual separately then groups will automatically be protected too. If no individual can be identified in the data set, then the assumption is that there is no risk of harm and the protective rights do not apply. It could be argued that human rights and research ethics have a similar focus on protecting individuals.

In the era of Big Data, the analytic focus is on identifying types of people who then can be the subjects of an action or a decision. It is the group that may benefit or be harmed by such decisions and so it is the group that must be protected.

> The individual sardine may believe that the encircling net is trying to catch it. It is not. It is trying to catch the whole shoal. It is therefore the shoal that needs to be protected, if the sardine is to be saved ... Sometimes the only way to protect the individual is to protect the group to which the individual belongs. Preferably before any disaster happens.[55]

2.4 PUBLIC INTERESTS

Research using linked data can lead to advances in disease prevention, diagnosis, treatment, and healthcare delivery. While individual research participants may receive no direct benefit from participation in a particular project, all members of society benefit indirectly from long-term improvements in health, health care, and equitable access to these benefits.

The previous sections discussed the interests of individuals and of collectives or groups in society. This section identifies the interests and concerns that affect the welfare of a broader collective, that is, the general public. What is in the public interest must benefit the collective rather than any particular individual or group within the broader collective. Individuals and groups in any collective will have competing interests, and if we are to recognise, respect, and promote public interests we must recognise that 'such policies promote the welfare, not of each, and not even necessarily of most, but of the public as a whole'.[56] It is important to consider whether

[54] L Floridi, 'Open Data, Data Protection, and Group Privacy' (2014) 27(1) *Philosophy & Technology* 1.

[55] Ibid 3.

[56] F Oppenheim, 'Self-Interest and Public Interest' (1975) 3(3) *Political Theory* 259, 265.

research using linked data is in the public interest in this sense, considering the relevant risks and benefits.

Initiatives to collect, link, and use data for research, and health research in particular, aim to improve:

- the general health and welfare of the community;
- the prevention, diagnosis, and treatment of disease; and
- the efficiency and equity of health care delivery.

Where research successfully contributes to these aims, the challenge is to ensure that the risks and benefits of the research are distributed justly and that all members of the community share in the results fairly. This does not mean that any particular individual or group in the community will directly benefit from a particular improvement in public health, diagnosis, and treatment of disease, or the increased efficiency of the healthcare system, but that the public, as a whole, will benefit.

The general community also has an interest in the data collections themselves and in other elements of the data linkage infrastructure. This is particularly clear in public health systems where the data collections contain data from all members of the community and the infrastructure is financed through public expenditure. The public have an interest in the creation of this public asset and in maximising its beneficial use, but it cannot be described as a 'public good' in the economic sense. Public goods are defined as goods that do not decrease by consumption (non-rivalrous) and from use of which no one can be excluded (non-excludable). While data collections may be non-rivalrous, they are not non-excludable since access to the data is strictly limited.[57] In contrast, it can be argued that the knowledge outcomes of the research are public goods in this sense if they are publicly available.

Privacy is commonly framed as a private good – akin to private property that is both rivalrous and excludable – and most privacy regulation is focused on protecting an individual's right to control access to information about themselves. However, the value of privacy goes beyond the individual because privacy harms can have an impact on a whole society. While ecological studies indicate that humans, like all animals, need some degree of seclusion for their well-being,[58] scholars also argue that privacy is essential for the healthy functioning of a society that promotes human flourishing and fosters creativity and innovation.[59]

> Part of what makes a society a good place in which to live is the extent to which it allows people freedom from the intrusiveness of others. A society without privacy

57 A Bialobrzeski, J Ried, and P Dabrock, 'Differentiating and Evaluating Common Good and Public Good: Making Implicit Assumptions Explicit in the Contexts of Consent and Duty to Participate' (2012) 15(5) *Public Health Genomics* 285.

58 Moore (n 13).

59 Cohen (n 15).

protection would be suffocating, and it might not be a place in which most would want to live.[60]

Clarke has expressed the view that it is a serious mistake to limit consideration of privacy to the personal sphere. Privacy is essential to flourishing societies, economies, and polities. Economically, individuals need to be free to innovate. As innovation may require deviation from the norm, individuals need privacy in which to experiment. Politically, individuals need to be free to think, argue, and act. Clarke's view is that surveillance has a chilling effect on these behaviours and thus has the potential to undermine democracy.[61]

One particular aspect of the public interest in privacy is its importance in health care. Privacy contributes to the trust in and quality of health services by ensuring that patients feel confident to confide in their health professionals. If patients are concerned about confidentiality, they may be less likely to visit health professionals or to share sensitive information. This can impact on the timing and effectiveness of health care, which has the potential to put an increasing burden on the health system. Thus, protecting privacy in the healthcare system benefits both the individual and the community.

The public interest in respecting privacy is recognised in ethics guidelines, the common law, and in data protection legislation that require a balance to be drawn between two conflicting public interests: the public interest in the disclosure and use of information on the one hand and the public interest in respecting individual privacy on the other hand.[62]

Legislation and policies governing the release of data without consent frequently require that the activity be in the 'public interest'. These public interest tests are generally imprecise, with very little guidance given to decision makers. What is in the public interest is contextual and will change over time and with societal customs, conventions, and values. It is understood as a normative test that requires evaluation of the impact of the activity and a conclusion that, overall, there will be a positive impact for the community or a segment of the community.[63] The public interest tests are usually expressed as a threshold test but are understood as a mechanism to identify and weigh competing claims.[64] In this context, the relevant

60 D Solove, '"I've Got Nothing to Hide" and Other Misunderstandings of Privacy' (2007) 44(4) *San Diego Law Review* 745, 762.

61 R Clarke, 'What's "Privacy"?' (Research Paper, Australian Law Reform Commission, 28 July 2006).

62 See, eg, *X* v. *Y* [1988] 2 All ER 648; National Health and Medical Research Council, 'Guidelines Approved Under Section 95A of the Privacy Act 1988' (2014) 23 [D.4]; *National Health Act* 1953 (Cth) s. 135A(3)(a).

63 The NSW Privacy Commissioner has defined 'in the public interest' to mean that 'the outcome of a research or statistical activity should have a positive impact on, or be relevant to, the community or a segment of the community as distinct from a matter of purely private or personal interest': Information and Privacy Commission, 'Statutory Guidelines on Research: *Health Records and Information Privacy Act 2002* (NSW)' (1 September 2004).

64 B Capps, 'Defining Variables of Access to UK Biobank: The Public Interest and the Public Good' (2013) 5(1) *Law, Innovation and Technology* 113.

claims would include not just public interests but also the individual and collective interests identified in this chapter.

2.5 MORAL LEGITIMACY IN DECISION MAKING

Research using linked data can make a significant contribution to the well-being of individuals and particular groups in society and can contribute to improving the health and well-being of the community as a whole, but it comes with risks to both individuals and collective and public interests. In the previous sections, we discussed the interests at stake. Decisions about data linkage and the use of data for research must take account of these interrelated interests. This is clearly a complex task. The moral claims that emerge from the interests discussed in the previous sections claims to:

- respect for dignity;
- respect for autonomy;
- respect for privacy;
- protection from harm (individual, collective, and community harms);
- promotion of human flourishing (individual, collective, and community flourishing); and
- fair distribution of burdens and benefits.

The ethical challenge of research using linked data is usually framed as an opposition between individual autonomy and the public interest, but, as can be seen in this chapter, the challenges are more complex. The interests are interwoven and interdependent. Individuals have an interest in autonomy and privacy but they, or the people about whom they care, also benefit from improvements in health care. Research into the causes and treatment of disease is a public benefit, but there is also a public interest in privacy and the maintenance of confidential relationships in health care. Individual, collective, and public interests cannot be neatly separated into a binary analysis. If decision making about data linkage and the use of data for research is to have moral legitimacy, then the individual, collective, and public interests must all be recognised and considered.

Traditional bioethical frameworks, developed in the context of clinical care and clinical research, place primary emphasis on protecting individual interests, such as autonomy and protection from harm, but there has been sustained criticism of this emphasis in the context of public health interventions, public health research, and in biobank and data-based research. The essence of the criticism is that the existing framework is too individualistic, ignoring the interconnectedness of people and the importance of cooperation and community for human flourishing. Highly individualistic approaches drawing on the Western liberal tradition stress the individual interests of those directly involved, such as research participants. In contrast, communitarian approaches prioritise the common good and well-being of the society as a whole and provide more scope to consider all those affected.[65] The authors consider that in relation to research using linked data a wide lens needs to be adopted to properly consider the interests of individuals, groups, and the community. In considering these issues, it is helpful to draw on existing thought in relation to public health ethics and the additional values of solidarity and reciprocity.

2.5.1 *Public Health Ethics*

It has been argued that the emphasis on consent and autonomy in traditional bioethics fails to adequately address the core ethical concerns in public health – the collective nature of public health and the legitimate use of the coercive power of the state – and provides very little guidance as to when it is ethical to override individual autonomy.[66] These are also the core ethical concerns for research using linked data.

First, research using linked data is a civil project dependent on collective activity. Just as public health improvements require collective action so too does research using linked data. The benefits of research using linked data cannot be realised without whole community involvement. The data collections and the linkage infrastructure are jointly created public assets. Administrative data is collected by government and includes information from the whole population. Significant public resources go into collecting and managing the data and into creating data linkage infrastructure.[67] The data itself is about individuals and many people see it as a part of themselves and as belonging to them; however, it can also be seen as jointly created by the data contributor and the collector.[68] The outcomes of research such as improved healthcare services are public benefits that are delivered to everyone irrespective of individual choice.[69]

There is also a parallel between public health and data linkage in the use of coercive powers. Public health initiatives include mandatory screening, treatment and vaccination, quarantine, and infectious diseases reporting to prevent the spread of disease. They also include mandatory regulation governing the safety of food and other products, water, and premises. Research using linked data, particularly

65 B Jennings, 'Relational Ethics for Public Health: Interpreting Solidarity and Care' (2019) 27(1) *Health Care Analysis* 4; M Sutrop, 'Viewpoint: How to Avoid a Dichotomy Between Autonomy and Beneficence: From Liberalism to Communitarianism and Beyond' (2011) 269(4) *Journal of Internal Medicine* 375.

66 N Kass, 'An Ethics Framework for Public Health' (2001) 91(11) *American Journal of Public Health* 1776; J Childress et al, 'Public Health Ethics: Mapping the Terrain' (2002) 30(2) *Journal of Law, Medicine & Ethics* 170; O O'Neill, 'Accountability, Trust and Informed Consent in Medical Practice and Research' (2004) 4(3) *Clinical Medicine* 269.

67 A Ballantyne and G Schaefer, 'Consent and the Ethical Duty to Participate in Health Data Research' (2018) 44(6) *Journal of Medical Ethics* 392.

68 A Sexton et al, 'The Role and Nature of Consent in Government Administrative Data' (2018) 5(2) *Big Data & Society* 1.

69 O'Neill, 'Informed Consent and Public Health' (n 29).

administrative data, relies on statutory authority rather than on the consent of the participants, so it too involves the coercive powers of the state. The autonomy of individuals is limited in order to pursue the public benefits of research.

The focus of public health ethics has been on how and when coercion is justified. The starting premise is that individual freedom and autonomy are highly valued and should be maximised. Interventions should minimise the infringement of individual liberty.[70] The use of the coercive powers of the state raises moral concerns at the heart of human rights discourse and public health ethics draws on this discourse through the concepts of proportionality and necessity. The principle of reciprocity, discussed in the section on reciprocity in this chapter, is also prominent in public health ethics, with an emphasis on minimising the impact on those who bear the burden of interventions and a fair distribution of burdens and benefits.[71]

Childress and colleagues describe the moral concerns of public health and cluster them into those relating to the goals of public health – 'producing benefits, preventing harms, and maximizing utility' – and those directed at justice and protecting individual liberty.[72] They suggest that the justificatory conditions relevant to resolving conflict between these concerns and to determining when public health goals justify overriding other moral concerns are effectiveness, proportionality, necessity, least infringement, and public justification.

Ballantyne proposes that this framework should be used to analyse the ethical issues in the use of health data because it focuses attention on justice, equity, and power. She identifies the core values as:

- public benefit (scientific integrity and social value);
- proportionality (necessity and least infringement);
- equity (solidarity and reciprocity);
- trust (engagement); and
- accountability (public justification and transparency).[73]

We agree that these values are central to resolving the ethical issues relating to research using linked data. They should inform the decisions about linking and using data and should be embedded in the decision-making processes. Limits on individual autonomy can only be justified where there is a worthwhile benefit that is proportional to the infringement on individual rights and interests. It can only be justified where there is no other way of achieving the benefit and where the infringement is minimised as much as possible. It is also essential that the benefits

70 A Dawson and B Jennings, 'The Place of Solidarity in Public Health Ethics' (2012) 34(1) *Public Health Reviews* 65.

71 A Viens, 'Public Health, Ethical Behavior and Reciprocity' (2008) 8(5) *American Journal of Bioethics* 1.

72 Childress et al (n 66).

73 Ballantyne (n 28) 357–8.

and burdens are distributed fairly overall. Not only the decisions but the decision-making processes must reflect these values. Those with a moral interest should be included in decision making and there should be accountability in the decision-making process and in the conduct of the research endeavour.

2.5.2 *Solidarity*

The concept of solidarity focuses on the interconnectedness of people, being 'bound together', and the interdependency of people and communities for their well-being.[74] Linking administrative data for research is a practice based on solidarity and depends on the recognition and acceptance of people's interdependence. Solidarity requires the recognition of shared attributes and concerns and identification with others. It is receiving increasing attention in bioethical writing and is seen as providing another perspective to balance the dominant concern with autonomy.

Dawson and Jennings capture the essential essence of solidarity in the idea of 'standing beside' others and suggest it requires a public act of identification. It is an act of concern for others motivated by 'sympathy and understanding'.[75] It indicates recognition of the others' moral worth and their claims to freedom, dignity, and consideration.[76]

Prainsack and Buyx emphasise bearing costs and describe solidarity as 'shared practices reflecting a collective commitment to carry "costs" (financial, social, emotional or otherwise) to assist others'.[77] In the context of research using linked data, the 'cost' is access to information about oneself and often the loss of the right to decide on that access. This cost is borne collectively in the expectation that improvements in medical treatment and health care will benefit others.

Prainsack and Buyx describe three tiers in the practice of solidarity: individual acts of solidarity at an interpersonal level; group practices where acts of solidarity become normalised and accepted as good conduct; and contractual or legal manifestations where solidarity practices solidify into legal arrangements such as social welfare.[78] This last tier would include statutory arrangements for the collection of data and the establishment of data linkage infrastructure. This tier suggests that solidarity practices, such as contribution to data-based research, can be coerced. Acts that are coerced in the face of reluctance cannot be seen as acts of solidarity by individuals; however, institutional and legal arrangements can be premised

74 B Prainsack and A Buyx, 'Thinking Ethical and Regulatory Frameworks in Medicine from the Perspective of Solidarity on Both Sides of the Atlantic' (2016) 37(6) *Theoretical Medicine and Bioethics* 489.

75 Dawson and Jennings (n 70) 74.

76 Jennings (n 65).

77 B Prainsack and A Buyx, *Solidarity: Reflections on an Emerging Concept in Bioethics* (Report, Nuffield Council on Bioethics, November 2011) 46 [5.3].

78 Ibid 47–9.

on solidarity and they may represent a collective practice of solidarity even if they include dissenting individuals.

The concept of solidarity clearly carries moral weight, but it is understood as a background condition rather than an ethical principle. It recognises humans' innate need for community and requires us to consider what connects us. Dawson and Jennings suggest that ethical analysis should start from the community rather than the individual – from an understanding that our concerns and interests are all interconnected rather than from an oppositional analysis of you versus me.[79] Harman says that 'solidarity demands common action ... to realise useful standards of decency and justice' and it 'emphasises the role of duties ... towards individuals and communities'.[80] He argues, therefore, that solidarity supports a duty to participate in research.[81]

When solidarity is regarded as an essential part of the nature of human beings it offers a different perspective on the development of policy and governance practices and has normative force. Prainsack and Buyx argue that policies and governance practices that recognise this willingness to identify with others and carry costs for others will be preferable to those that do not.[82] Policies and practices that support solidarity will strengthen the communities that are essential for our well-being.

The recognition at the heart of the concept of solidarity that individuals are embedded in social communities is particularly relevant to public health. The interrelationship between people and the impact of social conditions and structural inequities on health is the foundation of public health research and public health interventions. Research using linked data is particularly valuable in enriching our understanding of the relationship between health and social determinants. Data from different sources such as education, social welfare, justice, and housing can be linked to health data to investigate these relationships.[83]

The use of linked administrative data for research rests on the concept of solidarity. People accept the use of their information for research because they know that we all share a common goal of improving health care that can only be achieved collectively. However, there are dangers in overreliance on solidarity at the expense of individual interests and rights. There is particular danger in the context of top-down governance where assumptions are made about the willingness to bear costs for others. The maintenance of solidarity is crucial to the ongoing practice of data linkage for research. Factors that are likely to be critical to this include confidence

79 Dawson and Jennings (n 70).

80 S Harmon, 'Solidarity: A (New) Ethic for Global Health Policy' (2006) 14(4) *Health Care Analysis* 215. See also R Chadwick and K Berg, 'Solidarity and Equity: New Ethical Frameworks for Genetic Databases' (2001) 2(4) *Nature Reviews Genetics* 318.

81 Harmon (n 80).

82 B Prainsack and A Buyx, 'Understanding Solidarity (with a Little Help from Your Friends)' (2012) 5(2) *Public Health Ethics* 206.

83 L Roos et al, 'Poverty and Early Childhood Outcomes' (2019) 143(6) *Paediatrics* e20183426.

that benefits will in fact flow to those intended to benefit and adequate protection from individual and collective risks.[84] Adequate compensation or mitigation if harms eventuate is also essential before individuals can be expected to show solidarity.[85] Woods emphasises the importance of the active involvement of community voices in negotiating the governance practices to ensure that the claims of solidarity and the details of governance reflect community views.[86] Coerced participation based on statutory authority will undermine solidarity if it goes beyond the accepted norms of the community.

Solidarity is vital in maintaining flourishing societies and in our view is an appropriate measure for evaluating the legal and ethical frameworks and the decision making for research using linked data. This kind of research relies on solidarity and the regulatory regimes should sustain and foster community solidarity.

2.5.3 *Reciprocity*

Support for research using linked data, and indeed for participation in health research more generally, is often framed in terms of reciprocity. Since, at some stage, everyone benefits from improvements in medical treatment, healthcare delivery, and public health then it is fair that we all contribute to those benefits by participating in research.

Reciprocity requires that there should be a fair exchange of benefits and obligations. Members of a community incur obligations to others in the community because they will or have themselves received benefits. Social cooperation involves a mutual exchange and there should be a proportionate balancing between the benefits and burdens of the exchange.[87] Those who benefit from research should contribute and should not burden others disproportionately.

Reciprocity is a contractarian concept that takes its moral force from a hypothetical contract and mutual agreement. Social living requires cooperation and there must be agreement on the basic rules in order to benefit from that cooperation. Rational beings would be prepared to limit their individual freedom and interests to benefit from being part of the community.[88]

Where benefits can only be achieved collectively, then there is often considered to be an obligation to contribute to their creation, for example through taxation. These can be legal obligations, but they are also seen as a moral obligation based on

84 Chadwick and Berg (n 80).

85 B Prainsack and A Buyx, 'A Solidarity-Based Approach to the Governance of Research Biobanks' (2013) 21(1) *Medical Law Review* 71.

86 S Woods, 'Big Data Governance: Solidarity and the Patient Voice' in B Mittelstadt and L Floridi (eds), *The Ethics of Biomedical Big Data* (Springer International Publishing, 2016).

87 Viens (n 71).

88 *Stanford Encyclopedia of Philosophy* (online at 20 June 2020) 'Contractarianism' <https://plato.stanford.edu/archives/sum2018/entries/contractarianism/>.

fairness. Those who fail to contribute are termed 'free riders' as they unfairly receive the benefits without contributing. The use of people's information for research can be seen in the same way. The statutory authority for the release of information for research effectively imposes a legal duty to contribute to research but it can also be argued that reciprocity gives rise to a moral duty to contribute to research.[89]

While the benefits achieved through research using linked data are not always distributed equally, or equitably, we all benefit in some way from the advances in disease prevention, diagnosis and treatment, and improvements in health care. Since we accept these benefits, fairness requires that we ought to support and contribute to this research. An ethical duty to participate is also grounded in the principle of beneficence that encompasses an ethical duty to help others.[90] The 'rule of rescue' suggests that there is a moral obligation to help others where there is small personal risk of harm and a serious risk to others.[91]

Ballantyne and Schaefer argue that an obligation to participate in research is particularly relevant to the use of public health data in research because it is a public resource and that a moral duty to participate justifies the expansion of the secondary use of identifiable public health data for research without consent. They challenge the default position that consent is required on the grounds that there is an ethical obligation to share health information for research. They suggest that the 'impracticability of consent' test for a waiver of consent should be removed and the 'public good' test strengthened.[92]

The strength of reciprocity lies in a shared understanding of the benefits of community cooperation. It depends on agreement that community cooperation will produce benefits that are worth having and confidence that the benefits and burdens will be distributed fairly. The processes for linkage and the research use of linked data are not widely understood so robust community debate is essential to support the value of reciprocity. Human rights, legal and ethical frameworks, and the decision-making processes can play a role in ensuring that there is a fair exchange in research using linked data and that the community accepts that benefits and burdens are fairly distributed.

2.6 CONCLUSION

This chapter has considered how research using linked data affects the interests of individuals, groups, and the public; the way in which these interests are entwined; and ethical values that address this interrelationship. Those who are entrusted to

89 J Harris, 'Scientific Research Is a Moral Duty' (2005) 31(4) *Journal of Medical Ethics* 242; S Chan and J Harris, 'Free Riders and Pious Sons: Why Science Research Remains Obligatory' (2009) 23(3) *Bioethics* 161.

90 Ibid.

91 Ibid; Ballantyne and Schaefer (n 67).

92 Ballantyne and Schaefer (n 67).

make decisions about the linkage of data and its use for research need to recognise the full range of these diverse interests and values if their decisions are to have moral legitimacy.[93]

The decision-making frameworks, principles, and policies should support the transparent consideration of these multiple, divergent, and sometimes conflicting interests and values. There are two minimal requirements to achieve this. First, there should be explicit and transparent consideration of the conflicting interests, concerns, and consequences. This includes the contribution of the project to the welfare of the community and the impact on individuals and groups.[94] Second, decisions should be made in consultation with those with a morally relevant interest.[95]

This book focuses on countries where it has been accepted that the public interest can prevail over individual self-determination and that identifiable health information can be used for data linkage and research without individual consent. Decision makers must decide when this is justified. To do this, they should consider whether the likely benefit is justified by the infringement of individual rights and interests and whether the distribution of benefits and burdens is fair. The practice of research using linked data is supported by the values of solidarity and reciprocity. However, these values can only bear that weight if there is a shared understanding of common goals and if the use of individual information for research reflects contemporary norms about the flow of information. Robust community engagement and accountability are essential to obtain that shared understanding and to support the moral legitimacy of research using linked data.

In summary, our conclusions in this chapter are that:

1. The relevant interests are complicated and interwoven. There is not just a binary opposition of interests.
2. The decision-making regime should explicitly recognise and evaluate all interests.
3. Consent and anonymisation are no longer adequate to protect individual interests and ignore collective interests.
4. All those with a moral stake should be included in the decision making.
5. Decisions and decision making should be informed by public benefit, proportionality, equity, engagement, and accountability.
6. The human rights, legal, and ethical frameworks for decision making should support solidarity and reciprocity.

93 D Melé and J Armengou, 'Moral Legitimacy in Controversial Projects and Its Relationship with Social License to Operate: A Case Study' (2016) 136(4) *Journal of Business Ethics* 729.

94 Ibid.

95 R Anderson, *The Collection, Linking and Use of Data in Biomedical Research and Health Care: Ethical Issues* (Report, Nuffield Council on Bioethics, 2015) ch 5.

3

Social Licence

3.1 INTRODUCTION

Our social licence to operate as scientists needs to be founded on a continually renewed relationship of trust between scientists and society.[1]

Social licence is broadly understood as indicating ongoing community acceptance and support for an activity. It is an indicator that an enterprise is seen as legitimate, credible, and trustworthy and that it meets the expectations and demands of the community.[2] The term 'social licence' is used as a metaphor to contrast legal authorisation with social acceptance and suggests that enterprises

[1] D King, *Rigour, Respect, Responsibility: A Universal Ethical Code for Scientists* (United Kingdom Government Office for Science, 2007) 1.

[2] I Thomson and R Boutilier, 'The Social License to Operate' in P Darling (ed), *SME Mining Engineering Handbook* (Society for Mining, Metallurgy, and Exploration, 3rd ed, 2011) 1779 ('*The Social License to Operate*'); N Gunningham, R Kagan, and D Thornton, 'Social License and Environmental Protection: Why Businesses Go Beyond Compliance' (2004) 29(2) *Law & Social Inquiry* 307.

may need to go beyond legal and regulatory requirements to meet community expectations.[3]

The concept has been widely used in the resources industry since the late 1990s and it is now increasingly being used in the context of scientific research,[4] particularly data research.[5] The focus on social licence in the resources industry developed in the face of community resistance to mining projects and as a means of addressing the risks posed by this resistance.[6] Similarly, its use in the data field is emerging at a time when community concern and resistance to data use are increasingly evident. There is growing concern about data mining and the unfettered commercial use of data.[7] These concerns extend to the collection and use of data by governments. The acknowledgement that government data has a commercial value beyond its use in government programmes and attempts to exploit that commercial value have led to public resistance.[8] There is also public concern about the expansion of government use of data for security surveillance. Developments in the use of government-held data are supported by legislation but the criticism suggests that this is not enough to justify or sustain them. This leads to general questions about the extent of the social licence to use government data and more particularly to use government data for research using linked data.

Social licence has an earlier history stemming from the work of the sociologist Everett Hughes. He described a licence or privilege granted to an occupation or profession to do things that are not acceptable in wider society and a mandate to

3 Gunningham, Kagan, and Thornton (n 2).

4 R Boutilier, 'Frequently Asked Questions about the Social Licence to Operate' (2014) 32(4) *Impact Assessment and Project Appraisal* 263; R Boutilier, L Black, and I Thomson, 'From Metaphor to Management Tool: How the Social License to Operate Can Stabilise the Socio-Political Environment for Business' (Conference Paper, International Mine Management 2012 Conference, 20–21 November 2012).

5 M Dixon-Woods and R Ashcroft, 'Regulation and the Social Licence for Medical Research' (2008) 11(4) *Medicine, Health Care and Philosophy* 381; S Raman and A Mohr, 'A Social Licence for Science: Capturing the Public or Co-Constructing Research?' (2014) 28(3–4) *Social Epistemology* 258; P Carter, G Laurie, and M Dixon-Woods, 'The Social Licence for Research: Why care.data Ran into Trouble' (2015) 41(5) *Journal of Medical Ethics* 404; J Powles, 'There is No Social License for My Health Record: Australians Should Reject It', *Guardian* (online, 20 July 2018) <www.theguardian.com/commentisfree/2018/jul/20/there-is-no-social-license-for-my-health-record-australians-should-reject-it>; Australian Government, *Data Availability and Use* (Productivity Commission Inquiry Report No 82, March 2017) ('*Data Availability and Use*').

6 J Owen and D Kemp, 'Social Licence and Mining: A Critical Perspective' (2013) 38(1) *Resources Policy* 29.

7 P McGrath, C Blumer, and J Carter, 'Medical Appointment Booking App HealthEngine Sharing Clients' Personal Information With Lawyers', *ABC News* (online, 26 June 2018) <www.abc.net.au/news/2018-06-25/healthengine-sharing-patients-information-with-lawyers/9894114>; H Timms and J Heimans, 'Commentary: #DeleteFacebook Is Just the Beginning: Here's the Movement We Could See Next', *Fortune* (online, 17 April 2018) <https://fortune.com/2018/04/16/delete-facebook-data-privacy-movement/>.

8 A Pollock and P Roderick, 'Trust in the Time of Markets: Protecting Patient Information' (2014) 383(9928) *The Lancet* 1523.

establish the standards applicable to their domain.[9] He saw this as part of a bargain struck between a profession and society and the moral division of labour where a profession claims responsibility for particular functions because it is 'good for society'.[10] Hughes illustrates this with reference to the privilege granted to medical practitioners to handle the human body. In the past, medical practitioners also exercised a mandate to determine professional standards for both medical care and medical research. There is a clear parallel to researchers using people's sensitive health information in their work. In general, it is not acceptable to access personal health information, especially without the consent or knowledge of the person, for purposes other than their health care.[11] Researchers lay claim to a social licence to use people's health data in exchange for the beneficial outcomes produced by their research.

Social licence can play a role in clarifying the social dimensions of research using linked data and in bringing together the scientific and the social considerations. The world of data analysis, of numbers, codes, and algorithms, can appear devoid of human beings and deceptively value-free. The social licence framework draws attention to the social impact of research using linked data and invites consideration of the wider cultural and moral norms of the community.

We regard social licence as an essential analytical tool for developing and evaluating the decision-making framework for linking data and approving research using linked data. It is important to note, however, Owen and Kemp's view that social licence has not supported a collaborative development agenda in the resources industry because the substance and governance aspects of social licence have not been clearly articulated.[12] If social licence is to be valuable in the context of data linkage, then the challenge is to articulate the conditions that underpin community acceptance and support.

In this chapter, we consider the nature of social licence and its application to the research enterprise of linking data and using it for research. Our concern is not to determine whether there is currently evidence of a social licence for this enterprise, either generally or for particular projects, or to measure its strength. Our aim is to consider how the social licence concept can be used to design and evaluate the governance arrangements for research using linked data.

The first step is to understand community expectations of the conduct and outcomes of the research enterprise and the conditions under which they are likely to accept and support it. The governance structure itself must also be accepted and

9 E Hughes, 'The Dual Mandate of Social Science: Remarks on the Academic Division of Labour' (1959) 25(4) *Canadian Journal of Economics and Political Science/Revue Canadienne d'Economique et de Science Politique* 401.

10 Ibid 404.

11 P Gulliver et al, 'Qualitative Research: Surveys, Social Licence and the Integrated Data Infrastructure' (2018) 30(3) *Aotearoa New Zealand Social Work* 57.

12 Owen and Kemp (n 6).

have social licence. The second step, therefore, is to understand what the community expects of the governance mechanisms. The governance framework will need to address those conditions and meet those expectations to be trusted and accepted as legitimate.

3.2 WHAT IS SOCIAL LICENCE?

A social licence describes a relationship where the community accepts and supports an enterprise. It is built on past behaviour and interactions, on shared expectations and values, and the recognition of mutual benefits. Social licence is closely related to contractarian theories in that it relies on a notion of implicit agreement or exchange.[13] A project obtains the tacit agreement of the community because it is seen as beneficial. It is dependent on community perception that the organisation responsible for the project is trustworthy and a belief that it meets community expectations of how it should operate.[14] In this context, the word 'community' is used to include all the stakeholders in the enterprise.

The concept of social licence focuses attention on the social aspects of an enterprise. It draws attention to the nature of the privilege enjoyed by an enterprise and to its dependence on community support. In research using linked data, it draws attention to the privilege of access to and use of individual-level data and the individuals and communities that are involved. Gulliver and colleagues define social licence as 'societal acceptance that a practice that lies outside general norms may be performed by a certain agent, on certain terms' and add that 'it is the result of an ongoing process of negotiating terms with a wider societal group, and means that the practice can be performed by that agent without incurring social sanction'.[15]

The legal metaphor of a licence indicates the limits of legal regulation and points to the need to engage with the social context. It emphasises that legality is not necessarily enough to ensure community acceptance and the success of the enterprise. Enterprises may need to do more than comply with legal requirements to satisfy community expectations. However, the metaphor can be taken too far and can disguise the intangible and dynamic nature of the concept. There is no moment of permission and no power to grant permission. There are no fixed criteria, and the existence of a social licence is self-asserted. The idea that a social licence can be 'granted' by a society is clumsy because it draws attention away from the volatility of social licence, which fluctuates with changes in community perceptions and expectations and between different groups and stakeholders. Social licence is

[13] G Demuijnck and B Fasterling, 'The Social License to Operate' (2016) 136(4) *Journal of Business Ethics* 675.

[14] Gunningham, Kagan, and Thornton (n 2).

[15] Gulliver et al (n 11).

better understood as describing complex relationships that will constantly evolve and be re-evaluated.[16]

The concept of social licence recognises that enterprises and professions need the support of the community in which they operate. This is a truism that most businesses take for granted; however, where there is no direct relationship with the community as customers or clients, as is the case with the resources industry – and with much linked data research – the existence or absence of community support is not readily apparent. Because it is so intangible there is a danger that its existence is assumed and only discussed where there is overt opposition.[17] The default assumption is that social licence exists, and the rhetoric is directed at maintaining it. Where data linkage infrastructure is supported by statute the democratic process may lend some support to the assumption that the community supports the endeavour. This assumption is undermined where there is very little community knowledge, or public discussion, of the ways in which data is linked and used. Where there is no prior engagement or building of social licence then the public are likely to be engaged for the first time when concerns are raised.

Community opposition can take the form of boycotts, legal challenges, and media campaigns. Resistance may be organised by particular interest groups, such as privacy groups, or may be spontaneous, with social media enabling individuals to influence community opinion.[18] Internet-based communications and mobile apps allow anyone to distribute information and opinions and decrease the ability of organisations to influence opposition. The control of opinions and information is increasingly difficult in the contemporary media environment where anyone can speak to mass audiences.[19] The loss of social licence can have quantifiable costs to an enterprise through loss of reputation, increased regulation or enforcement of regulations, and loss of access to resources.[20]

If the community loses trust in the enterprise of data-based research or no longer sees it as legitimate, then the restrictions on data use, oversight, and regulatory hurdles may increase and funders may be reluctant to provide support. Individuals may be reluctant to participate in data-based studies when invited to do so and opt out if they can. Fears about the research use of data may undermine trust in the confidentiality of health information and patients may withhold information from healthcare providers. This has far-reaching consequences for the quality and efficiency of healthcare delivery.

16 M Dare, J Schirmer, and F Vanclay, 'Community Engagement and Social Licence to Operate' (2014) *Impact Assessment and Project Appraisal* 1; R Parsons and K Moffat, 'Constructing the Meaning of Social Licence' (2014) 28(3–4) *Social Epistemology* 340.

17 Parsons and Moffat (n 16).

18 See, eg, 'medConfidential: Keep Our Secrets', *medConfidential* (Web Page) <https://medconfidential.org/>.

19 J Gehman, L Lefsrud, and S Fast, 'Social License to Operate: Legitimacy by Another Name?' (2017) 60(2) *Canadian Public Administration* 293.

20 Parsons and Moffat (n 16); Gunningham, Kagan, and Thornton (n 2).

The failure of care.data – a National Health Service initiative in the United Kingdom (UK) to make primary health care information from general practitioners available for research through the national Health and Social Care Information Centre – has been explained in terms of loss of social licence. In considering the failure of this initiative, Carter, Laurie, and Dixon-Woods identified reciprocity, non-exploitation, and service of the public good as necessary conditions for social licence.[21] They noted that reciprocity must be based on a genuine engagement and dialogue. They concluded that there was inadequate prior consultation about care.data, leading to a lack of understanding of what was important to the public. The use of opt-out consent failed to provide the usual 'warrants of trust' and to assure people that they were protected from risk and exploitation. The information leaflet circulated in the community did not provide adequate information about how the data collected would be shared and used. The expectation that care.data would be used for research that would serve the public good and improve public health outcomes was confused by reference to efficiency and economic growth. The implementation of care.data illustrates how the lack of genuine community engagement can undermine the perceived legitimacy and community trust in a data-sharing project.

Several models of social licence have been developed in an effort to give the concept substance and describe the conditions required for social licence. Three normative components for social licence were identified by Thomson and Joyce in the context of resources industries: legitimacy, credibility, and trust.[22] Legitimacy is described as meeting established legal, social, and cultural norms. Credibility, or believability, is linked to the perception that the enterprise representatives listen, respond, and keep promises and it is dependent on effective community engagement.[23] Credibility then is a form of interactional trust that can deepen into institutional trust where the relationship is perceived to be one of mutual regard for each other's interests.[24] Boutilier and Thomson later refined their analysis to include four factors: economic legitimacy, socio-political legitimacy, interactional trust, and institutionalised trust.[25] Boutilier and Thomson saw these factors as a continuum reflecting different levels of social licence from mere acceptance to psychological identification with the project.[26]

[21] Carter, Laurie, and Dixon-Woods (n 5).

[22] I Thomson and S Joyce, 'The Social Licence to Operate: What It Is and Why Does It Seem So Difficult to Obtain?' (Convention Paper, Prospectors and Developers Association of Canada Convention, March 2008).

[23] D Jijelava and F Vanclay, 'Legitimacy, Credibility and Trust As the Key Components of a Social Licence to Operate: An Analysis of BP's Projects in Georgia' (2017) 140(P3) *Journal of Cleaner Production* 1077.

[24] Thomson and Boutilier (n 2).

[25] R Boutilier and I Thomson, 'Modelling and Measuring the Social Licence to Operate: The Fruits of a Dialogue Between Theory and Practice' (Conference Paper, International Mine Management, 2011).

[26] Thomson and Boutilier, *The Social License to Operate* (n 2).

Moffat and Zhang put community trust at the centre of their model of social licence and suggest that this will be dependent on how well the enterprise manages the impacts on the social infrastructure, the quantity and quality of community engagement, and the fairness of dealings with community members. The development of trust supports social acceptance of the enterprise.[27] In the context of the mining industry, surveys of public attitudes identify distributional fairness, procedural fairness, and confidence in governance as the key predictors of trust and social acceptance.[28]

Drawing on these theories we take trust and legitimacy to be the foundations of social licence.

3.3 FOUNDATIONS OF SOCIAL LICENCE

3.3.1 *Trust*

An enterprise that is trusted, that is perceived as reliable and responsive, and that has regard for a community's interests and well-being is more likely to attract community support. Rousseau and colleagues define trust as 'a psychological state comprising the intention to accept vulnerability based upon positive expectations of the intentions or behaviour of another'.[29] This definition captures the notion that trust presumes risk and imperfect knowledge.[30] Individual data subjects have little or no knowledge or control over the use of information about them. This is particularly the case with administrative data that is collected on a compulsory basis but is also true where data is provided with consent. Data subjects and communities are at risk from the mishandling of data but may accept that vulnerability because of a positive expectation that data custodians, linkage units, and researchers will protect their data and privacy and use the data for worthwhile purposes.

Rousseau's definition of trust emphasises an intention to accept vulnerability; however, for many data providers there is no real choice or intention. A patient who wants health care has no choice but to provide information to the healthcare provider and act as if they trust that the information they provide will be protected. A community with a public health system has little choice but to accept the collection of information necessary for the efficient operation of the health system. The choice is to forgo the service or accept the risk. Wynne notes that this dependency leads to 'as if' trust where a person accepts the risk and acts as if they trust.[31]

27 K Moffat and A Zhang, 'The Paths to Social Licence to Operate: An Integrative Model Explaining Community Acceptance of Mining' (2014) 39(1) *Resources Policy* 61.

28 K Moffat et al, 'The Social Licence to Operate: A Critical Review' (2016) 89(5) *Forestry* 477.

29 D Rousseau et al, 'Not So Different After All: A Cross-Discipline View of Trust' (1998) 23(3) *Academy of Management Review* 393, 395.

30 O O'Neill, 'Accountability, Trust and Informed Consent in Medical Practice and Research' (2004) 4(3) *Clinical Medicine* 269.

31 B Wynne, 'Public Engagement as a Means of Restoring Public Trust in Science: Hitting the Notes, but Missing the Music?' (2006) 9(3) *Community Genetics* 211.

The public are asked to trust that their information will be kept securely and their privacy protected, but they regularly see and hear stories of data breaches and violations. They are asked to trust that data custodians will find the right balance between using the data for the public good and keeping it safe, yet they may feel that they have no choice but to provide their information and no power to control how it is used.[32] In these circumstances, trust is hard-won and always likely to be ambivalent.

3.3.2 *Legitimacy*

Legitimacy is the second foundation stone of social licence. A legitimate enterprise is accepted because it conforms to the legal, cultural, and social norms of a society and where the entity responsible for the enterprise is regarded as acting in the best interests of the community. It is seen as proper and justified according to those norms. In organisational theory, legitimacy is described as 'a generalized perception or assumption that the actions of an entity are desirable, proper, or appropriate within some socially constructed system of norms, values, beliefs, and definitions'.[33] Research using linked data will be legitimate if the use of individuals' information is regarded as conforming to the society's norms.

Legitimacy can be regarded as either an instrumental or a normative concept. An instrumental approach relies on the perception of legitimacy and can be achieved where the community has in fact accepted that the activity is appropriate. Social licence is sometimes criticised because acceptance is possible even where people do not have a real understanding of the activity or are persuaded by manipulation. It can be regarded as merely a tool used to promote community acceptance, but this approach overlooks the necessity for moral content. A normative approach asks more than empirical acceptance and requires moral legitimacy based on the common good and substantive justice.[34] Moral legitimacy provides ethical support to social licence and takes it beyond a pragmatic concept. While it is feasible that social licence may be based on false perceptions, it will be a fragile licence if this is the case. A robust social licence will depend on intrinsic value and moral worth.

Moral legitimacy indicates that decisions should be made based on a shared understanding of the common good and substantive justice. However, in a diverse society there will be a range of views and interests and decisions taken may have negative consequences for some groups. The decision maker is faced with the

[32] A Sexton et al, 'A Balance of Trust in the Use of Government Administrative Data' (2017) 17 *Archival Science* 305; S Davidson et al, *Public Acceptability of Cross-Sectoral Data Linkage: Deliberative Research Findings* (Report, Scottish Government Social Research, 2012) ('*Public Acceptability of Cross-Sectoral Data Linkage*').

[33] M Suchman, 'Managing Legitimacy: Strategic and Institutional Approaches' (1995) 20(3) *Academy of Management Review* 571, 574.

[34] D Melé and J Armengou, 'Moral Legitimacy in Controversial Projects and Its Relationship with Social License to Operate: A Case Study' (2016) 136(4) *Journal of Business Ethics* 729.

problem of balancing partisan interests.[35] Decisions made based on the dominant or most powerful voice will not necessarily be morally legitimate. Decisions must be justified according to a broad consensus as to the common good.[36]

Research activity loses legitimacy where the norms followed by researchers diverge from those of the wider community. This was graphically illustrated by the Royal Liverpool Children's Inquiry that revealed that the tissue and organs of children were routinely retained after death for research purposes without the knowledge or consent of parents. The evidence of parents at the inquiry documents their outrage and sorrow on discovering that they had buried the bodies of their children without their organs. The inquiry found a vast gap between the research practices and the cultural and moral views of the community.[37]

Historically, medical practitioners and scientists exercised a mandate to set the standards of conduct in medical research and to determine what was acceptable.[38] The horrors of the experiments conducted under the Nazi regime undermined that mandate and revealed the weakness of self-regulation of medical research. The ethical guidelines for research and the requirements for research governance developed in the wake of those revelations have been premised on the need for independent oversight to ensure that the conduct of research aligned with the ethical values of the broader community. While the current regulation of research is criticised as being overly burdensome, the approval processes can help support a project's claims of legitimacy.[39] The research ethics review process involves independent oversight by a committee that includes a range of expertise and a cross section of society. This is one form of community consultation that ensures that decisions conform to society's norms. Community consultation on the establishment and linkage of data collections and community collaboration throughout the life of research projects will support legitimacy in the same way.

The focus in the social licence literature has been on social legitimacy and the need to go beyond legal legitimacy and compliance with the regulatory requirements. Jijelava and Vanclay describe social legitimacy as including respect for individuals and culture, fairness in dealings, benefiting the community, minimising harm, and upholding human rights.[40] These factors are reflected in findings of the qualitative studies discussed in this chapter that emphasise real benefits to the community and concerns about the security of data, the protection of privacy, and the potential for discriminatory impacts on minority or disadvantaged groups. They are also reflected in the desire for transparency and accountability.

[35] Owen and Kemp (n 6).
[36] Demuijnck and Fasterling (n 13).
[37] United Kingdom House of Commons, *The Royal Liverpool Children's Inquiry* (Report No MR/CJK071100, The Stationery Office, January 2001).
[38] Hughes (n 9).
[39] Dixon-Woods and Ashcroft (n 5).
[40] Jijelava and Vanclay (n 23).

The collection and linkage of administrative data for health research are largely done by government entities or publicly funded universities or research institutes in Australia, New Zealand, Canada, and the UK. In democratic countries such as these, claims of legitimacy are supported by democratic processes. Political legitimacy in democracies rests on the notion that decisions are made by us and for us. One would expect, therefore, that government law and policy would be aligned to the community's norms and values, but this alignment is weakened in rapidly changing spheres such as Big Data.[41] The law is often 'in the rear and limping' as it adjusts to scientific and technological developments.[42] Formal democratic processes may not be enough to ensure that the practice of research using linked data conforms to shared norms and values.

Legitimacy depends, in part, on the perception that citizens have been fairly engaged in the decision-making process and that their interests have been represented and understood.[43] It has a procedural element.[44] In the current climate of political cynicism, broad participation in the electoral process may be inadequate and other more informal, but more direct, methods of engagement may be necessary to ensure legitimacy. The failure of care.data in the UK is a clear illustration that legislative backing does not necessarily lead to social legitimacy. The passage of the *Health and Social Care Act 2012* (UK) through Parliament did not persuade the public that the collection, use, and disclosure of health information from general practitioners was legitimate. The implementation of care.data was seen as underhand and there was a perception that the public had not been told about it and that their views were not considered.[45] Legitimacy requires shared deliberation on how to achieve goals and benefits and compromise to resolve conflicting needs.

3.4 SOCIAL LICENCE FOR RESEARCH USING LINKED DATA

There are challenges in using the concept of social licence in the context of research using linked data. The development of social licence has occurred largely in the context of the resources industries where the focus is on local specific projects such as a mine or processing operation. Local community acceptance and support for the project are considered together with wider stakeholder concerns such as environmental interests.

In comparison, research using linked data involves a sequence of activities that may be conducted by different organisations. These include the original collection of the information from the individual, usually in the context of service delivery; the transfer of that data to a secondary data collection; the linkage of the data; the

[41] Gehman, Lefsrud, and Fast (n 19).
[42] *Mt Isa Mines* v. *Pusey* (1970) 125 CLR 383, 395 (Windeyer J.).
[43] M Smith and D Weinstock, 'Political Legitimacy and Research Ethics' (2019) 33(3) *Bioethics* 312.
[44] S Hershovitz, 'Legitimacy, Democracy and Razian Authority' (2003) 9(3) *Legal Theory* 201.
[45] Carter, Laurie, and Dixon-Woods (n 5); 'The Social Licence for Research'; M Taylor, 'Information Governance as a Force for Good? Lessons to be Learnt From care.data' (2014) 11(1) *SCRIPTed* 1.

extraction of linked data for a research project; the analysis of the linked data; the publication of the research; and the research translation. Different stakeholders will be involved at different stages and community acceptance is needed at all these stages (see Figure 3.1).

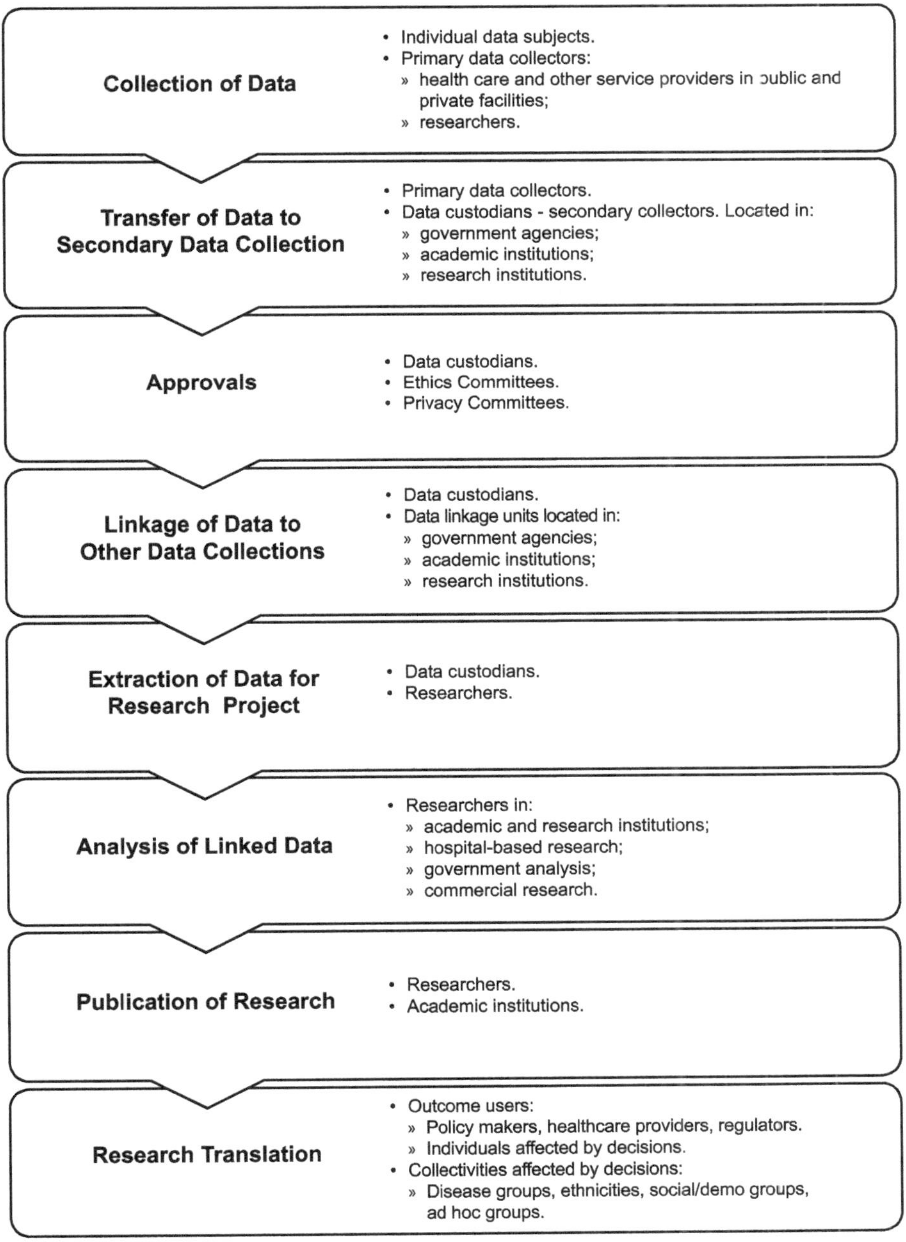

FIGURE 3.1 Stakeholders

Social licence needs to be considered in relation to each research project but, in addition, there needs to be community acceptance of the overall enterprise of linking data for research and the establishment of the infrastructure to support data linkage. This includes legislation mandating the collection of data and authorising its linkage and use for research; the establishment of data linkage units and repositories of linked data; the provision of secure access facilities; and the establishment of application and approval processes. The relevant stakeholders include political and social influencers such as traditional media providers, social media influencers, and professional lobby groups such as medical associations, consumer representative groups, civil rights groups, and privacy lobby groups.

There are other challenges in establishing and maintaining social licence for research using linked data. First, the benefits of research of this kind are diffuse and distant. The outcomes do not usually benefit individual participants in the way interventional studies can. The benefits are likely to be longer-term improvements in the diagnosis and treatment of illness and the delivery of health care that will benefit groups in the community or the whole community. Second, the data environment is volatile and rapidly changing. The social licence for data activities cannot be assumed to remain static and must evolve and be renegotiated with changing data uses. Third, general community concerns about the collection and use of data in a range of contexts provide a further challenge to the development of social licence for Big Data research. Concerns about the use of data for security surveillance and the commercial collection of data for marketing and political influencing will affect attitudes to research use of data. Reports of misuse of data, lost data, and security breaches also colour community perceptions.

3.5 PUBLIC VIEWS ON RESEARCH USING LINKED DATA

There is a growing body of empirical research exploring public views on the use of data in research generally and data-linkage research in particular. This research consistently reports general but conditional support for data-based research. The conditions for this support must be closely considered to understand when the community is likely to accept data linkage for research and what governance arrangements will develop and maintain social licence. We reviewed qualitative studies that considered the public views on research using linked data and research using administrative data to identify the conditions likely to support social licence.

The complexity of public views in this field is difficult to capture in quantitative studies but qualitative studies are better able to explore this complexity. For this reason, we limited our review of the literature to qualitative studies. A variety of qualitative methods have been adopted to explore attitudes to data sharing and data linkage for research, including focus groups, interviews, and deliberative democracy approaches. Deliberative methods where information is provided to participants are particularly appropriate in this context where public knowledge and understanding is low and the subject matter is complex.[46]

Careful attention needs to be paid to the context in which studies are conducted because public views are finely nuanced and demonstrate the balancing of competing concerns in different contexts.[47] There are many studies of public and patient attitudes in the context of genetic information and longitudinal biobanks and on the sharing of data collected by researchers; however, in these studies consent is a dominant theme. Consent and control are clearly very important to people, but studies adopting a deliberative methodology have found that people recognise the challenges of seeking consent and are prepared to accept data use without consent under some conditions.[48] In light of this, and the nature of research using linked data, it is important to focus on the conditions that enable community support when consent is not sought.

There are a number of studies that focus on linked data and on the secondary use of administrative or service data where a waiver of consent is the norm. These studies were the focus of our review. We considered fourteen studies published between 2010 and 2020 that investigated public views in relation to research using either linked data or administrative data, or both, in Canada, New Zealand, the UK, or Australia.[49] We also included four systematic or narrative reviews in our analysis. These include a

46 D Cameron, S Pope, and M Clemence, *Dialogue on Data: Exploring the Public's Views on Using Administrative Data for Research Purposes* (Ipsos MORI Social Research Institute, 2014); P Paprica, M de Melo, and M Schull, 'Social Licence and the General Public's Attitudes toward Research Based on Linked Administrative Health Data: A Qualitative Study' (2019) 7(1) *CMAJ Open* E40; G Moody and F Lugg, 'Public Understanding of, and Attitudes towards, Data Linkage in Research' (2017) 1(1) *International Journal of Population Data Science* 73; K Doherty, A Hawkins, and M Burgess, 'Involving Citizens in the Ethics of Biobank Research: Informing Institutional Policy through Structured Public Deliberation' (2012) 75(9) *Social Science & Medicine* 1604.

47 V Xafis, 'The Acceptability of Conducting Data Linkage Research without Obtaining Consent: Lay People's Views and Justifications' (2015) 16 *BMC Medical Ethics* 79.

48 Ibid; Ipsos MORI Social Research Institute, *The One-Way Mirror: Public Attitudes to Commercial Access to Health Data* (Report prepared for the Wellcome Trust, March 2016) ('*The One-Way Mirror*'); M Aitken et al, 'Public Responses to the Sharing and Linkage of Health Data for Research Purposes: A Systematic Review and Thematic Synthesis of Qualitative Studies' (2016) 17(1) *BMC Medical Ethics* 73 ('*Public Responses to the Sharing and Linkage of Health Data for Research Purposes*').

49 M Aitken, *Linking Social Care, Housing and Health Data: Social Care Clients' Views* (Scottish Government Social Research, 2011) ('*Linking Social Care, Housing and Health Data*'); M Aitken, S Cunningham-Burley, and C Pagliari, 'Moving from Trust to Trustworthiness: Experiences of Public Engagement in the Scottish Health Informatics Programme' (2016) 43(5) *Science and Public Policy* 713; M Aitken et al, 'Public Preferences Regarding Data Linkage for Health Research: A Discrete Choice Experiment' (2018) 3(1) *International Journal of Population Data Science* 429; Davidson et al, *Public Acceptability of Cross-Sectoral Data Linkage* (n 32); S Davidson et al, *Public Acceptability of Data Sharing Between the Public, Private and Third Sectors for Research Purposes* (Report, Scottish Government Social Research, 2013); Wellcome Trust, *Summary Report of Qualitative Research into Public Attitudes to Personal Data and Linking Personal Data* (Report, Wellcome Trust, July 2013); Cameron, Pope, and Clemence (n 46); G Moody and F Lugg (n 46); J Hobbs, M Tully, and I Ali, 'Exploring Public Attitudes towards Data Sharing and Linkage in Health and Social Care' (2018) 3(4) *International Journal of Population Data Science* 932; NatCen Social Research, *Public Attitudes to*

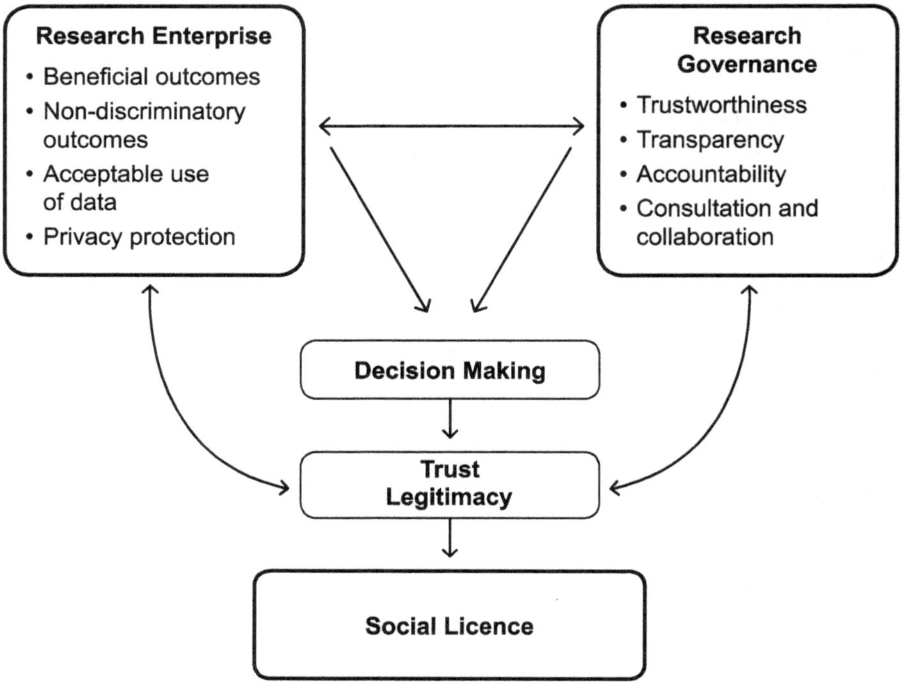

FIGURE 3.2 Conditions for social licence

broader range of studies covering other jurisdictions, different kinds of research data, and quantitative studies.[50] The analysis identified several recurrent themes that point to the conditions that will support social licence for research based on linked data.

First, there are substantive conditions that relate to the conduct and outcomes of the research enterprise. Support is confined to research that is seen as producing clear beneficial outcomes. There are concerns that research might result in negative outcomes for some people or that the data might be misused. Concerns about the impact on privacy are evident in all the studies of public views. These concerns

Data Linkage (Report, University College London, 2018); Xafis (n 47); Paprica, de Melo, and Schull (n 46); J Teng et al, 'Sharing Linked Data Sets for Research: Results from a Deliberative Public Engagement Event in British Columbia, Canada' (2019) 4(1) *International Journal of Population Data Science* 1103; Gulliver et al (n 11).

50 Aitken et al, 'Public Responses to the Sharing and Linkage of Health Data for Research Purposes' (n 48); N Howe et al, 'Systematic Review of Participants' Attitudes towards Data Sharing: A Thematic Synthesis' (2018) 23(2) *Journal of Health Services Research & Policy* 123; S Kalkman et al, 'Patients' and Public Views and Attitudes towards the Sharing of Health Data for Research: A Narrative Review of the Empirical Evidence' (2019) *Journal of Medical Ethics* 10.1136:1–11; E Waind, 'Trust, Security and Public Interest: Striking the Balance. A Narrative Review of Previous Literature on Public Attitudes towards the Sharing, Linking and Use of Administrative Data for Research' (2020) 5(3) *International Journal of Population Data Science* 1368.

relate to the entire research enterprise, including individual research projects as well as the infrastructure supporting data linkage such as linkage units, data repositories, and data access facilities. Support is conditional on adequate protection of privacy.

Second, there are procedural conditions that relate to the governance of research using linked data. These include the trustworthiness of those involved and the desire for transparent and accountable governance. They also include public consultation and collaboration as well as involvement in decision making. The decision-making framework will need to meet all these conditions for the community to support research using linked data. These themes are interrelated and support the foundational components of social licence identified in this chapter – legitimacy and trust (see Figure 3.2).

3.6 CONDITIONS FOR SOCIAL LICENCE

The empirical research discussed so far in this chapter has identified a range of conditions that relate to the conduct and outcomes of any potential project using linked data. In addition to these conditions, several process or governance issues were identified that are necessary to establish and maintain community support both in relation to a particular project and in relation to the general enterprise of data linkage for research.

3.6.1 *The Research Enterprise*

The conditions discussed in this section relate to the conduct and outcomes of research using linked data. These conditions include that the research leads to outcomes that benefit the community; the research does not result in discriminatory treatment; data is only used in acceptable ways; and privacy is adequately protected.

3.6.1.1 Beneficial Outcomes

The strongest theme emerging from studies of public attitudes was the importance of beneficial outcomes from the use of data. There was strong support for research using linked data where there was perceived to be a real benefit to the community.[51] Participants valued the benefits of research to the broad community and demonstrated that they were prepared to forgo control of their personal information and some level of privacy if they believed there would be real benefits in terms of improved medical treatments, delivery of health services, and community well-being.[52] Some people saw administrative data as an asset that should

[51] Aitken et al, 'Public Responses to the Sharing and Linkage of Health Data for Research Purposes' (n 48); Paprica, de Melo, and Schull (n 46); Teng et al (n 49); Howe et al (n 50).

[52] Xafis (n 47); Aitken et al, 'Public Responses to the Sharing and Linkage of Health Data for Research Purposes' (n 48); Davidson et al, *Public Acceptability of Cross-Sectoral Data Linkage* (n 32).

be used for the public benefit.[53] However, there was also concern that different people may have different values and that data may be used in ways that did not match their values.[54]

Legislation, policy, and ethical review principles generally require decision makers to assess the public interest, and this means that they need to evaluate the balance between risk and beneficial outcomes. Therefore, it is important that there is agreement between decision makers and the community on what benefits are valued when this assessment is made. Aitken and colleagues used deliberative discussion with mini publics in Scotland to explore understandings and expectations of public benefit from data-intensive research. Participants understood 'the public' very broadly and wanted the benefits to reach as widely as possible. However, they also recognised that projects that assisted vulnerable groups, such as particular disease groups, were particularly important and felt that they ultimately benefited the whole community. The nature of 'benefits' was also very broadly conceived, with participants being more concerned about the realisation of tangible benefits in ways that improved people's lives.[55]

3.6.1.2 Non-discriminatory Outcomes

Participants in some studies expressed concern that the outcomes of research may have negative impacts on some sections of the community. There were fears that people might be treated as categories rather than individuals and that negative labelling may lead to discrimination in the provision of services.[56] There was concern that there may be harmful impacts on vulnerable or marginalised groups such as seniors, LGBTIQA people, and people with high engagement with social services.[57] This was of particular concern to Indigenous people who feared that the historical and social context of the data would be lost and negative stereotyping reinforced.[58] A Māori woman in the study by Gulliver and colleagues said 'it's going to highlight our problems … It is often used just to prove cultural deficits'.[59] Engagement and collaboration with communities are essential to alleviate these concerns and avoid discriminatory outcomes.

53 Paprica, de Melo, and Schull (n 46).

54 Davidson et al, *Public Acceptability of Cross-Sectoral Data Linkage* (n 32).

55 M Aitken et al, 'Who Benefits and How? Public Expectations of Public Benefits from Data-Intensive Health Research' (2018) 5(2) *Big Data and Society* 1–12.

56 Aitken, *Linking Social Care, Housing and Health Data* (n 49); Aitken et al, 'Public Responses to the Sharing and Linkage of Health Data for Research Purposes' (n 48); Davidson et al, *Public Acceptability of Cross-Sectoral Data Linkage* (n 32).

57 Davidson et al, *Public Acceptability of Cross-Sectoral Data Linkage* (n 32); Paprica, de Melo, and Schull (n 46); Gulliver et al (n 11).

58 Gulliver et al (n 11); Teng et al (n 49).

59 Gulliver et al (n 11), 64.

3.6.1.3 Acceptable Use of Data

Several studies revealed concerns about the misuse of data.[60] Concerns documented included the use of data to justify political positions and government surveillance of citizens.[61] These concerns are likely to vary between countries and political systems and to reflect the history of government use of data. The increasing levels of electronic surveillance in many countries, for example, is likely to have an impact on the level of trust in government use of data.

The use of data by commercial entities that are primarily driven by profit was frequently raised as a concern by study participants. However, there was also recognition of the mingling of private and public interests and the dependence on commercial entities for research funding.[62] Concerns were expressed about the use of data to identify individuals or the potential use for purposes that had not been properly approved.[63] There was also concern that data may be sold or fall into the hands of banks, insurers, or employers.[64]

Social licence will be dependent on trust that the linked data will not be misused. Decision makers need to understand what uses the community regards as acceptable and decisions should transparently reflect that shared understanding.

3.6.1.4 Privacy Protection

The most common concerns identified in studies on public attitudes to data linkage for research relate to privacy.[65] Social licence is dependent on trust that individual privacy is adequately protected. There was acceptance that some trade-off is required between individual privacy and the beneficial outcomes offered by research using linked data but that trade-off was dependent on acceptance of the level of protection offered.[66]

One aspect of privacy protection is the security of individual data, and this was a ubiquitous concern in the studies on public views.[67] Stories of lost and leaked data

60 Aitken et al, 'Public Responses to the Sharing and Linkage of Health Data for Research Purposes' (n 48).

61 Ibid; Davidson et al, *Public Acceptability of Cross-Sectoral Data Linkage* (n 32).

62 Aitken et al, 'Public Responses to the Sharing and Linkage of Health Data for Research Purposes' (n 48); J Street et al, 'Sharing Administrative Health Data with Private Industry: A Report on Two Citizens' Juries' (2021) *Health Expectations* <https://doi.org/10.1111/hex.13268>.

63 Ibid.

64 Davidson et al, *Public Acceptability of Cross-Sectoral Data Linkage* (n 32).

65 Aitken, *Linking Social Care, Housing and Health Data* (n 49); Davidson et al, *Public Acceptability of Cross-Sectoral Data Linkage* (n 32); Paprica, de Melo, and Schull (n 46); Cameron, Pope, and Clemence (n 46).

66 Xafis (n 47).

67 Aitken, Cunningham-Burley, and Pagliari (n 49); Davidson et al, *Public Acceptability of Cross-Sectoral Data Linkage* (n 32); Cameron, Pope, and Clemence (n 46); Hobbs, Tully, and Al (n 49); Paprica, de Melo, and Schull (n 46); Teng et al (n 49).

and breaches of security fuel concerns about data security and have led to public scepticism about the feasibility of security and the competence of those looking after data.[68] These fears are exacerbated by the growth of data brokers and a market trading in individuals' information where data is a valued commodity. Loss of trust in the security of data in commercial hands can impact on trust in other sectors.[69] The protection of data with effective security measures remains a fundamental public concern. It is also a principal preoccupation of data custodians and there seems to be very little evidence of security breaches in relation to research data.[70] Despite this, a lack of trust in the security of data is a significant obstacle to social licence for data-based research. Community acceptance requires demonstrated competence in protecting the security of data and accountability if there are breaches.

The studies of public views demonstrate that security of data was not the only aspect of privacy that was regarded as important. In their systematic review of qualitative studies in 2016, Aitken and colleagues found that assurances about confidentiality were crucial to public support.[71] The degree of identifiability of data was clearly important.[72] Aitken found that support for data linkage of service data was dependent on anonymisation.[73] Cameron and colleagues also concluded that de-identification was a primary condition of support for linkage of administrative data.[74] Xafis found that participants did not regard de-identified information as having the same value or importance as identified information and regarded it as acceptable that researchers use de-identified information without consent.[75] In other studies, some participants recognised the challenges of de-identification and noted that individuals may be recognisable even if the obvious identifying variables such as names, addresses, and birth dates were removed.[76] Aitken and colleagues noted that there were concerns about negative impacts if insurers or employers had access to identifiable data from research.[77] While it is no longer possible to claim that any individual-level

[68] Davidson et al, *Public Acceptability of Cross-Sectoral Data Linkage* (n 32); Cameron, Pope, and Clemence (n 46); N Patterson, '19 Years of Personal Data Was Stolen from ANU: It Could Show Up on the Dark Web', *The Conversation* (online, 5 June 2019) <https://theconversation.com/19-years-of-personal-data-was-stolen-from-anu-it-could-show-up-on-the-dark-web-118265>.

[69] Paprica, de Melo, and Schull (n 46).

[70] G Laurie et al, *A Review of Evidence Relating to Harm Resulting from Uses of Health and Biomedical Data* (Report, Nuffield Council on Bioethics and Wellcome Trust, 30 June 2014).

[71] Aitken et al, 'Public Responses to the Sharing and Linkage of Health Data for Research Purposes' (n 48).

[72] NatCen Social Research (n 49); Gulliver et al (n 11).

[73] Aitken et al, 'Public Responses to the Sharing and Linkage of Health Data for Research Purposes' (n 48).

[74] Cameron, Pope, and Clemence (n 46).

[75] Xafis (n 47). See also Davidson et al, *Public Acceptability of Cross-Sectoral Data Linkage* (n 32); Cameron, Pope, and Clemence (n 46).

[76] Aitken, *Linking Social Care, Housing and Health Data* (n 49); Davidson et al, *Public Acceptability of Cross-Sectoral Data Linkage* (n 32); Gulliver et al (n 11); Cameron, Pope, and Clemence (n 46).

[77] Aitken et al, 'Public Responses to the Sharing and Linkage of Health Data for Research Purposes' (n 48).

information is completely anonymous, it is clear that concerns about identifiability should be taken seriously and that identifiability should be minimised as much as possible by role separation and minimising variables and access to the data. Social licence will be dependent on practices that maximise privacy; however, the community is unlikely to trust that privacy is protected without a better understanding of these practices.

The concerns about discriminatory impact and unacceptable uses, discussed in this section, also relate to privacy and reflect concerns about individuals' capacity to control information about themselves. Where there is no consent for the use of the information, individuals lose control of their information and cannot ensure that it is only used in ways that are consistent with their own values.

3.6.2 *Research Governance*

The conditions discussed in the previous section relate to the conduct and outcomes of research using linked data. The conditions discussed in this section focus on the governance arrangements regulating the use of data for research, including decision making that leads to the restriction or release of data for research. These conditions include demonstration of trustworthiness by decision makers and the various parties to the research; transparency and accountability of decision making and in the conduct of research; and consultation and collaboration with the community.

3.6.2.1 Trustworthiness

While trust is one of two foundational concepts supporting social licence, it is not possible to generate inter-relational trust between parties without some demonstration that the parties are trustworthy.[78] The qualities of trustworthiness include competence, honesty, integrity, and benevolence.[79] Those engaged in the various stages of collection, linkage, and use of data, including decision makers, need to consistently demonstrate these qualities in order to generate trust.

In this context, competence would include the ability to effectively protect the security of data and maximise privacy and the ability to create and use data effectively to achieve beneficial outcomes. It would also include competent decision-making that is efficient and reliably produces good decisions. Honesty and integrity require telling the truth about the risks and benefits of the collection and use of data without embellishment or understatement and keeping promises about the way it

[78] Aitken, Cunningham-Burley, and Pagliari (n 49).

[79] S Grimmelikhuijsen et al, 'The Effect of Transparency on Trust in Government: A Cross-National Comparative Experiment' (2013) 73(4) *Public Administration Review* 575; L Poppo and D Schepker, 'Repairing Public Trust in Organizations' (2010) 13(2) *Corporate Reputation Review* 124.

is handled and used. Benevolence requires a commitment to the beneficial use of data and to the well-being of people and communities. It includes avoiding uses that the community regards as unacceptable, such as surveillance that is not related to health.

Access to the data by commercial organisations, including banks, insurance companies, and pharmaceutical companies, needs to be very carefully considered in light of the obligation of corporations to maximise profit for shareholders rather than to act in the broader public interest. This may not be consistent with benevolence in all cases.[80]

Transparency and accountability measures, discussed in the sections that follow, were raised by participants in qualitative research on the basis that they could help to demonstrate trustworthiness and foster trust.[81]

3.6.2.2 Transparency

Openness about the way data is used and handled has been identified as essential to maintaining public trust in data linkage for research.[82] The qualitative studies available indicate that members of the public sought more transparency in relation to the use of their data for research. Teng and colleagues found that participants wanted information to be available on what data was shared and with whom.[83] Davidson and colleagues found that people wanted access to information on the outcomes of research using linked data.[84] They also wanted decision-making transparency and requested accessible information on the procedures and processes around data linkage, including the requirements that must be met by applicants and the way applications were evaluated.[85] Transparency is also important to other stakeholders, such as data applicants, who need to know the processes and criteria that will be used to assess their application.

This evidence from the qualitative studies reflects the widely held view that transparency will support trust in government. The relationship between transparency and trust is not straightforward, however. Transparency requires frank and impartial information. If communication materials are inadequate or insincere, then they can trigger scepticism rather than trust. There is circularity in the relationship between transparency and trust in that trust may be a prerequisite for transparency to be seen as adequate and genuine.[86] The impact of transparency may depend on the existing

[80] Ipsos MORI Social Research Institute, *The One-Way Mirror* (n 48).

[81] Aitken, Cunningham-Burley, and Pagliari (n 49).

[82] Davidson et al, *Public Acceptability of Cross-Sectoral Data Linkage* (n 32); Aitken et al, 'Public Responses to the Sharing and Linkage of Health Data for Research Purposes' (n 48); NatCen Social Research (n 49); A Ferretti et al, 'Ethics Review of Big Data Research: What Should Stay and What Should Be Reformed?' (2021) 22 *BMC Medical Ethics* 51.

[83] Teng et al (n 49).

[84] Davidson et al, *Public Acceptability of Cross-Sectoral Data Linkage* (n 32).

[85] Ibid; Aitken, Cunningham-Burley, and Pagliari (n 49).

[86] Aitken, Cunningham-Burley, and Pagliari (n 49).

levels of trust and is likely to reflect political and cultural norms of trust in government and institutions.[87]

It is clear, however, that lack of transparency can undermine trust. Media revelations about the use of data can significantly undermine trust where people are unaware of the use of their data. Where there is no transparency, it can lead to a sense that the use of data is hidden and sinister. One aim of transparency should therefore be to avoid surprises.

Transparency is also important because it is disrespectful not to tell people how their information is being used.[88] This is particularly problematic for the use of administrative data collected during service and care delivery where there is no consent or knowledge of secondary uses. Transparency is important in maintaining a shared understanding about the acceptable use of data and it can support confidence that the data is being used for the public good and not misused.

There is a danger, however, that informational transparency alone is seen as the solution to lack of trust. This reflects the 'deficit model' of public engagement that sees the public as passive recipients of information who just need to understand science in order to trust it.[89] While it is one component of a trustworthy relationship, it is insufficient on its own and needs to be part of a reflexive relationship that includes accountability and collaboration.

3.6.2.3 Accountability

Oversight and accountability have been identified as important to participants in studies of public attitudes.[90] Aitken and colleagues found that high levels of accountability were a crucial factor in participants support.[91] In a 2012 deliberative study in Scotland, Davidson and colleagues explored the safeguards for overcoming concerns about linking personal data for research. Participants recommended an oversight body including professionals and lay members and also sought clear lines of accountability through ministerial responsibility or an independent official.[92] Participants in a study in New Zealand (NZ) by Gulliver and colleagues also thought there should be an independent body to oversee the access and use of the data.[93]

There is widespread scepticism about the ability of data custodians and data users to protect the security and privacy of data. In the face of these risks, there is a strong

87 Grimmelikhuijsen et al (n 79).

88 N Kass and R Faden, 'Ethics and Learning Health Care: The Essential Roles of Engagement, Transparency, and Accountability' (2018) 2(4) *Learning Health Systems* e10066:1–3.

89 Sexton et al (n 32).

90 Davidson et al, *Public Acceptability of Cross-Sectoral Data Linkage* (n 32); Aitken, Cunningham-Burley, and Pagliari (n 49); Howe et al (n 50).

91 Aitken, Cunningham-Burley, and Pagliari (n 49).

92 Davidson et al, *Public Acceptability of Cross-Sectoral Data Linkage* (n 32).

93 Gulliver et al (n 11).

desire for accountability and transparency in governance. Accountability means taking responsibility, particularly when things go wrong, and requires clear definition of where responsibility lies. Misconduct needs to be met with investigation and appropriate penalties. Decision-making processes and criteria need to be clearly established and publicly available, and there needs to be independent oversight. O'Neill has been critical of managerial accountability as overly burdensome and as a misconceived attempt to replace trust.[94] However, appropriate systems of governance and independent scrutiny can support trust by reassuring the public that data custodians and researchers are not simply free to do what they like.[95] Good governance also supports those who must make decisions by providing clear decision-making frameworks. Strong standards of accountability and oversight are essential in governance arrangements to support social licence.

3.6.2.4 Consultation and Collaboration

A number of studies identified public involvement in the development and oversight of data linkage for research as an important factor in community support.[96] Davidson and colleagues found a 'strong appetite' for public involvement in the development of the Data Linkage Framework in Scotland.[97] Participants in the study by Cameron and colleagues agreed that there should be some public involvement in running the Administrative Data Research Centres in the UK, with one person saying '[i]f you know there are a couple of members of Joe public in that committee … then you'll know your voice is going to be spoken for'.[98] However, there is also suspicion that consultation can be merely a rubber stamp and offer no real opportunity for the public to have input or to participate in decisions.[99]

Social licence is sometimes criticised for being a risk management tool used to avoid the costs of opposition and for valuing community perceptions of an enterprise over real engagement with communities. If it is too closely associated with risk management, then it can obstruct a genuine engagement with the community.[100] The danger is that it can become an exercise in marketing to sell the enterprise to the community rather than a collaborative endeavour to build a project based on shared values and objectives.[101] Raman and Mohr highlight the difference between seeking public support for a project that has already been determined and the co-creation of

[94] O'Neill (n 30).

[95] Dixon-Woods and Ashcroft (n 5).

[96] Aitken et al, 'Public Responses to the Sharing and Linkage of Health Data for Research Purposes' (n 48); Howe et al (n 50).

[97] Davidson et al, *Public Acceptability of Cross-Sectoral Data Linkage* (n 32).

[98] Cameron, Pope, and Clemence (n 46) 55.

[99] Davidson et al, *Public Acceptability of Cross-Sectoral Data Linkage* (n 32); Paprica, de Melo, and Schull (n 46).

[100] Owen and Kemp (n 6).

[101] Ibid.

the project. Attempts to 'capture the public' are likely to fail if they are not based on shared understandings of the benefits and common values and goals.[102]

What is needed is meaningful consultation that leads to collaboration with the community.[103] It should be a real two-way conversation and be intended to produce change.[104] Collaboration recognises the value of lay knowledge and incorporates it in the shared endeavour. It requires a sharing of power at all stages of that endeavour.[105] Collaboration could include community and consumer participation in:

- the design of data linkage infrastructure and policy;
- decisions about the linkage of new data collections and access to linked data;
- ethics committees and privacy committees;
- setting research agendas and advising on the design and conduct of specific research projects; and
- the publication and implementation of research outcomes.

Community engagement and collaboration in research using linked data is challenging because of the large numbers of people whose data is involved. It is also particularly important for that reason and because there is no direct contact between researchers, data custodians, and participants. Community members are currently included in the required membership of ethics committees and some privacy committees. There is also a growing recognition of the need and the value of including community members and consumers in the design and conduct of research projects.[106]

Community support depends on a common perception that the research and the outcomes are genuinely beneficial and justify using individuals' information without their consent. It also depends on the level of privacy and security being accepted. Researchers and data custodians who focus closely on the analysis of the data may overlook the social context and be unaware of collective interests and potential

[102] Raman and Mohr (n 5).

[103] R McWhirter et al, 'Community Engagement for Big Epidemiology: Deliberative Democracy as a Tool' (2014) 4(4) *Journal of Personalized Medicine* 459.

[104] M Aitken et al, 'Consensus Statement on Public Involvement and Engagement with Data-Intensive Health Research' (2019) 4(1) *International Journal of Population Data Science* 586 ('*Consensus Statement on Public Involvement and Engagement*').

[105] S Cunningham-Burley, 'Public Knowledge and Public Trust' (2006) 9(3) *Public Health Genomics* 204.

[106] J Gordon, S Franklin, and S Eltringham, 'Service User Reflections on the Impact of Involvement in Research' (2018) 4(1) *Research Involvement and Engagement* 11; M de Wit et al, 'Involving Patient Research Partners Has a Significant Impact on Outcomes Research: A Responsive Evaluation of the International OMERACT Conferences' (2013) 3(5) *BMJ Open* e002241:1–11; Consumers Health Forum of Australia, *Statement on Consumer and Community Involvement in Health and Medical Research* (National Health and Medical Research Council, 2016); C Fisher et al, *Family and Domestic Violence Priority Setting Partnership Project Report* (Report, University of Western Australia School of Population Health, Telethon Kids Institute, Kulunga Aboriginal Research Development Unit, Consumer and Community Health Research Network, Anglicare WA, and Crowe Associates, 2016).

negative impacts on vulnerable groups. Collaboration should involve those affected by the outcomes of the research. Decision makers need to be closely attuned to changing community values in the volatile arena of Big Data that demand ongoing engagement. Consultation and collaboration should aim at the development of shared values and goals that are essential for the legitimacy of the research using linked data. Meaningful collaboration with community stakeholders is therefore central to building and maintaining social licence.[107]

3.6.3 *The Role of Decision Makers*

There is clear public support for the use of individual-level data for research that produces beneficial outcomes, but this is conditional on reassurance that data will not be misused and that outcomes will not be discriminatory. It is also conditional on acceptable privacy protection. Decision makers who approve the linkage and use of data for research play a central role in ensuring that research using linked data meets these conditions. The decision makers must assess the risks and benefits and evaluate the various interests at stake. They are required to make a decision in the public interest, that is, a decision that promotes the welfare of the community as a whole rather than the welfare of particular individuals, or even the majority of individuals, in the community.[108]

Decisions need to be based on careful consideration of all the competing interests. They need to be informed by community consultation and collaboration to ensure that decision makers understand the interests of all the stakeholders and understand and share the goals and norms of the community. They need to understand what outcomes the community values and what uses and outcomes the community will not accept. They need to understand what loss of privacy community members are prepared to accept in the pursuit of improved health and welfare.

The decision-making processes must also meet the conditions identified in this chapter if the community is to support research using linked data. Decision making must be transparent, and the evaluation of competing interests should be explicit and based on criteria that reflect the interests of all stakeholders. Decision makers must be accountable for decisions and be able to give reasons for their decisions. There should be oversight of decisions, including some level of review of decisions or the decision-making process.

Governance arrangements supporting social licence should ensure that the decisions are made by those who are trusted to understand the interests of all the stakeholders and to act honestly, beneficently, and without any conflict of interest or bias.

[107] Aitken et al, *Consensus Statement on Public Involvement and Engagement* (n 104).

[108] See Chapter 2 'Individual, Collective, and Public Interests'.

3.7 CONCLUSION

In this chapter, we have considered how the concept of social licence applies to research using linked data and the governance arrangements that regulate such research. Community acceptance underpins the social, political, and financial support necessary for the potential of linked data to be realised. However, recognising the need for social licence does not advance the development of data linkage if we do not understand the conditions under which the community will support data linkage.

The empirical evidence examined in this chapter indicates that the community will support research using linked data where the benefits achieved are valued and the protection from risks is sufficient. Social licence depends on the outcomes and conduct of research meeting the following substantive conditions:

- beneficial outcomes – tangible benefits for the community or for particular groups;
- non-discriminatory outcomes;
- acceptable uses; and
- protection of privacy and security of data.

The governance structure for linking data and approving research using linked data should be directed to achieving these conditions. Decision makers are required to evaluate the risks and benefits of linking data and using it for research and to make decisions that promote the welfare of the community. Decisions should be based on an explicit evaluation of these conditions and they should be clearly embedded in the decision-making framework.

In addition, the governance arrangements themselves must also have community support. The empirical evidence examined indicates that the governance under which decision makers and those conducting research operate must meet certain conditions to support social licence. The following conditions have been identified as critical to community support:

- trustworthiness – decision making and collection, linkage, and use of data seen as competent, honest, and benevolent;
- transparency – about the use of data, research outcomes, and decision making;
- accountability – independent oversight, clear lines of responsibility, investigation of and penalties for misconduct; and
- consultation and collaboration – to develop shared values and goals.

The governance of research using linked data needs to demonstrate these attributes if it is to be accepted and supported by the community. Research using linked data must meet conditions relating to the conduct and outcomes of the research enterprise and conditions relating to the governance arrangements to attain the trust and legitimacy at the heart of social licence.

Trust is inter-relational and grows with experience of trustworthiness. The trust relationship between those involved in research using linked data and members of the community are usually abstract relationships.[109] There are generally no direct interactions on which trust can be built. Data may be initially collected in a face-to-face relationship, for example with a healthcare provider, but it becomes disembodied through coding, linking, extraction, and analysis as it passes through a faceless system.[110]

Trust in such an abstract system requires markers of trustworthiness. The system must demonstrate competence, honesty, integrity, and benevolence. It will depend on decision makers and researchers demonstrating that they have the competence to achieve beneficial outcomes and provide protection from harms. The community must be confident that decision makers, who are part of that system, are acting in the broad public interest.

The desire for transparency and accountability discussed in this chapter are further indicators of the qualities that an abstract system needs if it is to be trusted. The work of decision makers and researchers must be transparent and honest and there must be oversight and accountability, particularly where harms occur. Trust will also be built by developing collaborative relationships with communities through open deliberation on the goals, risks, and benefits of research using linked data and the choices they entail.

Legitimacy is dependent on acceptance that research using linked data conforms to community values and norms. The qualitative data available suggests that research using linked data will only be regarded as legitimate if it produces demonstrable benefits that are valued by the community and if data uses that the community regards as unacceptable are avoided. Data security will also need to meet community expectations and privacy protection will need to match community norms on information sharing and use. Consultation and collaboration lead to a shared understanding of common goals and accepted norms about the flow of information and of the risks that are acceptable. This in turn ensures that decisions are made in the public interest. This shared understanding also supports the concepts of solidarity and reciprocity discussed in Chapter 2 and is central to the moral legitimacy of research using linked data. It is also essential that the governance and processes of decision making are regarded as legitimate. The qualitative data examined indicates that transparency, accountability, and participation in decision making all support the legitimacy of governance.

In the following chapters, we describe the governance systems that support decision making about linked data for research in selected jurisdictions. We consider whether the current regimes enable decisions that are directed to the essential conditions identified in this chapter and whether they demonstrate the qualities necessary to support social licence.

109 A Giddens, *The Consequences of Modernity* (Polity Press, 1990).

110 Sexton et al (n 32).

PART II

Frameworks for Decision Making

Governments hold vast collections of information about individuals that is collected on a mandatory basis, for example to administer public health insurance or pharmaceutical benefits schemes, to register births and deaths, and to record public hospital admissions and discharges. This is sensitive individual-level information that is generally subject to a high level of moral and legal protection. However, governments routinely use and disclose this information for research without the consent, and often without the knowledge, of the individuals to whom the information relates. On what basis do they do so? Is this practice morally and legally acceptable?

Part II focuses on the three regulatory frameworks that govern the use of individual-level government-held data for research: human rights law, research ethics, and domestic legal arrangements. It is important to ensure that these three frameworks and other relevant areas of the law work together in a way that adequately protects the rights and interests of individuals without raising unjustified barriers to the conduct of beneficial research. Annas notes that

> bioethics, health law and human rights are overlapping and interrelated in ways that are not always either articulated or understood. Rather than antagonistically competing for their own influence, these fields can most constructively be viewed as complementary and synergistic. Thus, for example, human rights strongly support the medical ethics principle of informed consent, and medical ethics supports the human rights concept of the right to health.[1]

1 G Annas, 'Bioethics, Health Law and Human Rights' in Y Joly and B Knoppers (eds) *Routledge Handbook of Medical Law and Ethics* (Routledge, 2014) 11, 11.

It is important to acknowledge that these regulatory frameworks have moral normative foundations. Human rights law and research ethics both have their foundations in moral philosophy. Whether or not the law allows governments to use personal information in this way, the accompanying question is, should they do so? It may be that conforming to human rights norms and ethical principles more broadly – as well as complying with the law – will assist with building and maintaining social licence. As discussed in Chapter 3 on social licence, there is instrumental and normative value in respecting human rights norms and ethical principles in the conduct of research.

In Part II, we identify those human rights norms and ethical principles most relevant to research using individual-level data without consent. We explore how these rights and principles have been translated into the regulatory landscape, focusing on three jurisdictions where the use of government-held data for research is well established: Australia, Canada, and the United Kingdom. We discuss whether this has resulted in regulatory frameworks that adequately consider and protect the full range of interests and values at play in the context of research using linked data identified in Part I.

In Chapter 4, we consider the human rights relevant to research using linked data without consent; how these rights come into tension with each other and other relevant interests; and how these tensions should be considered and resolved. We note the emphasis placed in the West on civil and political rights, such as the right to privacy, and the lack of attention to economic, social, and cultural rights, such as the right to health, and how this has resulted in an unbalanced approach to the regulation of research.

In Chapter 5, we describe how the various international research ethics guidelines frame the ethical issues involved in research using linked data. We use a hypothetical research project to analyse the differences between them and go on to discuss how the core ethical values of research merit and integrity, justice, beneficence, and respect can be reinterpreted to encompass the ethical concerns raised by research using linked data.

In Chapter 6, we consider the legal basis on which this information is used and disclosed in the three jurisdictions under consideration. The bodies of law relevant to research using individual-level data without consent are examined. We consider how these bodies of law regulate the use of such data and balance the relevant private and public interests in play. The chapter critiques these bodies of law in terms of clarity and consistency, including consistency with the human rights norms and ethical principles discussed in previous chapters.

4

Human Rights

4.1 INTRODUCTION

> These are not easy questions, but if rights mean anything, then the government cannot simply assume answers that justify its conduct.[1]

International human rights law – like the principles of research ethics[2] and the rules of domestic law[3] – is one of the regulatory frameworks that govern the use of individual-level information for research. It provides a particularly useful framework of internationally agreed standards in the field of research using linked data as we contemplate the importance of cross-jurisdictional and international linkage to address global concerns such as COVID-19.

Modern international human rights law developed in the aftermath of World War II (WWII), drawing inspiration from the moral philosophy of human rights. This chapter will touch on those moral foundations but will focus on how

[1] R Dworkin, *Taking Rights Seriously* (Duckworth, 1977) 202.

[2] Considered in Chapter 5 'Research Ethics'.

[3] Considered in Chapter 6 'Law'.

the international law of human rights can be used to assess whether research using individual-level data without consent is acceptable and to reconcile relevant rights when they come into tension in that context. Our contention is that the balance suggested by international human rights law is not appropriately reflected in domestic law and policy in the three jurisdictions under consideration – Australia, Canada, and the United Kingdom (UK) – and that the right to health, in particular, warrants further consideration in the legal and policy debates on this issue.

The chapter will consider why human rights and human rights law are important; what human rights are relevant in the context of using individual-level information for research without consent; how we find an appropriate balance between rights when they come into tension; how individual rights must be considered against broader public interests, such as supporting and promoting advances in population health; and how compliance with human rights moral and legal norms is likely to impact on the social licence underpinning research using individual-level information without consent.

4.2 WHAT ARE HUMAN RIGHTS?

4.2.1 *What Is a Right?*

Before considering the specific human rights involved in providing access to individual-level information for research, it is important to consider what is meant by the term 'right' in the context of human rights. This is because defining something as a right provides guidance on how it should be weighed against other rights and interests involved in a particular moral, legal, or policy debate.

In his seminal work *Taking Rights Seriously*,[4] Dworkin discusses the importance of the idea that individuals have fundamental moral rights that may come into conflict with the authority of the state and the public interest. He emphasises, in the quote set out at the beginning of this chapter that, if rights mean anything, governments cannot simply ignore them on the basis that it is in the public interest to do so. They are matters of fundamental importance and in part act to protect individuals not only from abuse by governments but also from the 'tyranny of the majority'. This is why we must stop and carefully consider the basis on which we say that sensitive individual-level data may be used *without consent* for research.

Chapter 2 considers the range of interests at play in the research context. Rights function to protect those interests that we all share and that are necessary for humans to lead a minimally good life. Scanlon has noted that rights often take their names

[4] Dworkin (n 1).

from the important interests they protect – for example, the right to privacy – but that they are different. Rights are more than mere interests having special force and imposing duties on States to protect them.[5]

4.2.2 *Moral and Legal Rights*

Human rights may exist as moral or legal rights, or both, but it is important to distinguish between the two. Moral philosophy is concerned with distinguishing between good and bad and right and wrong and helping us to decide what we should do and how we should live in relation to others. Moral rights are one element of this philosophical framework and human rights are a subset of moral rights. They are fundamental in the sense that they cannot be taken away and, while they may be recognised in the law, they do not depend on the law for their existence. All humans possess these rights, which is why they are referred to as universal human rights.

In discussing moral rights more broadly, Dworkin acknowledges that there is great uncertainty on what rights amount to fundamental moral rights and that there is room for reasonable people to disagree on the matter. In addition, there is uncertainty and controversy about the limits of such rights.[6] In terms of translating moral rights into legal rights:

> It is part of the job of governing to 'define' moral rights through statutes and judicial decisions, that is, to declare officially the extent that moral rights will be taken to have in law.[7]

Human rights may be recognised and encoded – in part or in full – into law at the international, national, or subnational level and this is the focus of the following discussion. A broad range of human rights has become part of the modern international legal framework, beginning with the Universal Declaration of Human Rights (UDHR) in 1948.[8] As a 'declaration', the UDHR was not intended to be binding in international law when it was first adopted, although many of its provisions have come to form part of customary international law or have been translated into legally binding instruments over time.

This chapter will consider the rights as set out in two of these binding international instruments that were developed based on the UDHR: the *International Covenant on Civil and Political Rights* (UN ICCPR) 1966;[9] and the *International*

5 T Scanlon, 'Rights and Interests' in K Basu and R Kanbur (eds), *Arguments for a Better World: Essays in Honor of Amartya Sen* (Oxford University Press, 2009) 68, 75.

6 Dworkin (n 1) 197.

7 Ibid.

8 *Universal Declaration of Human Rights*, GA Res 217A (III), UN GAOR, UN Doc A/810 (10 December 1948) ('UDHR').

9 *International Covenant on Civil and Political Rights*, opened for signature 16 December 1966, 999 UNTS 171 (entered into force 23 March 1976) ('UN ICCPR').

Covenant on Economic, Social and Cultural Rights (UN ICESCR) 1966.[10] The UDHR, the UN ICCPR, and the UN ICESCR are together referred to as the International Bill of Rights. Australia, Canada, and the UK are all members of the United Nations (UN), and all voted in favour of adopting the UDHR in 1948. The three countries are also party to both international treaties and, as a consequence, are bound in international law to protect and promote the human rights set out in these instruments. Both treaties are very widely accepted among the States making up the international community and represent a significant global consensus.[11] It is on this basis that they can be used to develop international standards for activities that engage and potentially infringe rights. Certain rights in these treaties – including the right to privacy[12] and the right to the highest attainable standard of physical and mental health[13] – are central to the question of research using individual-level data without consent.

Human rights are also enshrined at the international regional level, for example in instruments negotiated by the Council of Europe (COE); the European Union (EU); the Organization of American States (OAS); and the African Union. This chapter will draw on regional instruments where relevant and instructive, particularly in the area of data protection where the COE and the EU have a more developed approach than the UN.

Council of Europe treaties, such as the *Convention for the Protection of Human Rights and Fundamental Freedoms* ('*COE Convention on Human Rights*')[14] and the *European Social Charter*[15] are directly relevant to the UK as a member of the COE.[16] The treaties of the OAS – such as the *American Convention on Human Rights*[17] – are directly relevant to Canada as a member of the OAS. Australia is not a member of an international regional organisation; however, Australian law and policy are influenced by developments in other international organisations such as the Organisation for Economic Co-operation and Development (OECD) and indirectly by developments in Europe.

10 *International Covenant on Economic, Social and Cultural Rights*, opened for signature 16 December 1966, 993 UNTS 3 (entered into force 3 January 1976) ('UN ICESCR').

11 The UN ICCPR has 173 and UN ICESCR 170 States parties from among the 193 States that make up the membership of the UN.

12 UN ICCPR (n 9) art 17.

13 UN ICESCR (n 10) art 12.

14 *Convention for the Protection of Human Rights and Fundamental Freedoms*, opened for signature 4 November 1950, 213 UNTS 221 (entered into force 3 September 1953).

15 *European Social Charter (revised)*, opened for signature 3 May 1996, CETS No 163 (entered into force 1 July 1999).

16 Although the UK is no longer a member of the EU, the *EU General Data Protection Regulation* has been incorporated into UK domestic law and is discussed in Chapter 6 'Law'.

17 *American Convention on Human Rights*, opened for signature 22 November 1969, 1144 UNTS 143 (entered into force 18 July 1978).

4.2.3 *Why Are Human Rights Important?*

The drafters of the UDHR drew on the normative precepts of moral philosophy in developing a response to the atrocities and oppression of WWII, including the use of torture in the name of 'research'. The Preamble to the UDHR also underlines the instrumental importance of the Declaration, stating that 'recognition of the inherent dignity and of the equal and inalienable rights of all members of the human family is the foundation of freedom, justice and peace in the world'.[18]

In becoming a party to an international human rights treaty – such as the UN ICCPR or the UN ICESCR – States voluntarily take on the legal obligation to respect, protect, and fulfil the rights set out in the treaty. The obligation on States to *respect* rights requires States to refrain from interfering directly or indirectly with the enjoyment of a right. The obligation to *protect* requires States to take measures that prevent third parties from interfering with rights. The obligation to *fulfil* requires States 'to take appropriate legislative, administrative, budgetary, judicial and other measures towards the full realization of such rights'.[19]

Human rights legal obligations are owed *erga omnes*, that is, they are obligations owed to the entire international community. The *Vienna Declaration and Programme of Action*, adopted by the World Conference on Human Rights in Vienna in 1993, underlined that the promotion and protection of human rights are a matter of priority for the international community and emphasised the responsibility of all States to develop and encourage respect for human rights.[20] Frédéric Mégret has discussed the extent to which international human rights treaties may be considered constitutional in character so as to form part of the normative foundations of international communities.[21] Beitz describes the practice of human rights as part of the global normative order.[22] Compliance with international human rights legal obligations demonstrates respect for these normative foundations.

Acting in compliance with human rights norms also supports social licence. As discussed in Chapter 3, the social and moral legitimacy of a project relies in part on demonstrating respect for individuals and the community, and this includes upholding human rights. The responsibility for ensuring that research – and the stakeholder community involved in research – is appropriately regulated lies with States

18 UDHR (n 8) Preamble.

19 Committee on Economic, Social and Cultural Rights, *The Maastricht Guidelines on Violations of Economic, Social and Cultural Rights*, UN ESCOR, 24th sess, Agenda Item 3, UN Doc E/C.12/2000/13 (2 October 2000) 17 [6].

20 World Conference on Human Rights, *Vienna Declaration and Programme of Action*, GA Res 48/121, UN GAOR, 8th sess, 85th plen mtg, UN Doc A/CONF.157/23 (12 July 1993) 2 ('*Vienna Declaration and Programme of Action*').

21 F Mégret, 'Nature of Obligations' in D Moeckli et al (eds), *International Human Rights Law* (Oxford University Press, 3rd ed, 2018) 86, 91.

22 C Beitz, *The Idea of Human Rights* (Oxford University Press, 2009) 209.

under the international human rights regime. However, other stakeholders in the research context – including research institutions and researchers themselves – also have responsibility to ensure that they are complying with human rights norms in order to establish and maintain their social licence to conduct research.

4.3 WHAT RIGHTS ARE RELEVANT?

The international community has attempted to define and articulate a list of rights in the context of developing the international human rights law regime. This chapter will initially consider the relevant rights separately. It is, however, significant that rights are described as 'universal, indivisible and interdependent and interrelated'.[23] This requires States to promote and protect all human rights 'on the same footing, and with the same emphasis'.[24]

In this context, it is important to consider whether civil and political rights (first-generation rights) – such as the right to privacy – are categorically different from economic, social, and cultural rights (second-generation rights) – such as the right to health. The UDHR does not draw a distinction between the two sets of rights, and the decision to draft two separate treaties was a controversial one, reflecting ideological and political differences in the decades following WWII between the East and West.

There are some differences between the two treaties in terms of the obligations imposed on States and the enforcement mechanisms provided but these do not impact on the obligation to positively consider all relevant rights in an integrated way in developing law and policy. More recent treaties, such as the UN *Convention on the Rights of the Child*[25] and the UN *Convention on the Rights of Persons with Disabilities*,[26] recognising the fundamental importance of both sets of rights to human dignity, have reintegrated them. While it remains the case that Western industrialised nations tend to give first-generation rights more prominence in their constitutional and legal arrangements, this does not reflect modern human rights discourse.

While a wide range of rights is relevant to research using linked data, the rights most relevant to research using linked administrative health data are as follows:

- the right to privacy (UN ICCPR article 17);
- the right to enjoy the highest attainable standard of physical and mental health (UN ICESCR article 12); and
- the right to enjoy the benefits of scientific progress (UN ICESCR article 15).

[23] *Vienna Declaration and Programme of Action* (n 20) [5].
[24] Ibid.
[25] *Convention on the Rights of the Child*, opened for signature on 20 November 1989, 1577 UNTS 3 (entered into force 2 September 1990).
[26] *Convention on the Rights of Persons with Disabilities*, opened for signature 30 March 2007, 2525 UNTS 3 (entered into force 3 May 2008).

4.3.1 The Right to Privacy

The right to privacy in international human rights law protects a broad array of interests, including one's private life, family life, home, and correspondence.[27] The right to privacy of one's personal data is one element of this broader right and the one most directly impacted by research using linked data. The right to privacy imposes a duty on States to respect and protect the privacy of the personal data they collect and hold in administrative data collections. That duty is higher in relation to sensitive data, such as personal health data, in recognition that unjustified disclosure of such data may seriously impact on a person's private and family life, as well as their social and employment situation, and on their confidence in health professionals and services.[28]

Where direct access to research participants is possible and practicable, data can, and generally should, be collected for research on the basis of fully informed and voluntary consent. In this way, individuals can shape the scope of their right to privacy by voluntarily sharing, or consenting to the sharing, of information with others. Consent is not, however, always required in international human rights law where the use or disclosure of personal data is subject to other appropriate safeguards. Where there is no direct access to research participants and gaining their consent is not practicable – as is the case with much research using linked data – governments may limit the right to privacy of individuals by, for example, allowing the use of individual-level data for research without consent.

This is justified on the basis that, like most human rights, the right to privacy is not absolute. The UN Human Rights Committee – which administers the UN ICCPR and monitors State compliance – has made clear that '[a]s all persons live in society, the protection of privacy is necessarily relative'.[29] Any 'interference' with, or limitations imposed on, the right to privacy must meet certain criteria. If these criteria are met, the interference with privacy becomes a 'permissible limitation' on the right rather than a violation of the right to privacy.

The UN ICCPR does not prohibit all interferences with privacy. It prohibits unlawful and arbitrary interferences with privacy. This means that any interference must be based on law and that even those limitations imposed by the law must not be arbitrary, that is, they must comply with the provisions, aims, and objectives of the UN ICCPR and be reasonable in the circumstances. The Human Rights Committee has explained that the test of reasonableness implies that any interference with privacy must be proportional to the end sought to be achieved and

[27] See, eg, UN ICCPR (n 9) art 17; COE *Convention on Human Rights* (n 14) art 8; *Convention for the Protection of Individuals with Regard to Automatic Processing of Personal Data*, opened for signature 28 January 1981, 25702 UNTS 65 (entered into force 1 October 1985).

[28] European Court of Human Rights, *Health-Related Issues in the Case-Law of the European Court of Human Rights* (Thematic Report, European Court of Human Rights, June 2015) 27.

[29] Human Rights Committee, *General Comment No 16: Article 17 (Right to Privacy)*, 32nd sess, UN Doc HRI/GEN/1/Rev 1 (8 April 1988) ('*General Comment No 16*').

necessary to achieve those ends.[30] These requirements of necessity and proportionality are also reflected in public health ethics and discussed in Chapter 2.

All of the relevant international instruments[31] have been interpreted to require that any 'interference' with privacy must meet four criteria in order to be a permissible limitation: legitimate aim; legality; necessity; and proportionality. The jurisprudence around these terms is more developed in the context of the *COE Convention on Human Rights* and so the following discussion draws heavily on the decisions of the European Court of Human Rights, which adjudicates disputes under the Convention. The principles discussed in what follows are, however, widely understood and accepted, including by the relevant UN human rights treaty bodies.

4.3.1.1 Legitimate Aim

The first criterion is that any interference with privacy must be necessary to achieve a *legitimate* aim.[32] Article 17 of the UN ICCPR, which protects the right to privacy, does not expressly articulate what these aims might be and so they are potentially quite broad. An indication of legitimate aims is set out in a number of other provisions and sources. The UN *Guidelines for the Regulation of Computerized Personal Data Files*,[33] for example, state that a departure from the privacy principles set out in the Guidelines may be authorised if it is necessary to protect, amongst other things, public health or the rights and freedoms of others. Article 8 of the *COE Convention on Human Rights* provides that any interference with privacy by a public authority must be in pursuit of certain specific interests, including the protection of health or the rights and freedoms of others.[34] The protection of public health or the health of the community and the protection of the rights and freedoms of others are almost certainly legitimate aims in international human rights law.

The law and practice of allowing research to proceed using sensitive individual-level data without consent are often implicitly, and sometimes explicitly, linked to the protection of the health of the community. Would laws that are framed more broadly, for example to allow research more generally, also meet the legitimate aim test?

30 Human Rights Committee, *Views: Communication No 488/1992*, 50th sess, UN Doc CCPR/C/50/D/488/1992 (31 March 1994) [8.3] ('*Toonan v Australia*').

31 The UN ICCPR (n 9), the *COE Convention on Human Rights* (n 14), and the *American Convention on Human Rights* (n 17).

32 Human Rights Committee, *General Comment No 31: The Nature of the Legal Obligations Imposed on States Parties to the Covenant*, 80th sess, UN Doc CCPR/C/21/Rev.1/Add.13 (26 May 2004).

33 L Joinet, *Guidelines for the Regulation of Computerized Personal Data Files: Final Report Submitted by Mr Louis Joinet Special Rapporteur*, UN ESCOR, 40th sess, Agenda Item 11, UN Doc E/CN.4/Sub.2/1988/22 (21 July 1988) annex.

34 Interestingly, 'health' is not an interest identified in art 9 'Exceptions and Restrictions in the Council of Europe' *Convention for the Protection of Individuals with Regard to the Automatic Processing of Personal Data* (n 27). However, art 9(3) of the Convention does allow restrictions on some of the privacy requirements imposed where personal data is to be used 'for statistics or for scientific research purposes when there is obviously no risk of an infringement of the privacy of the data subject'.

Research more broadly is contemplated in some international instruments including, for example, the OECD *Guidelines on the Protection of Privacy and Transborder Flows of Personal Data*[35] – which, although not binding, reflect an international consensus on the handling of personal data and have been influential in the development of privacy principles in all three jurisdictions. The OECD has noted that 'data which may have been collected for purposes of administrative decision-making may be made available for research, statistics and social planning'.[36] The *European Union General Data Protection Regulation* (EU GDPR)[37] – which is not directly binding on any of the three jurisdictions but which has been incorporated into UK law – provides that sensitive information may be processed without consent for 'scientific or historical research purposes or statistical purposes' subject to certain safeguards. These provisions envisage research that is much broader than health research.

All the international instruments provide for the right to privacy to be limited to protect the rights and freedoms of others and this includes the right to health as well as other rights such as the right to education and the right to work.

We would argue that a very broad range of research is compatible with even the relatively limited aim of 'protecting health' or the 'right to health'. The World Health Organization (WHO), for example, recognises that research into areas such as the social determinants of health – 'the conditions in which people are born, grow, work, live, and age and the wider set of forces and systems shaping the conditions of daily life'[38] – is essential and that these determinants may be more important than healthcare or lifestyle choices in health outcomes. For this reason, we argue that research using linked data should not be legally confined in authorising legislation or in data protection legislation to 'medical research' or even 'health research', which may be given a more restrictive meaning. A broad range of research using linked administrative data will meet the test of legitimate aim.

4.3.1.2 Legality

The principle of legality is well established in international human rights law, as well as domestic law, and requires that any restrictions imposed on the right to privacy are 'envisaged by the law'[39] and, in addition, that the law is clear, accessible, and predictable. The Human Rights Committee has stated that, in relation to

35 OECD, *Recommendation of the Council Concerning Guidelines on the Protection of Privacy and Transborder Flows of Personal Data* (23 September 1980). The Guidelines were updated in 2013.

36 OECD, *The OECD Privacy Framework* (OECD Publishing, 2013) 57.

37 *Regulation (EU) 2016/679 of the European Parliament and of the Council of 27 April 2016 on the Protection of Natural Persons with Regard to the Processing of Personal Data and on the Free Movement of Such Data, and Repealing Directive 95/46/EC* (General Data Protection Regulation) [2016] OJ L 119/1 ('EU GDPR').

38 WHO, 'Social Determinants of Health', *Health Topics* (Web Page, 2021) <www.who.int/health-topics/social-determinants-of-health#tab=tab_1>.

39 *General Comment No 16* (n 29).

interferences with privacy, 'relevant legislation must specify in detail the precise circumstances in which such interferences may be permitted'.[40] These requirements must be met from the perspective of all stakeholders in the research enterprise, from the general public to researchers to those charged with making decisions under the law, such as government data custodians. The requirements for clarity, accessibility, and predictability extend to the criteria that data custodians and other decision makers rely on to decide whether to release data for research.

The European Court of Human Rights has also indicated that there will be a violation of the right to privacy where domestic law does not indicate with sufficient clarity the scope and manner of exercise of the discretion conferred on the domestic authorities.[41] It is critical, therefore, that law and policy relating to the sharing of administrative data for research are as clear and transparent as possible and that the decision-making criteria used by government data custodians are specified and on the public record.

The European Court of Human Rights has also stated that a State cannot absolve itself of responsibility under the *COE Convention on Human Rights* by delegating its obligations – for example, the obligation to decide that the right to privacy should be limited in a particular context – to private bodies or individuals.[42] It is on the basis of this principle, to ensure appropriate political accountability, that we conclude in Chapter 8 that the final decision to release data from administrative data collections for research should rest with government data custodians.

Chapter 6 considers the legal arrangements for the use of individual-level data without consent for research and concludes that there is room for improvement in terms of these criteria. Suggestions for reform, including making the relevant laws clearer and more accessible and predictable, are discussed in Chapter 8.

4.3.1.3 Necessity

The principle of necessity requires that any limitation on the right to privacy must be necessary in a democratic society to achieve the relevant legitimate aim, for example, the protection of health or the rights and freedoms of others. The European Court of Human Rights has stated that to be necessary the limitation must meet a 'pressing social need' rather than something that is merely useful or desirable.[43] The Court has also expressed the view that State authorities are generally in a better position than international judges to determine what is necessary for a particular democratic society in the pursuit of a legitimate aim.[44] States are given a 'margin of discretion'[45] to decide these matters.

40 Ibid.

41 European Court of Human Rights, *Guide to the Case-Law of the European Court of Human Rights: Data Protection* (31 December 2020) [70].

42 Ibid.

43 *Handyside* v. *United Kingdom* (1976) 24 Eur Court HR (ser A) 17.

44 Ibid.

45 Referred to as a 'margin of appreciation' in international law.

Imposing limitations on the right to privacy – by allowing the use of individual-level data without consent for research – is a practical necessity to allow research using linked administrative data to proceed. Without those limits, such research could not proceed. We would argue that research using linked data has the potential to meet a plethora of pressing social needs. It is the task of ethics committees to consider each specific project and to decide whether the limitation on the right to privacy – that is, a waiver of consent – is justified by beneficial outcomes. The test of pressing social need indicates that, where research proceeds on the basis of a waiver of consent, these benefits must be significant.

The limitations imposed on the right must also be 'necessary' in the sense that they are the least restrictive measure available to achieve the legitimate aim. One of the common criteria for approving research using linked data is that seeking consent is impracticable or not feasible. If seeking consent is practicable – and a waiver of consent is not, therefore, the least restrictive measure available to allow the research to proceed – a waiver will not be approved.

Some might argue that using an opt-out approach to participation in research using linked data would be less intrusive or restrictive on the right to privacy. We are of the view, however, that opt-out approaches suffer from the same practical and ethical problems as consent in this context. This issue is discussed in detail in Chapters 6 and 8.

The European Court of Human Rights relies on the requirements set out in article 5 of the *Convention for the Protection of Individuals with Regard to Automatic Processing of Personal Data* to refine their approach to what is 'necessary in a democratic society'.[46] These requirements are that the personal data is obtained and processed fairly and lawfully; that the data is stored for specified and legitimate purposes and not used in a way that is incompatible with those purposes; that the data is adequate, relevant, and not excessive in relation to the purposes for which they are stored; that the data is accurate and, where necessary, kept up to date; and that the data is preserved in a form which permits identification of the data subject for no longer than is required for the purpose for which the data is stored.

All of these requirements are relevant in the context of research using linked data, but some requirements are not as well met as others. Transparency is a foundational principle required to support the social licence for research using linked administrative data. The requirement that data is stored for *specified* purposes and not used in ways that are incompatible with those purposes is one element of transparency and a common protection provided in privacy principles. Chapter 8 suggests there is more work to be done to 'specify' or make clear to the community that administrative data is collected, used, and disclosed for research purposes in all three jurisdictions.

Article 6 of the *Convention for the Protection of Individuals with Regard to Automatic Processing of Personal Data* provides that sensitive personal data, including health

[46] *Convention for the Protection of Individuals with Regard to Automatic Processing of Personal Data* (n 27).

data, may not be processed unless domestic law provides appropriate safeguards but does not specifically mention consent. The EU GDPR – discussed further in Chapter 6 in relation to the UK – includes consent as one of the legal bases for processing personal data, including sensitive health data, but includes a range of other grounds, for example that the processing is necessary for reasons of substantial public interest or for scientific research or statistical purposes, so long as the processing meets the tests of legitimate aim, legality, and proportionality and is subject to appropriate safeguards for the rights and freedoms of the data subjects. This is consistent with the approach that we have taken in this book to consent, which may be an appropriate safeguard in some circumstances but not in relation to most research used linked administrative data.

4.3.1.4 Proportionality

Any limits placed on the right to privacy must also be proportionate to the aims to be achieved. The principle of proportionality requires a consideration of the balance between the benefits and burdens created by the limitation. It is necessary to consider the impact on the right to privacy and to balance this against the benefits to be gained by restricting the right to privacy. The principle of proportionality is closely linked to the principle of necessity in that an interference with rights that is found to be disproportionate is also likely to be assessed as not necessary in a democratic society.

The European Court of Human Rights has stated that, in order to determine whether a particular measure or limit on a right meets the test of proportionality, the Court will assess the legislative choices underlying the measure. This assessment will include consideration of the safeguards that have been provided to the individual in the regulatory framework.[47]

It is for this reason, we argue, that in the absence of consent there must be other safeguards in place to respect and protect the privacy, dignity, and autonomy of individual research participants as well as the individual's relationship of trust with health professionals. The safeguards discussed throughout this book, including the use of privacy-preserving techniques, are essential to the consideration of proportionality. If the risk to the individual is contained as much as possible – through applying best-practice data handling and linkage principles – and the benefits to the community are significant, it is our view that restrictions on the right to privacy will meet the proportionality test.

4.3.1.5 The Right to Be Forgotten

One development in relation to the right to privacy that has the potential to impact on the use of administrative data for research is the right to have personal data erased or the 'right to be forgotten'. This right has been developed in the context of

[47] European Court of Human Rights, *Guide on Article 8 of the European Convention on Human Rights: Right to Respect for Private and Family Life, Home and Correspondence* (31 December 2020) [28].

the EU GDPR[48] and provides that data subjects have the right to request that their data be erased in some circumstances. This right is not absolute and applies in a defined range of circumstances, for example when the data is no longer necessary for the purpose an organisation originally collected it. The right does not operate when the data is being used to perform a task that is being carried out in the public interest or the data represents important information that serves the public interest, scientific research, or statistical purposes and where erasure of the data would be likely to impair or halt progress towards these goals. We would argue that it is consistent with the principles of legitimate aim, legality, necessity, and proportionality to protect administrative collections of individual-level data from a 'right to be forgotten' and that such collections should remain intact given their value to the public interest and scientific research.

4.3.1.6 Conclusion

In conclusion, the right to privacy in international law allows the use of personal data without consent to protect health or the rights and freedoms of others so long as legal, policy, and practice arrangements meet the tests of legitimate aim, legality, necessity, and proportionality. The following section considers a number of the other rights that are directly relevant in the context of the use of individual-level data for research that may provide justification for limiting an individual's right to privacy in this way.

4.3.2 *The Right to Health*

The right to health emerged in the aftermath of WWII as a response to humanitarian concerns as well as in response to a growing recognition of the need for States to take greater responsibility for responding to public health challenges.[49] American President Franklin D. Roosevelt discussed the obligation to broaden access to adequate medical care and to ensure a healthy life for all in his 1941 Annual Message to Congress: the 'Four Freedoms Speech'.[50] The right to 'the highest attainable standard of health' subsequently found expression in the 1948 *Constitution of the World Health Organization*[51] and in the UDHR as one element of the right to an adequate standard of living.[52] The COE *European Social Charter*, finalised in 1961, included

48 EU GDPR (n 37) art 17.

49 J Tobin, *Right to Health in International Law* (Oxford University Press, 2012) 38.

50 87 *Congressional Record* 46 (Franklin D Roosevelt) (1941, Joint Session of the House of Representatives and the Senate).

51 *Constitution of the World Health Organization*, opened for signature 22 July 1946, 14 UNTS 185 (entered into force 7 April 1948) Preamble.

52 UDHR (n 8) art 25.

the right for everyone 'to benefit from any measures enabling him to enjoy the highest possible standard of health attainable'.[53]

The UN ICESCR was finalised and adopted in 1966 and required States to recognise 'the right of everyone to the enjoyment of the highest attainable standard of physical and mental health' and to take a number of steps, including those necessary 'to prevent, treat, and control epidemic, endemic, occupational and other diseases'.[54] The *Universal Declaration on Bioethics and Human Rights* also recognises that 'the enjoyment of the highest attainable standard of health is one of the fundamental rights of every human being'.[55]

The right to health does not establish a right to be healthy but a right to the 'highest attainable standard' of health given individual and State-specific circumstances.[56] While States cannot provide protection against every possible cause of human ill health, they are required to provide 'a variety of facilities, goods, services and conditions necessary for the realisation of the highest attainable standard of health'.[57]

Article 2 of the UN ICESCR recognises that fulfilling this right is a progressive exercise, requiring each State to take steps 'to the maximum of its available resources, with a view to achieving progressively the full realisation' of the right. States must, however, make every possible effort, within available resources, to realise the right to health. The Committee on Economic, Social and Cultural Rights (Committee on ESC Rights) – which administers the UN ICESCR and monitors State compliance – has expressly recognised that the right to health is not confined to the right to health care and embraces a wide range of socio-economic factors that promote conditions in which people can lead a healthy life.[58]

The Committee on ESC Rights has also made clear that:

> The obligation to fulfil requires States parties, inter alia, to give sufficient recognition to the right to health in the national political and legal systems, preferably by way of legislative implementation, and to adopt a national health policy with a detailed plan for realizing the right to health … The obligation to fulfil (promote) the right to health requires States to undertake actions that create, maintain and restore the health of the population.[59]

53 *European Social Charter*, opened for signature 18 October 1961, 529 UNTS 89 (entered into force 26 February 1965) art 11.

54 UN ICESCR (n 10) art 12.

55 *Universal Declaration on Bioethics and Human Rights*, 33rd UNESCO General Conference (October 2005) art 14(2).

56 Committee on Economic, Social and Cultural Rights, *General Comment No 14: The Right to the Highest Attainable Standard of Health (Article 12 of the International Covenant on Economic, Social and Cultural Rights)*, UN ESCOR, 22nd sess, Agenda Item 3, UN Doc E/C.12/2000/4 (11 August 2000) [8].

57 Ibid [9].

58 Ibid [4].

59 Ibid [37].

The Committee goes on to state that such obligations include the promotion of research and the provision of information.[60] The Committee expressly suggests 'using and improving epidemiological surveillance and data collection on a disaggregated basis'[61] as one strategy to control disease. Research using linked administrative data is a cost-effective and efficient way to move towards ensuring the right to enjoy the highest attainable level of health for everyone.

One element of the right to health is access to information, that is, 'the right to seek, receive and impart information and ideas concerning health issues'.[62] The Committee on ESC Rights notes, however, that such accessibility 'should not impair the right to have personal health data treated with confidentiality'.[63] This reflects the concern that research using linked administrative health data should be constrained by appropriate safeguards including the imposition of a duty of confidence on researchers who are given access to such information.

The Committee also notes that States sometimes use issues of public health as grounds for limiting the exercise of other fundamental rights, for example public health concerns have prompted limits on freedom of movement in response to COVID-19.[64] The Committee notes that any such restrictions

> must be in accordance with the law, including international human rights standards, compatible with the nature of the rights protected by the Covenant, in the interest of legitimate aims pursued, and strictly necessary for the promotion of the general welfare in a democratic society.[65]

In addition, 'such limitations must be proportional, that is, the least restrictive alternative must be adopted where several types of limitation are available'.[66] This mirrors the views of the Human Rights Committee and the jurisprudence of the European Court of Human Rights in relation to the right to privacy. Of interest in terms of social licence, the Committee on ESC Rights states that one aspect of the right to health is 'the participation of the population in all health-related decision-making at the community, national and international levels'.[67]

Finally, the obligation on States to respect, protect, and fulfil all human rights, including the right to health, free from discrimination, is enshrined in all the relevant human rights instruments.[68] Research using linked administrative data helps to ensure that research is conducted using comprehensive population-wide data

60 Ibid.
61 Ibid [16].
62 Ibid [12(b)].
63 Ibid [12(b)(iv)].
64 Ibid [28].
65 Ibid.
66 Ibid [29].
67 Ibid [11].
68 See, eg, UN ICCPR (n 9) art 2; UN ICESCR (n 10) art 2.

collections, an inclusive research method with less tendency to bias, and produces results that are relevant across those populations.

4.3.3 *The Right to Enjoy the Benefits of Scientific Progress*

The right to enjoy the benefits of scientific progress was articulated for the first time by the OAS in the *American Declaration of the Rights and Duties of Man* of 1948.[69] Article 13 of the Declaration provides that every person has the right 'to participate in the benefits that result from intellectual progress, especially scientific discoveries'. The right was also included in article 27 of the UDHR, which provides that 'everyone has the right … to share in scientific advancement and its benefits'.[70] In 1966, it was given binding legal form in article 15 of the UN ICESCR, which provides that States party to the Covenant recognise the right of everyone to 'enjoy the benefits of scientific progress and its applications'.[71]

In 2020, the Committee on ESC Rights published *General Comment* 25 on article 15 acknowledging that the development of science and technology has many benefits for the enjoyment of economic, social, and cultural rights but that, at the same time, there are risks, including the risk of unequal distribution of benefits and risks.[72] In its General Comment, the Committee emphasises the importance of community participation in decisions about the direction of scientific progress, noting that the orientation of scientific research or the adoption of certain technical advancements should be subject to public scrutiny and citizen participation. This is apposite in relation to research projects and methods that make use of administrative data collections for linkage without consent. Community consultation and participation are essential to support the social licence underpinning such research. It is also one way to help ensure that such research proceeds based on respect for human rights.

General Comment 25 also emphasises the importance of developing national action plans to promote scientific progress and to disseminate research results and products to all, without discrimination. Such plans should 'support public trust and support for sciences in the society, particularly through a vigorous and informed democratic debate on the production and use of scientific knowledge, and a dialogue between the scientific community and society'.[73] This is particularly relevant

[69] OAS, Ninth International Conference of American States, *American Declaration of the Rights and Duties of Man*, OAS Res XXX (2 May 1948) art 13.

[70] UDHR (n 8) art 27(1).

[71] UN ICESCR (n 10) art 15(1)(b).

[72] Committee on Economic, Social and Cultural Rights, *General Comment 25 on Science and Economic, Social and Cultural Rights (Article 15(1)(b), (2), (3), and (4) of the International Covenant on Economic, Social and Cultural Rights)*, UN ESCOR, 67th sess, UN Doc E/C.12/GC/25 (30 April 2020) [1].

[73] Ibid [87].

to research using linked administrative data, where individual-level data collected from the community on a mandatory basis is used, without consent, for research.

4.4 BILLS OF RIGHTS IN DOMESTIC LAW

Before discussing how best to resolve the tension between the rights discussed in this chapter, it is of interest to reflect on how these rights have been incorporated into the constitutional arrangements in the three jurisdictions under consideration in this book. This is significant because constitutional laws and bills or charters of rights – which sometimes form part of a state's constitutional arrangements – provide the broad framework for national regulatory regimes, including the regulation of research using linked data.

Human rights are generally referred to as indivisible, interdependent, and interrelated. In addition, as noted in Section 4.3, first- and second-generation rights – which are divided in the UN ICCPR and the UN ICESCR – are brought together on an equal footing in more recent international instruments. This development is not, however, reflected in the constitutional arrangements of the three jurisdictions under consideration.

Canada is the only jurisdiction under consideration to have in place a constitutional bill or charter of rights. The *Canadian Charter of Rights and Freedoms* focuses on those rights and freedoms essential to preserving democracy and equality in Canada and does not explicitly address the right to privacy or the right to health. The Canadian Supreme Court has, however, recognised the role of privacy in a liberal, democratic state and accepts that privacy interests are protected by the Charter, noting that 'society has come to realize that privacy is at the heart of liberty in a modern state'.[74] The Court also noted, however, that claims to privacy must be balanced against other societal needs. Quebec is the only province that has a *Charter of Rights and Freedoms* that covers a broader range of human rights issues, including civil and political rights, such as the right to privacy, and some social and economic rights, although these do not explicitly include the right to health.[75]

The UK does not have a bill of rights as part of its constitutional arrangements. However, the *COE Convention on Human Rights*[76] – which has been described as a 'constitutional instrument of European public order in the field of human rights'[77] – has been incorporated into UK domestic law by the *Human Rights Act 1998* (UK).[78]

74 *R* v. *Dyment* [1988] 2 RCS 417, 427–8.

75 *Charter of Human Rights and Freedoms*, CQLR, c C-12.

76 *COE Convention on Human Rights* (n 14).

77 *Bosphorus Hava Yollari Turizm ve Ticaret Anonim Sirketi* v. *Ireland* [2005] VI Eur Court HR 107, 110.

78 The *Human Rights Act 1998* (UK) ('*UK Human Rights Act*') is an ordinary law of the Parliament and does not have the same status or protection as a bill of rights incorporated into a nation's constitutional arrangements. The Act can therefore be repealed or amended simply by another Act of Parliament. This is unlikely to happen, however, while the UK remains a Member State of the COE.

The *Human Rights Act 1998* provides that primary and subordinate legislation must, so far as possible, be read and given effect in a way that is compatible with the rights set out in the Convention[79] and that it is unlawful for a public authority to act in a way that is incompatible with those rights, unless, because of the law, they 'could not have acted differently'.[80] As discussed, the *COE Convention on Human Rights* addresses civil and political rights, including the right to privacy, but does not expressly protect the right to health.

Australia does not have bills or charters of rights as part of its constitutional arrangements at the federal or state level. There are, however, legislative charters of rights in two states – Victoria and Queensland – and one territory – the Australian Capital Territory (ACT).[81] These legislative charters address a range of civil and political rights, including the right to privacy,[82] and some social and economic rights, including, in Queensland, the right to health services.[83]

It is noteworthy that the constitutional arrangements in Australia, Canada, and the UK include only limited express protection for the above-discussed human rights, including the right to health and the right to privacy. Express protection of rights, where it exists, is for the most part limited to civil and political rights and, with only one exception, does not include economic, social, and cultural rights such as the right to health. The broad right to privacy is implicitly protected at the constitutional level under the *Canadian Charter of Rights and Freedoms* and explicitly at the legislative level by the *Human Rights Act 1998* (UK). It is also protected under some Australian and Canadian provincial, state, and territory legislative bills of rights. One element of the right to privacy, that is, the right to protect personal information, is provided by legislation in all three jurisdictions and this is discussed in detail in Chapter 6.

The right to health, however, does not make an appearance in the constitutional arrangements in any of the three jurisdictions. While this may reflect perceived difficulties with the justiciability of economic, social, and cultural rights, a survey conducted in 2011 found that 36 per cent of constitutions around the world guaranteed the right to health, with 14 per cent of constitutions around the world specifically guaranteeing the right to public health and another 11 per cent aspiring to protect the right to public health.[84] The advantage of having rights reflected in the constitutional or legislative rights arrangements is that such rights may then be justiciable

79 *UK Human Rights Act* (n 78) s 3.

80 Ibid s 6.

81 *Human Rights Act 2004* (ACT) ('*ACT Human Rights Act*'); *Charter of Human Rights and Responsibilities Act 2006* (Vic) ('*Victorian Charter of Human Rights and Responsibilities Act*'); *Human Rights Act 2019* (Qld) ('*Qld Human Rights Act*').

82 *ACT Human Rights Act* (n 81) s 12; *Victorian Charter of Human Rights and Responsibilities Act* (n 81) s 13; *Qld Human Rights Act* (n 81) s 25.

83 *Qld Human Rights Act* (n 81) s 37.

84 J Heymann et al, 'Constitutional Rights to Health, Public Health and Medical Care: The Status of Health Protections in 191 Countries' (2013) 8(6) *Global Public Health* 639, 645.

in domestic courts and tribunals and, perhaps more importantly, may exert more direct influence on law and policy making.

The right to privacy is given significantly more legal force and visibility in constitutional and legislative rights arrangements than the right to health in the three jurisdictions under consideration. It may be that this contributes to a 'leaning' in the direction of the right to privacy in law and policy making that does not adequately take into account other rights such as the right to health.

It is important to remember, however, that the governments in Australia, Canada, and the UK have accepted obligations in international law to protect all the relevant rights by becoming parties to international human rights treaties. There is, therefore, an obligation in international law on all three jurisdictions to respect, protect, and fulfil the full range of rights relevant to the collection, use, and sharing of individual-level data for research and to ensure that these rights are appropriately reflected and protected in relevant law, policy, and decision making.

4.5 CONCLUSION

The right to be free from torture is one of the few human rights considered absolute, that is, a right that cannot be limited for any reason or in pursuit of any public interest. Article 7 of the UN ICCPR provides that:

> No one shall be subjected to torture or to cruel, inhuman or degrading treatment or punishment. In particular, no one shall be subjected without his free consent to medical or scientific experimentation.

This right to consent to scientific or medical experimentation must not be set aside even in pursuit of a significant public interest in the results of the proposed research. The distinction between interventional and observational research is significant – using linked administrative data for research is a form of observational research that usually does not involve direct contact with participants – and is discussed in Chapter 5. During drafting of article 7 of the UN ICCPR, a proposal for an exception to the principle of consent where the health of the community was affected was rejected on the grounds that it might lead to abuse.[85]

Most human rights, however, are not absolute in the same way. This is a result of the principles of indivisibility, interdependence, and interrelatedness. Because rights are linked in this way, fulfilling one right may support the achievement of another right. Realising the right to education will support achievement of the right to health. However, fulfilling one right may also come into tension with achieving another right. Realising the right to enjoy the highest attainable standard of health may come into tension with the right to privacy. Because rights are also universal,

85 M Bossuyt, *Guide to the 'Travaux Preparatoires' of the International Covenant on Civil and Political Rights* (Martinus Nijhoff, 1987) 152.

this tension may arise between an individual's own rights and between one person's rights and another person's rights or between the rights of groups of individuals.

Under international human rights law, States can place limits on most rights in order, for example to protect certain important interests or the rights and freedoms of others. The UDHR states that any such limitations must be 'determined by law solely for the purpose of securing due recognition and respect for the rights and freedoms of others and of meeting the just requirements of morality, public order and the general welfare in a democratic society'.[86] Similar tests are set out in other international instruments. In order for research to be consistent with international human rights obligations, the arrangements put in place, and any limits placed on a particular right by these arrangements, must meet the tests of legitimate aim, legality, necessity, and proportionality.

The use of the principle of proportionality to define 'permissible limitations' on rights has been criticised for resulting in a balancing exercise and losing sight of the fundamentally protective nature of rights.[87] It is important in discussing proportionality not to reduce the discussion to a utilitarian approach only concerned with maximising public good. Adopting a utilitarian approach, we would simply say that the use of individual-level data without consent for research would maximise the public benefit to be gained from the information and is therefore the right thing to do.

In order to give appropriate weight to rights, however, we must keep their fundamental moral foundations in mind. Dworkin's view is that governments may only act to limit a moral right when there is a compelling reason to do so and that this reason cannot simply be that there is a cost to protecting the right. There is always a cost to protecting rights, but there is also a point where the cost of protecting a right is too high and cannot be justified.[88]

Whether privacy is considered a moral or a legal right, some limits on the right are necessary in order to live in society. The privacy of personal data is certainly worth protecting, for the reasons discussed in Chapter 2. However, it is not justifiable to prevent research using linked administrative data when the impost on the right to privacy is limited and the research is conducted subject to safeguards that aim to protect the interests that underpin the right to privacy. Consent is not the only safeguard available to protect data privacy rights. Other safeguards provide better protection for privacy rights and interests in the context of research using linked data.

It is the role of governments and other stakeholders, including the community, to resolve the tensions that arise between rights in particular contexts. Where

86 UDHR (n 8) art 29.

87 Y Arai-Takahashi, 'Proportionality' in D Shelton (ed), *The Oxford Handbook of International Human Rights Law* (Oxford University Press, 2013) 446.

88 Dworkin (n 1) 200.

the right to privacy, for example, comes into tension with the right to health and the right to enjoy the benefits of scientific progress – as it may do in the context of research using linked administrative data – it is necessary to consider how to resolve that tension. One of the aims of this book is to highlight how all these rights can be better respected and protected in the conduct of research using linked data.

There are, of course, a wide range of other rights set out in international human rights law that would support the use of administrative data collections for research: the right to equality; the right to work; the right to education; the right to an adequate standard of living. Although these rights have not been discussed in detail here, a similar approach to resolving tensions could be adopted. This is one reason we suggest that research exceptions in data protection legislation need not be confined to 'health research'. It is a matter for governments and the community to decide where the balance lies between privacy and these other rights and whether a broader range of research would find an acceptable level of support, or social licence, in the community.

Taking a rights-based approach to using government-held data for research is necessary to ensure that law, policy, and practice in this area do not infringe human rights and that progress continues to serve human needs and interests. This is not a simple task as it is necessary to consider the full range of relevant rights on the basis that rights are indivisible, interdependent, and interrelated. This is, in the first instance, the task of governments, which must decide how best to integrate rights in particular contexts, such as the use of administrative data collections for research, and how to reflect that understanding in law, policy, and government decision making. In undertaking this task, it is critical for governments, and other stakeholders, to recognise and consider all relevant rights and to avoid focusing on one right, such as the right to privacy, to the detriment or exclusion of other fundamental rights such as the right to health.

5

Research Ethics

5.1 INTRODUCTION

Bioethics is that branch of moral philosophy that considers ethical problems in the life sciences, including health research. As with human rights, discussed in Chapter 4, international organisations have incorporated certain elements of theoretical bioethics – including the foundational principles of research merit and integrity, justice, beneficence, and respect – into a practical regulatory framework around the conduct of research. States have drawn on the principles articulated by these international actors to regulate research at the national level.

These principles originated primarily from concern about the conduct of interventional medical research and the resulting harms to research participants. Over the decades, research methods and interests have evolved. The huge and ever-increasing computing and data storage capacity now available to researchers means that research is now a data-intensive activity. Very important research can be conducted with data collected for purposes other than research. It does not require researchers to have any personal contact with research participants and often it is impracticable to obtain informed consent.

In this chapter, the following issues are considered:

- What are the internationally agreed ethical values and principles that guide the use of data for research?
- Are these values and principles 'fit for purpose' for this type of research?

5.2 INTERNATIONAL RESEARCH ETHICS GUIDELINES

Human research can be divided into two main categories, interventional and observational research. Interventional research is where the investigator assigns the participants to a treatment or other intervention and measures the outcomes. Observational research is where the investigator observes the participants and measures the outcomes but does not intervene in the services or treatments they receive.[1] Research involving linked data is usually observational research. In population-level, data-driven observational research, the research team will not usually have any contact with the participants.

The risks involved in interventional research – for example, physical harms from experimental drugs – are mainly borne by the individual participants. Interventional research may also be of direct benefit to the participants as well as the wider community. Observational research tends to be of low risk to individual participants and often of no direct benefit to them. Both types of research can result in significant benefits to the community as well as harms to the community, for example the stigmatisation of minority groups. Despite these differences, both types of research are regulated by the same international ethical guidelines.[2] In this chapter, the international ethics guidelines are reviewed to assess whether they are fit for purpose for health data research.

Research ethics guidelines were first developed at the international level and drew heavily on a long tradition of medical ethics that governed the relationship between physician and patient. This has resulted in a strong focus on interventional research and the protection of individual research participants from harm.

International ethics guidelines are not legally binding, but they are authoritative and drive consistent practice across the world. Transnational organisations, such as the World Medical Association (WMA) and the Council for International Organizations of Medical Sciences (CIOMS), have enormous influence over the development and promulgation of ethics guidelines and ethical research practices

1 M Thiese, 'Observational and Interventional Study Design Types; an Overview' (2014) 24(2) *Biochemia Medica* 199.

2 Research ethics guidance documents are referred to by a variety of names including 'guidelines', 'declarations', 'statements', 'resolutions', or 'frameworks'. In this book, all such documents will be referred to generally as 'guidelines'. This term indicates that these documents are advisory but are not legally binding.

at the national level. The influence of the guidelines published by these organisations extends well beyond the membership of these organisations. For example, the WMA primarily represents physicians, but the reach of the *Declaration of Helsinki: Ethical Principles for Medical Research Involving Human Subjects* ('Declaration of Helsinki') extends beyond physician behaviour, to 'others who are involved in medical research involving human subjects'.[3]

The Nuremburg Code 1947 ('Nuremburg Code') – a set of ten ethical principles for the conduct of medical research on humans – was developed in response to atrocities committed during World War II.[4] The Nuremburg Code focuses on the protection of research participants – including the requirement for informed and voluntary consent – and the responsibilities of researchers. Several international groups and organisations have developed ethics guidelines aimed at different audiences and heavily influenced by the Nuremburg Code. They have also been influenced by the *Belmont Report: Ethical Principles and Guidelines for the Protection of Human Subjects of Research* ('Belmont Report') published by the National Commission for the Protection of Human Subjects in Biomedical and Behavioural Research in the United States of America (USA) in 1979.[5] This report was developed in response to shocking misconduct in research studies in the USA. It identified three ethical principles – respect for persons, beneficence, and justice – that should be the basis for ethical conduct in human research.

There are currently three main international human research ethics guidelines of general application. These are:

- WMA, *Declaration of Helsinki*;[6]
- United Nations Educational, Scientific and Cultural Organization (UNESCO), *Universal Declaration on Bioethics and Human Rights* ('*UNESCO Declaration*');[7]
- CIOMS, *International Ethical Guidelines for Health-related Research Involving Humans* ('*CIOMS Guidelines*').[8]

3 M Smith and D Weinstock, 'Political Legitimacy and Research Ethics' (2018) 33 *Bioethics* 312; *World Medical Association Declaration of Helsinki – Ethical Principles for Medical Research Involving Human Subjects*, 64th WMA General Assembly (October 2013).

4 Nuremburg Military Tribunals, *Trials of War Criminals before the Nuremberg Military Tribunals under Control Council Law No. 10: Nuremberg, October 1946 – April 1949* (United States Government Printing Office, 1949–1953), vol. 2, 181–2.

5 National Commission for the Protection of Human Subjects of Biomedical and Behavioural Research, *The Belmont Report: Ethical Principles and Guidelines for the Protection of Human Subjects of Research* (United States Department of Health, Education, and Welfare, April 1979).

6 *World Medical Association Declaration of Helsinki – Ethical Principles for Medical Research Involving Human Subjects*, 64th WMA General Assembly (October 2013).

7 *Universal Declaration on Bioethics and Human Rights*, 33rd UNESCO General Conference (October 2005).

8 CIOMS, *International Ethical Guidelines for Health-Related Research Involving Humans* (CIOMS, 4th ed, 2016).

The WMA developed the *Declaration of Helsinki* in 1964. The Declaration has been regularly updated and revised and continues to provide the foundations for modern ethical review of medical research.[9] The most recent version was adopted in 2013. While the *Declaration of Helsinki* has had an extremely important impact on medical research ethics worldwide, its primary audience is medical practitioners.

The UNESCO Bioethics Programme developed the *UNESCO Declaration* in response to the large number of developing countries in the United Nations (UN) that did not have human research ethics committees. It differs from other ethics guidelines, like those published by the WMA, in that it combines bioethics and human rights principles.[10]

The CIOMS, established by the World Health Organization (WHO) and UNESCO, developed the *CIOMS Guidelines*.[11] The *CIOMS Guidelines* are written for a broad audience involved in health and related research. These guidelines include more detailed guidance than the *Declaration of Helsinki* on how to implement the ethical principles and rules described.

Four core values are common to each of these guidelines:

- research merit and integrity;
- justice;
- beneficence;
- respect.

The scope of all three guidelines extends to the use of individual-level information in research. However, only the *CIOMS Guidelines* include specific guidance on the issues surrounding the use of data for research.[12]

Each of these guidelines has a strong focus on individual consent and the protection of individual research participants. Close adherence to the *Declaration of Helsinki* and the *UNESCO Declaration* would preclude much population-based, data-intensive research due to the stringent consent requirements. The *CIOMS Guidelines* also require informed consent to be the default for the use of personal information in research. However, these Guidelines are more permissive than the WMA approach and state that:

> A research ethics committee may approve a modification or waiver of informed consent to research if:

9 D Chalmers, 'Medical Research' in Y Joly and B Knoppers (eds), *Routledge Handbook of Medical Law and Ethics* (Routledge, 2014) 303, 305.

10 H Wolinsky, 'Bioethics for the World: UNESCO's Universal Declaration on Bioethics and Human Rights Has Far-Reaching Goals, and Has Met with Widespread Opposition' (2006) 7(4) *EMBO Reports* 354.

11 *CIOMS Guidelines* (n 8).

12 Ibid.

- the research would not be feasible or practicable to carry out without the waiver or modification;
- the research has important social value; and
- the research poses no more than minimal risks to participants.[13]

The *CIOMS Guidelines* also differ from the *Declaration of Helsinki* and the *UNESCO Declaration* in the acknowledgement and guidance on collective interests that must be taken into consideration in ethical review of research:

> Proactive and sustained engagement with the communities from which participants will be invited to participate is a way of showing respect for them and the traditions and norms that they share. Community engagement is also valuable for the contribution it can make to the successful conduct of research. In particular, community engagement is a means of ensuring the relevance of proposed research to the affected community, as well as its acceptance by the community. In addition, active community involvement helps to ensure the ethical and social value and outcome of proposed research.[14]

Rapid advances in computing and data science and the sequencing of the human genome mean that there is now exponentially more data that can be used for research. Data can be combined and used in new ways that may raise different ethical issues than envisaged in the past. Millions of people can now be included in a research project and no direct contact with them is required. In these circumstances, informed consent is impracticable and would have an adverse impact on the research methodology as discussed in Chapter 1. The acknowledgement of these new ethical challenges has resulted in the development of new ethics guidelines that attempt to address these data-specific issues.

The *Declaration of Helsinki* refers to research on identifiable human material and data; however, the WMA recognised that new research strategies and models, as well as new predictive types of research, required more specific guidance.[15] In October 2002, the WMA adopted the *Declaration of Taipei on Ethical Considerations Regarding Health Databases and Biobanks* ('*Declaration of Taipei*').[16] The *Declaration of Taipei* acknowledges the benefits of research using databases of identifiable information, noting that such research 'represents a common good that is in the interest of individual patients, as well as the population and the society'.[17] Despite this recognition, the *Declaration of Taipei* takes an even more conservative approach to the use of data without consent than the *Declaration of Helsinki*. It only allows the requirement for consent

13 Ibid Guideline 10.

14 Ibid Commentary Guideline 7.

15 WMA, 'Declaration of Taipei: Research on Health Databases, Big Data and Biobanks', *Declaration of Taipei* (Web Page) <www.wma.net/what-we-do/medical-ethics/declaration-of-taipei/>.

16 *World Medical Association Declaration of Taipei on Ethical Considerations Regarding Health Databases and Biobanks*, 67th WMA General Assembly (October 2016).

17 Ibid [5].

to be waived in exceptional cases to protect the health of the population.[18] In comparison, the *Declaration of Helsinki* requires that where consent would be impossible the requirement for consent can be waived with the approval of an ethics committee.

The *Declaration of Taipei* continues to take a very individualistic approach to the use of data and contains only a brief mention of collective interests. It does not include any guidance on the risks of collective harms such as discrimination, stigmatisation, or adverse cultural impacts and makes no mention of consultation or collaboration with affected communities.

All of the ethics guidelines acknowledge that there are benefits that can arise from the conduct of research. However, none of the guidelines mention the possibility that there may be risks associated with not conducting research. For observational research, where only existing data will be used to conduct the research, there may be projects where the risks of not conducting the research are greater than the risks to the individual privacy of the participants. For example, population-level analysis of outcomes after the use of a new pharmaceutical may result in the removal of unsafe pharmaceuticals from the market.[19]

The development of DNA sequencing techniques and the completion of the first human genome sequence signalled a shift in international ethics guidelines. Specific genomic and genetic guidelines were developed because this type of data was considered special. It is unique to each person and encodes detailed information about a person's current and potential future health as well as information about their relatives. Unavoidably, there are familial and collective interests in the conduct and results of genetic and genomic research.

Four guidelines specifically address the use of genomic and genetic data in research:

- UNESCO, *Universal Declaration on the Human Genome and Human Rights*;[20]
- UNESCO, *International Declaration on Human Genetic Data*;[21]
- Human Genome Organisation (HUGO) International, *Statement on Human Genomic Databases*;[22]
- Global Alliance for Genomics and Health, *Framework for the Responsible Sharing of Genomic and Health-related Data*.[23]

18 Ibid [16].

19 J Allen et al, 'Privacy Protectionism and Health Information: Is There Any Redress for Harms to Health?' (2013) 21(2) *Journal of Law & Medicine* 473; K Jones et al, 'The Other Side of the Coin: Harm Due to the Non-Use of Health-Related Data' (2017) 97 *International Journal of Medical Informatics* 9.

20 *Universal Declaration on the Human Genome and Human Rights*, 29th UNESCO General Conference (November 1997).

21 *International Declaration on Human Genetic Data*, 32nd UNESCO General Conference (October 2003).

22 HUGO Ethics Committee, 'Statement on Human Genomic Databases, December 2002' (2003) 14(3–4) *Journal International de Bioethique* 207.

23 Global Alliance for Genomics and Health, 'Framework for the Responsible Sharing of Genomic and Health-Related Data' (Web Page, 9 December 2014) <www.ga4gh.org/genomic-data-toolkit/regulatory-ethics-toolkit/framework-for-responsible-sharing-of-genomic-and-health-related-data/>.

All of these international genetic and genomic guidelines recognise that there are benefits and risks, not only just to the individual participants but also to their families and communities. Despite this clear acknowledgement of collective interests, these guidelines are all based on informed, individual consent. For example, both the *Universal Declaration on the Human Genome and Human Rights* and the *International Declaration on Human Genetic Data* require that 'in all cases, the prior, free and informed consent of the person concerned shall be obtained'.[24] Neither of these instruments include an option for the requirement for consent to be waived in any circumstance.

The HUGO and the Global Alliance for Genomics and Health are international organisations of scientists and others involved in genomic and genetic research. Both organisations have developed more detailed statements to assist their members in responsible and ethical handling of this type of data. These statements build on the *Universal Declaration on the Human Genome and Human Rights* and accept the requirement for informed consent for the collection of genomic/genetic data. However, the HUGO *Statement on Human Genomic Databases* has a very broad interpretation of consent which 'may include notification of uses (actual or future), or opting out, or, in some cases, blanket consent'.[25] Some may consider this inconsistent with the *Universal Declaration on the Human Genome and Human Rights.* These approaches provide participants with little or no information about what their data will be used for, so it is difficult to describe consent as informed under these conditions.

5.3 CASE STUDY

In this section, we consider a hypothetical example of a research project to understand whether the international guidelines are suitable for research involving linked data.

CASE STUDY

Background: At the end of 2017 there were 121,837 refugees, 40,365 pending asylum cases, and 97 stateless persons in the United Kingdom (UK).[26] Owing to premigration and migration trauma, refugees may be at higher risk of mental health disorders. To plan and implement appropriate treatment and services for this group, a better understanding of the risks of mental health disorders is required.

Aim: To investigate the risk of mental health disorders among refugees compared with that among UK-born citizens.

Method: A case-control study using UK immigration records linked with mental health, hospital, general practice, and death records from across the UK

[24] *Universal Declaration on the Human Genome and Human Rights* (n 20) art 5(b).

[25] HUGO Ethics Committee (n 22) cl 4(a).

[26] United Nations High Commissioner for Refugees, 'Global Trends Forced Displacement in 2017', *UNHCR The UN Refugee Agency* (Web Page, 2017) <www.unhcr.org/globaltrends2017/>.

(England, Wales, Scotland, and Northern Ireland). Cases will be age- and sex-matched 1:4 with UK-born citizen controls. In order to inform service planning, the geographic locations of the participants will be included in the analysis. Date of arrival in the UK for the cases will be required to adjust for length of time living in the UK. Country of origin will also be collected to determine whether risks vary by nationality.

This study will require approximately 600,000 participants. Many of the participants will not speak English or English will be their second language. Contact details for some participants will not be up to date. Access to identifiable information (name, address, date of birth, sex) will be required to conduct the linkage. Names, addresses, and full birth date will not be provided to the analysts. The analysts will have access to year of birth, country of origin, geographic location in UK, mental health records, hospitalisations (all cause), and general practice records.

It will clearly be impractical to gain consent from each participant for this study due to the large number of participants. Would this study be granted a waiver of consent and approved under the international guidelines? Table 5.1 indicates how these guidelines would apply to a waiver of consent in this case study.

Table 5.1 demonstrates a spectrum of approaches to the waiver of consent in data-intensive health research. The approaches range from limiting waiver to circumstances of immediate threat only (*Declaration of Taipei*) to providing clear criteria for assessing and granting waivers of consent (*CIOMS Guidelines*).

Assuming that this study is conducted with appropriate levels of data security, the risks to individual participants will be minimal. There will likely be no benefits for the individual participants from the use of their information. However, there is the potential for significant community benefits as the study will result in a better understanding of the extent to which refugees suffer mental health disorders, which refugees are most at risk of mental health disorders, and the types of mental health disorders they are likely to suffer from. This information can be used by health practitioners for early diagnosis and to plan and implement appropriate mental health services in the most needed locations. Good mental health care for refugees will assist them in integrating into their new country. It will also reduce the burden on the community and health system of undiagnosed and untreated people with mental health conditions.

While the risks to individual participants in this study may be low, there are risks to the refugee community as a whole as well as subgroups of this community. A finding that a particular nationality or ethnic group is more at risk of mental health disorders could result in stigmatisation of that group. This could have broad-reaching effects on all people in this community and their ability to be accepted into the wider community.

The project in the case study could have a significant impact on particular communities as well as individuals. Would these collective interests be taken into account under the provisions of the international guidelines? Table 5.2 considers

TABLE 5.1 *Comparison of international guidelines for waiver of consent*

International guideline	Relevant provisions	Could a waiver of consent be granted?
Declaration of Helsinki	Article 32: 'There may be exceptional situations where consent would be impossible or impracticable to obtain for such research.'	It would be impracticable, if not impossible, to obtain consent for this study given the numbers involved. However, this study is not an exceptional situation. It is a very common design for population data research. Different ethics committees are likely to interpret this clause differently. Some would grant a waiver of consent and some would not.
UNESCO Declaration	Article 2: 'Scientific research should only be carried out with the prior, free, express and informed consent of the person concerned.' Article 2: 'Exceptions can be made to this principle as long as they are in accordance with ethical and legal standards adopted by State.'	It is not possible to carry out this study with the prior, free, express, and informed consent of the participants given the numbers involved. The *UNESCO Declaration* does recognise exceptions to this principle. However, the Declaration does not give any guidance on when a waiver is ethical. Some states have ethical and legal standards that would permit a waiver. In the UK, where this case study is located, there are legal provisions permitting a waiver but no domestic ethical guidelines that give ethics committees guidance on waiver of consent.
CIOMS *Guidelines*	Guideline 10: 'A research ethics committee may waive informed consent if it is convinced that the research would not be feasible or practicable to carry out without the waiver, the research has important social value, and the research poses no more than minimal risks to participants.'	A waiver of consent could be granted if an ethics committee determined that these criteria were met.
Declaration of Taipei	Article 16: 'In the event of a clearly identified, serious and immediate threat where anonymous data will not suffice, the requirements for consent may be waived to protect the health of the population. An independent ethics committee should confirm that each exceptional case is justifiable.'	This research study could not be considered a response to a serious and immediate threat so a waiver would not be granted.

TABLE 5.2 *Comparison of international guidelines in relation to collective interests*

International guideline	Relevant provisions	Would the collective interests in this project be taken into account?
Declaration of Helsinki	Article 8: 'While the primary purpose of medical research is to generate new knowledge this goal can never take precedence over the rights and interests of individual research subjects.' Article 17: 'All medical research involving human subjects must be preceded by careful assessment of predictable risks and burdens to the individuals and groups involved in the research in comparison with foreseeable benefits to them and to other individuals or groups affected by the condition under investigation.'	The foundational premise of the *Declaration of Helsinki* is the protection of the patient or research participant and that their interests should have precedence over other goals. However, the Declaration does provide clear direction that the risk–benefit analysis at the heart of beneficence must include group interests as well as individual interests. Assuming appropriate levels of data security were in place, the risks to individual participants and the foreseeable benefits to individuals would both be low. The foreseeable benefits to the refugee community would be timely diagnosis of mental health issues and provision of appropriate services. The risks to the refugee community in general and subsets of the community may include stigmatisation and subsequent discrimination based on assumptions about poor mental health. Any determination of whether the benefits outweigh the risks may depend on proposed approaches to mitigate the risks of stigmatisation.
UNESCO Declaration	Article 2: 'The interests and welfare of the individual should have priority over the sole interest of science or society.' Article 4: 'In applying and advancing scientific knowledge, medical practice and associated technologies, direct and indirect benefits to patients, research participants and other affected individuals should be maximized and any possible harm to such individuals should be minimized.'	The *UNESCO Declaration* prioritises individual interests over those of society. It acknowledges that there are potential effects on individuals other than those who participate and requires that the benefits to them be maximised and the harms minimised. It requires protection of vulnerable groups and asserts that individuals and groups should not be stigmatised.

(continued)

TABLE 5.2 *(continued)*

International guideline	Relevant provisions	Would the collective interests in this project be taken into account?
	Article 8: 'Individuals and groups of special vulnerability should be protected and the personal integrity of such individuals respected.' Article 11: 'No individual or group should be discriminated against or stigmatized on any grounds, in violation of human dignity, human rights and fundamental freedoms.'	It may be difficult to approve the Case Study applying the *UNESCO Declaration* as it may be difficult to demonstrate that some refugee groups would not be stigmatised.
CIOMS Guidelines	Guideline 4: 'The potential individual benefits and risks of research studies must be evaluated in consultation with the communities to be involved in the research.' Commentary 4: '[R]esearch results in certain fields (for example, epidemiology, genetics, and sociology) may present risks to the interests of communities, societies, families, or racially or ethnically defined groups. For example, results could indicate – rightly or wrongly – that a group has a higher than average prevalence of alcoholism, mental illness or sexually transmitted disease ... Plans to conduct such research should be sensitive to these considerations and minimize risks to groups.' Guideline 7: 'Researchers, sponsors, health authorities and relevant institutions should engage potential participants and communities in a meaningful participatory process that involves them in an early and sustained manner in the design, development, implementation, design of the informed consent process and monitoring of research, and in the dissemination of its results.'	The *CIOMS Guidelines* recognise community interests and provide the most detailed guidance for their consideration. They provide clear guidance on the kinds of collective risks that projects like the case study may generate and require protection of vulnerable groups. Importantly, they indicate that researchers and others should consult with relevant communities in order to demonstrate respect and to understand the risks. If substantial engagement and support from the refugee community was demonstrated and this case study and the dangers of stigmatisation were addressed and minimised, then it would meet the requirements of these guidelines.

	Commentary 7: 'Proactive and sustained engagement with the communities from which participants will be invited to participate is a way of showing respect for them and the traditions and norms that they share … In particular, community engagement is a means of ensuring the relevance of proposed research to the affected community, as well as its acceptance by the community. In addition, active community involvement helps to ensure the ethical and social value and outcome of proposed research. Community engagement is especially important when the research involves minorities or marginalized groups, including persons with stigmatizing diseases such as HIV, in order to address any potential discrimination.' Guideline 15: 'When vulnerable individuals and groups are considered for recruitment in research, researchers and research ethics committees must ensure that specific protections are in place to safeguard the rights and welfare of these individuals and groups in the conduct of the research.'	
Declaration of Taipei	Article 17: 'The interests and rights of the communities concerned, in particular when vulnerable, must be protected, especially in terms of benefit sharing.'	The *Declaration of Taipei* acknowledges that there are collective interests; however, it focuses solely on protection and does not address the wider ethical significance of community interests. The researchers would need to propose a feasible approach to preventing or minimising the risk of stigmatising refugee communities to meet the *Declaration of Taipei* requirement in this case study.

the extent to which the international guidelines provide ethical guidance for the consideration of collective interests.

The international guidelines are not consistent in the guidance they provide for the ethical review of the case study. The main areas of inconsistency concern:

- Whether there are circumstances in which the use of data without consent is ethical and, if so, in what circumstances.
- How collective interests should be considered and balanced with the protection of individual interests.

These inconsistencies are likely to result in confusion and variation in how the guidelines are applied in practice and how they are adopted and reflected in domestic guidelines.

5.4 UPDATING THE ETHICS FRAMEWORK FOR THE DATA ERA

Some authors have suggested that the ethics frameworks described in this chapter do not meet the needs of modern data-driven research.[27] It is unsurprising that researchers are confused about what constitutes ethical uses of data for research given the number of international guidelines and the discrepancies between them. The existing frameworks, which are built around the four core values (research merit and integrity, justice, beneficence, and respect), have been criticised for focusing primarily on individual interests and for an overemphasis on informed consent. Alternative frameworks have been proposed, including a public health ethics framework.[28] We propose that the four core values of the current ethics frameworks can be re-envisaged and made fit for purpose. In this section, we consider how the core values should be applied to research using linked data.

5.4.1 *Research Merit and Integrity*

Research involving humans has merit and is ethically justifiable if it produces valuable knowledge: knowledge that is reliable and useful.[29] This is acknowledged in

[27] A Ballantyne, 'Adjusting the Focus: A Public Health Ethics Approach to Data Research' (2019) 33(3) *Bioethics* 356; N Kass, 'An Ethics Framework for Public Health' (2001) 91(11) *The American Journal of Public Health* 1776; J Childress et al, 'Public Health Ethics: Mapping the Terrain' (2002) 30(2) *Journal of Law, Medicine and Ethics* 170.

[28] Ballantyne (n 27); Kass (n 27); S Leonelli, 'Locating Ethics in Data Science: Responsibility and Accountability in Global and Distributed Knowledge Production Systems' (2016) 374(2083) *Philosophical Transactions, Series A, Mathematical, Physical, and Engineering Sciences* 20160122; G Laurie et al, 'Delivering a Practical Framework for Ethical Decision-Making Involving Big Data in Health and Research' (2019) 11(3) *Asian Bioethics Review* 223.

[29] I Pieper and C Thomson, 'Contextualising Merit and Integrity within Human Research' (2011) 29(4) *Monash Bioethics Review* 15(1); J van Delden and R van der Graa, 'Social Value' in G Laurie et al (eds), *The Cambridge Handbook of Health Research Regulation* (Cambridge University Press, 2021) 37.

most of the international ethics guidelines. For example, the first guideline in the *CIOMS Guidelines* states:

> The ethical justification for undertaking health-related research involving humans is its scientific and social value: the prospect of generating the knowledge and the means necessary to protect and promote people's health … Therefore, researchers, sponsors, research ethics committees, and health authorities, must ensure that proposed studies are scientifically sound, build on an adequate prior knowledge base, and are likely to generate valuable information.[30]

A research project that has scientific value starts with an appropriate research question and uses a study design that can answer the question.[31] The methods used are based on accepted scientific principles and a comprehensive knowledge of the relevant scientific literature. A number of the guidelines also recognise that research should be conducted with integrity. It should only be carried out by people who are appropriately trained and experienced. A project should also have social value in the sense that it has the potential to contribute to improving individual or community well-being. The research must be relevant and useful and must be capable of producing reliable and valid results. Research that does not meet these standards will not contribute valuable knowledge and so it is not ethically justifiable to use human participants and expose them to risks or inconvenience.

There are several issues that may impact on the merit of research projects using linked data, including the quality of the data to be linked. This is particularly pertinent if the information has not been collected specifically for research purposes, for example administrative data. This data may not be fit for purpose for some research objectives. Any research design will need to take into account the limited data variables available, changes in coding or data collection practices over time, and the accuracy of data collection and input.[32] Consideration must also be given to the quality of the linkage. There can be concerns about errors in linked data, especially if cases are not linked accurately. Different linkage methods will produce different levels of precision and will be influenced by the number and type of identifying fields and the accuracy of the recording of the data.

The case study presented earlier in the chapter would not be ethical unless it could be demonstrated that the quality of the data and the analysis methods proposed could deliver valid results. In addition, the research team would need to include members with appropriate skills and experience in the analysis of population-level administrative data.

30 *CIOMS Guidelines* (n 8) Guideline 1.

31 R Rhodes, 'Rethinking Research Ethics' (2005) 5(1) *American Journal of Bioethics* 7.

32 M Bietz et al, 'Opportunities and Challenges in the Use of Personal Health Data for Health Research' (2016) 23(e1) *Journal of the American Medical Informatics Association* e42; L Jorm, 'Routinely Collected Data As a Strategic Resource for Research: Priorities for Methods and Workforce' (2015) 25(4) *Public Health Research and Practice* 30.

Research merit is necessary but not sufficient for research to be ethical. Researchers must also behave with integrity. To conduct research with integrity researchers must be transparent and honest about all their interests in the research and do everything in their power to minimise bias by being scientifically disinterested.

While most researchers undoubtedly wish to see the results of their research translated into improvements in the health and well-being of the wider community, they may also have a range of other interests in the conduct and outcomes of the research. These interests may be financial or non-financial and the researcher may or may not be aware of any bias that results from them. Financial interests include things like grant funding, commercial sponsorship, consultancies, and advisory board memberships. Non-financial interests include a wide range of matters from religious or political beliefs to career advancement and a personal relationship with a person with the disease being studied.[33] There is good evidence that financial interests can influence the outcomes of clinical trials and systematic reviews.[34] Non-financial interests are also strong drivers of human behaviour as people are highly motivated to protect family, avoid social disapproval, and seek status or fame.[35] There is some evidence that these interests also can affect health research.[36]

Adherence to scientific method is supposed to ensure unbiased results and that researchers are neutral actors in the scientific process. It is important for decision makers to be aware and to take into consideration the range of interests that individual researchers may have in requesting access to linked data for research.

5.4.2 *Justice*

Justice in research requires that the benefits and burdens of research are fairly distributed. It includes both distributive justice and procedural fairness in the recruitment and treatment of participants. Initially, the focus on justice in ethics guidelines was directed at protecting vulnerable people from exploitation and reflected the history of incidents of research exploitation of the poor, the institutionalised, and the marginalised.[37] Justice requires that participants are only selected for scientific reasons, not based on convenience or dependence, and that those who are unlikely to benefit

33 L Bero and Q Grundy, 'Why Having a (Nonfinancial) Interest Is Not a Conflict of Interest' (2016) 14(2) *PLoS Biology* e2001221.

34 Ibid.

35 M Wiersma et al, 'Should We Try to Manage Non-Financial Interests?' (2018) 361 *BMJ* k1240; M Wiersma et al, 'Status, Respect, and Stigma: A Qualitative Study of Non-financial Interests in Medicine' (2020) 17 *Bioethical Inquiry* 203.

36 M Viswanathan et al, 'A Proposed Approach May Help Systematic Reviews Retain Needed Expertise While Minimizing Bias from Nonfinancial Conflicts of Interest' (2014) 67(11) *Journal of Clinical Epidemiology* 1229; H Abdoul et al, 'Non-Financial Conflicts of Interest in Academic Grant Evaluation: A Qualitative Study of Multiple Stakeholders in France' (2012) 7(4) *PLoS One* e35247.

37 I Pieper and C J Thomson, 'Justice in Human Research Ethics' (2013) 31(1) *Monash Bioethics Review* 99.

as a group should not bear the burden disproportionately. Where retrospective data is used and there is no direct recruitment the issues of dependence and convenience are less likely to be problematic. Where there are scientific reasons for focusing on particular groups or communities, care must still be taken not to overburden them with research participation.

The emphasis on protection of vulnerable people led to concerns that the benefits of research were not being fairly distributed. The exclusion of the disadvantaged and vulnerable, particular ethnicities, and women and children from research projects can mean that the results of research are not applicable to these groups and can exacerbate inequalities in health care. It can also exclude these groups from the direct benefit of participation in some forms of research, such as drug trials, where participation can provide access to treatment that is not otherwise available.

International ethics guidelines now generally include justice principles that cover both the protection of the vulnerable from unjust burdens and the fair inclusion of all. The *Declaration of Helsinki*, for example, includes the following clauses:

> 13. Groups that are underrepresented in medical research should be provided appropriate access to participation in research....
>
> 20. Medical research with a vulnerable group is only justified if the research is responsive to the health needs or priorities of this group and the research cannot be carried out in a non-vulnerable group. In addition, this group should stand to benefit from the knowledge, practices or interventions that result from the research.[38]

Research using linked data addresses the concerns associated with justice in research by enabling the inclusion of participants from the whole population and, hence, the just distribution of burdens and benefits. Direct recruitment often excludes the most disadvantaged members of the community from research. Language difficulties, transitory accommodation, mental illness, and other health issues may all be obstacles to participation in research. Research based on linked administrative data can minimise these difficulties and include vulnerable groups. In countries with universal public health care, administrative data can include the entire population and are likely to be more inclusive, representative, and unbiased. For example, refugees are likely to be difficult to recruit directly for research because of language barriers, high mobility, and distrust of authority. The study design in the case study in this chapter includes all refugees in the UK and so the burdens would be distributed among all refugees, not just a selected group or nationality. This would also mean that the benefits are more likely to be accurate and relevant to all refugees in the UK.

The results from research using linked data of this kind include those that are often excluded from intervention studies and can be used to target the health needs

[38] *Declaration of Helsinki* (n 6).

of marginalised groups.[39] However, it is always important to consider whether a particular data collection reflects the diversity of the target population.[40] Some large data collections are not representative of all societal groups and their use in research may raise issues of justice. For example, many existing genomic data collections predominantly contain samples of European origin. The analysis of this data is likely to miss disease risk variants that are common among non-European groups and may distort effect size estimates.[41]

The individual risks involved in research using linked data can be fairly spread across whole populations. They are generally low and do not include physical risks. This helps to mitigate concerns about unfairly burdening individual members of vulnerable groups. However, there are other risks that may have a particular and potentially unfair impact on vulnerable groups such as stigmatisation, discrimination, and impacts on cultural values. While applying the value of justice requires the fair distribution of risks and benefits, the value of beneficence requires the identification of risks and benefits and a decision about whether the potential benefits of research projects outweigh any risks. This is discussed further in the following section.

5.4.3 *Beneficence*

A beneficent act is one that is done to promote the well-being of others, but in the research context, the beneficence principle must take into account the risks of harm associated with the research. It is framed as a utilitarian enquiry requiring the balancing of benefits and risks of the project.[42] The burdens and potential risks must be justified by the likely benefits of the research. All the international guidelines capture this. For example, the *Declaration of Helsinki* states:

> Medical research involving human subjects may only be conducted if the importance of the objective outweighs the risks and burdens to the research subjects.[43]

To demonstrate beneficence, researchers must demonstrate not only the benefits of their research but also how they will minimise any risks.

In research involving direct contact with participants, the focus is usually on the immediate impact on the people participating. In research using linked data,

39 A Ballantyne and G Schaefer, 'Consent and the Ethical Duty to Participate in Health Data Research' (2018) 44(6) *Journal of Medical Ethics* 392.

40 S Malanga et al, 'Who's Left Out of Big Data? How Big Data Collection, Analysis, and Use Neglect Populations Most in Need of Medical and Public Health Research and Interventions' in I Cohen et al (eds), *Big Data, Health Law and Bioethics* (Cambridge University Press, 2018) 98.

41 E Cohn, G Henderson, and P Appelbaum, 'Distributive Justice, Diversity, and Inclusion in Precision Medicine: What Will Success Look Like?' (2017) 19(2) *Genetics in Medicine* 157.

42 I Pieper and C Thomson, 'Beneficence As a Principle in Human Research' (2016) 34 *Monash Bioethics Review* 117.

43 *Declaration of Helsinki* (n 6) [16].

beneficence requires a wider focus and recognition that the risks and benefits are long term and can include whole communities as well as individuals.

In data-based research, it is unusual for there to be any immediate concrete benefit to the individuals whose data is used. The improved understanding of the causes and risks of diseases and the impacts of healthcare delivery gained through data-based research lead to broad outcomes. The benefits are generally longer-term changes to health care, policy, and practices that benefit either specific groups in the community or the whole community. The principle of beneficence requires that researchers maximise the benefits of their research. This encompasses not only the design and conduct of the research but also the application of the results. There is growing recognition that health researchers have an ethical obligation to promote the translation of their research outcomes into concrete benefits through the dissemination of their research, not just through academic channels but directly to participant groups, policy makers, and healthcare decision makers.[44] For example, the case study described earlier in the chapter would not be ethical unless the results of the study were conveyed to refugee groups in languages and formats accessible to these groups and translated into improved and relevant mental health services for the refugee community in the UK.

Research using linked data rarely involves any physical risks for the participants, but the use of linked data for research is not without individual risks. The common risk shared by all projects using individual-level health information is the risk to privacy. The exposure of private information can cause psychological and social harms, as well as economic risks, through stigmatisation and discrimination. Malicious access to personal details exposes people to the risk of fraud, theft, or other crimes. As the volume and detail of data increase and the analytic power and expertise improve, the risks of re-identification increase. Seemingly innocuous, unrelated, or anonymous data can be used to determine very specific things about individuals. Big Data involving accumulations of individual-level information, or 'profiling', can also build very detailed and intrusive pictures about individuals. The information does not necessarily have to be 'personal' to be revealing. For example, Stanford researchers were able to infer from telephone metadata (telephone number and length of call) that a person likely suffered from cardiac arrhythmia.[45]

Researchers have an ethical obligation to minimise these risks by minimising identifiability and access to the data and by implementing a suitable information security plan and meticulous information governance. Ethics review committees need to assess the likelihood of harm eventuating from disclosure and the seriousness

44 M Aitken, S Cunningham-Burley, and C Pagliari, 'Moving from Trust to Trustworthiness: Experiences of Public Engagement in the Scottish Health Informatics Programme' (2016) 43(5) *Science and Public Policy* 713.

45 J Mayer, P Mutchler, and J Mitchell, 'Evaluating the Privacy Properties of Telephone Metadata' (2016) 113(20) *Proceedings of the National Academy of Sciences* 5536.

of the likely consequences. This assessment requires expertise in information technology and security that may not be available in the membership of committees. Committees tasked with reviewing Big Data research will need to add this expertise to their membership or seek external advice.[46]

The international research guidelines have traditionally focused on protecting participants from abuse and have been expressed in terms of potential risks to individual participants in research.[47] In Big Data research, it is important to consider the community-based risks as well as individual risks. Some of the more recent international guidelines provide guidance on group risks, for example the *CIOMS Guidelines*.

Health research using linked data aims to understand the impact of factors such as disease, health care, environment, and socio-demographics on populations. The results reveal patterns about particular groups in society and may have both a beneficial and a negative impact on the group. Ethical consideration should be sensitive to the risks that the outcomes of research may lead to discrimination or stigmatisation of specific groups and may impinge on cultural beliefs.[48] These risks can result from the publication and implementation of results of research projects and must be weighed against the potential harm from not conducting, publishing, or implementing the research. Community risks of this kind are not eliminated by de-identifying or aggregating data.[49]

In the case study discussed in this chapter, the publication of results that indicate a prevalence of mental illness in the refugee community could lead to stigmatisation and discrimination in housing and employment. These risks must be weighed against the potential to improve the provision of health care and the harm to individuals and society if good health care is not provided.

5.4.4 *Respect*

Respect in research requires that the human value of all participants is recognised. Research should be conducted in a way that acknowledges that value.[50] The well-being, feelings, and interests of participants should be considered, and they should be treated with dignity. People's cultural and social context should be recognised and respected, and their ability to live according to their own values and wishes should be supported.[51]

46 M Ienca et al, 'Considerations for Ethics Review of Big Data Health Research: A Scoping Review' (2018) 13(10) *PLoS ONE* e0204937.

47 B Mittelstadt and L Floridi, 'The Ethics of Big Data: Current and Foreseeable Issues in Biomedical Contexts' (2015) 22(2) *Science and Engineering Ethics* 303.

48 M Mello and L Wolf, 'The Havasupai Indian Tribe Case: Lessons for Research Involving Stored Biologic Samples' (2010) 363(3) *New England Journal of Medicine* 204.

49 Ballantyne (n 27); Mittelstadt and Floridi (n 47).

50 N Dickert, 'Re-Examining Respect for Human Research Participants' (2009) 19(4) *Kennedy Institute of Ethics Journal* 311.

51 Pieper and Thomson, 'Justice in Human Research Ethics' (n 37).

Respect is prominent in all international research ethics guidelines. The *Declaration of Helsinki*, for example, states:

> Medical research is subject to ethical standards that promote and ensure respect for all human subjects and protect their health and rights.[52]

The *CIOMS Guidelines* state:

> All research with humans must be carried out in ways that show respect and concern for the rights and welfare of individual participants and the communities in which research is carried out.[53]

Respect links all the core values of research ethics. Research cannot be respectful unless it has research merit, it is just in the distribution of risks and benefits, there is proper protection of participants, and the risks justify the likely benefits of the project.

Respect for individual autonomy is a key component in the principle of respect in human research. It requires respecting a person's freedom to decide for themselves whether to participate according to their own values and priorities. Informed consent is the practical tool used to protect autonomy and ensure that people have a free and real choice.

In practice, respect is often equated with respect for autonomy and informed consent.[54] Lysaught attributes this narrowing of the concept to the influence of *The Principles of Biomedical Ethics,* first published in 1979.[55] There, Beauchamp and Childress explicitly limit the principle of respect to respect for autonomy. Respect is described as respecting an individual's freedom to choose for themselves whether or not to participate in research.

The centrality of consent is explicable in the historical context of abuses and the focus of early guidelines on research involving clinical interventions. Informed consent was understood as a mechanism that enabled people to protect themselves from harm and exploitation. However, if respect is simply conflated with informed consent, then it is a very thin version of respect that ignores other important ways of demonstrating respect and has little relevance to most research using linked data. While some of the international and national guidelines include a broader description of respect, the detailed guidance provided is largely confined to informed consent.

52 *Declaration of Helsinki* (n 6) [7].

53 *CIOMS Guidelines* (n 8) 2.

54 I Pieper and C Thomson, 'The Value of Respect in Human Research Ethics: A Conceptual Analysis and a Practical Guide' (2014) 32(3–4) *Monash Bioethics Review* 232; N Kass and R Faden, 'Ethics and Learning Health Care: The Essential Roles of Engagement, Transparency, and Accountability' (2018) 2(4) *Learning Health Systems* e10066; R Faden et al, 'An Ethics Framework for a Learning Health Care System: A Departure from Traditional Research Ethics and Clinical Ethics' (2013) 43(s1) *Hastings Center Report* S16.

55 M Lysaught, 'Respect: Or, How Respect for Persons Became Respect for Autonomy' (2004) 29(6) *Journal of Medicine and Philosophy* 665; T Beauchamp and J Childress, *Principles of Biomedical Ethics* (Oxford University Press, 1979).

If respect focuses only on consent, then it has no application to people who do not have decision-making capacity and no application to research where seeking consent is impracticable. This includes most research using linked data. A narrow view of respect fails to acknowledge and value the contribution of participants in this kind of research. Insistence on consent may not demonstrate respect if it denies people, who may want to contribute to society, the ability to act according to their values.[56] If the principle of respect is to have any value in the ethical evaluation of research using linked data, then it needs to be re-conceptualised and guidance is needed on other ways of demonstrating respect.

A further criticism of the emphasis on consent is that it is overly individualistic and is reduced to a libertarian principle of non-interference.[57] It ignores the interrelatedness and interdependence of individuals in communities. This is significant for three reasons.

First, as discussed, the risks associated with Big Data are often group risks, such as discrimination and stigmatisation, rather than individual risks, and can harm people who are not participants in the research. While consent enables individual participants the opportunity to decide whether they wish to take the risk of harm, it cannot protect others in their community who may also bear the risk. Consent does not give other members of the affected community autonomy.

Second, the expansion of whole-of-population, data-based and genetic research and the recognition of the collective nature of these endeavours as well as their shared risks and benefits have led to a shift to a more communitarian approach to bioethics. The central position given to the protection of individual rights and autonomy is being challenged, with a growing understanding of the entwined interests of individuals, groups, and the public discussed in Chapter 2 and by calls to consider the social and political implications of the research that is done and the research that is not done.[58]

Third, an overemphasis on individuality and liberty ignores other values that play an important role in some people's decisions to participate in research, such as altruism. This is particularly pertinent where consent is impracticable and individuals cannot choose for themselves how they prioritise those values. While a desire for autonomy and the ability to decide for themselves is clearly important to most people, it is not necessarily or always the most important preference. Nor is self-interest

[56] R Rhodes, 'Rethinking Research Ethics' (2010) 10(10) *American Journal of Bioethics* 19 ('Rethinking Research Ethics 2010').

[57] Lysaught (n 55).

[58] B Knoppers and R Chadwick, 'Human Genetic Research: Emerging Trends in Ethics' (2005) 6(1) *Nature Reviews Genetics* 75; G Williams, 'Bioethics and Large-Scale Biobanking: Individualistic Ethics and Collective Projects' (2005) 1(2) *Genomics, Society and Policy* 1; K Berg and R Chadwick, 'Solidarity and Equity: New Ethical Frameworks for Genetic Databases' (2001) 2(4) *Nature Reviews Genetics* 318.

always the sole or dominant motivation. If this is ignored, then there is a failure to properly respect the values and preferences of the people concerned.[59]

Where individual consent is impracticable, the decision to permit the use of linked data is made collectively by ethics or privacy committees who are asked to approve a waiver of consent. These substitute decision makers have the difficult task of making a decision that reflects the community's views and preferences on the use of linked data without consent.

All the international guidelines make some provision for a waiver of consent, however, as the case study in this chapter demonstrates, not all would permit a waiver of consent in a research project with a typical design using linked data. The *CIOMS Guidelines* provide the most appropriate guidance for this kind of research.[60]

The domestic ethics guidelines examined in Chapter 7 permit a waiver of consent, with ethics committee approval, where consent is impracticable. Those guidelines that provide detailed guidance or criteria for the granting of a waiver of consent generally include a requirement of minimal risk,[61] and some also require consideration of the public benefit from the research.[62] This guidance is framed as a utilitarian exercise of balancing risks and benefits and reflects the principle of beneficence. In our view, minimal risk and the prospect of real benefit are the bare essentials for a waiver of consent to use linked data in research. There are other ways of demonstrating respect to research participants who are unable to decide for themselves that should also be considered.[63] Ethics committees making decisions to waive consent for the use of linked data need further guidance on how respect is applicable to these decisions.

Where research using linked data is conducted without consent, guidance on respect should also include the following considerations:

- *Impracticability*: A waiver of consent limits individuals' autonomy and cannot be respectful if seeking consent is practicable. Where researchers have a direct relationship with participants, for example where they are using data that they have collected directly from participants themselves, then consent for the research using linked data should normally be obtained.
- *Consultation and collaboration*: Researchers should consider the ways in which they can seek the views of the relevant community on the conduct

59 Rhodes, 'Rethinking Research Ethics 2010' (n 56).

60 *CIOMS Guidelines* (n 8) Guideline 10.

61 National Health and Medical Research Council, Australian Research Council and Universities Australia, *National Statement on Ethical Conduct in Human Research* (National Health and Medical Research Council, 2018 ed, 2007) ('*National Statement*'); Canadian Institutes of Health Research, Natural Sciences and Engineering Research Council of Canada, and Social Sciences and Humanities Research Council, *Tri-Council Policy Statement Ethical Conduct for Research Involving Humans* (Document No TCPS2 2018, December 2018).

62 *National Statement* (n 61).

63 Dickert (n 50).

of the project, for example through community reference groups or public consultation. Ethics committees should consider evidence of the views and preferences of the relevant community. In particular, the following should be considered:
  - Waiver of consent: What is the community view on the use of linked data without consent?
  - The aims of the project: Does the community value this research? Does it address an issue that they regard as important? Has there been collaboration with the relevant community to identify the research questions they would like investigated?
  - The methods: Has there been consultation and collaboration with the community on the way the project will be conducted and the dissemination of the results?
- *Protection*: Ethics committees should consider whether the researchers have understood and acknowledged both the individual risks to participants and any group risks and have taken appropriate steps to minimise those risks.
- *Acknowledgement*: Researchers and ethics committees should consider whether conduct of the project and the subsequent publication of the outcomes provides appropriate acknowledgement of the contribution of the participants.
- *Dissemination of the results to the participants*: Researchers and ethics committees should consider how the participants can be informed of the outcomes of the research. This could include local media outlets, social media, and direct meetings with the relevant community.
- *Research translation*: Ensuring that outcomes are translated into real benefits for the participants, the participants' community, or the wider public. Ethics committees and researchers should consider the appropriate role for researchers in ensuring that research outcomes are translated into improved practice and policy.

To demonstrate respect in the case study presented in this chapter, the researchers would need to demonstrate a detailed plan that covers the points in the above list. As approximately 600,000 participants are required, it is likely that obtaining individual consent is impracticable. In addition to an appropriate data management plan, a significant community involvement programme would be required prior to the research project to assess whether there is community support for the project, to obtain the advice of the community on the conduct of the project, and to develop a clear plan to inform the participants of the results and translate the results into improved refugee mental health services.

5.5 CONCLUSION

National human ethics guidelines and practices arise from and are influenced by international ethics guidelines. International ethics guidelines also have an impact on how ethics committees make decisions about whether individual research projects are ethical or not. Therefore, it is important that the international guidelines explicitly address the issues associated with data-intensive research.

Some authors have suggested that the current internationally agreed framework for ethical conduct in human research (research merit and integrity; justice; beneficence; respect) is not fit for purpose for data-intensive research and should be replaced.[64] The current international guidelines are not consistent in their approach to the use of data for research. Some guidelines take a relatively permissive approach to waiving the requirement for consent; others take a very restrictive approach. There are also differences in how collective interests are considered and balanced with the protection of individual interests. More consistency is required in the international guidelines, but this does not mean that an entirely new international data ethics framework is necessary. The current overarching ethics framework is valuable but is often too narrowly interpreted. The principles of research merit and integrity, justice, beneficence, and respect can be applied to the use of individual-level data for research, particularly if the differences between interventional and observational research are acknowledged.

If a new interpretation of the existing ethics framework is to be successfully implemented for data-intensive research, it will require both researchers and ethics committees to have skills and experience in data science and data management to evaluate the research merit of data projects and to assess the risks of data breaches and privacy risks.[65] They will also need an understanding of the aims and methods of engaging and collaborating with the community in the development and conduct of research.

In summary, our conclusions in this chapter are:

1. International research ethics guidelines should be re-drafted so that they are consistent and provide useful guidance for the ethical consideration of research using linked data. They should recognise that research without consent can be ethical in circumstances where consent is not practicable, the risks are minimal, and the research has important value. They should also consistently recognise the potential for risks as well as the benefits to individuals and collectives who are not participants in the research.
2. The four core values (research merit and integrity, justice, beneficence, respect) should be retained as the foundation of ethical review and should be interpreted for data-intensive research. In particular, the interpretation of the value of respect must extend beyond informed consent and the autonomy of participants. The value of respect should include respect for the multiple, divergent, and sometimes conflicting rights, interests, and values of the relevant individuals and groups.

64 Ballantyne (n 27).
65 Ienca et al (n 46).

3. Additional guidance on interpreting the core values for data-intensive research should be developed. This should include guidance on respect that goes beyond consent, on the evaluation of the range of individual and collective interests, and on consultation and collaboration with the relevant communities.
4. Ethics committees require the necessary skills and experience in data science, data management, and community involvement to assess applications for data-intensive research. The use of specialist data ethics committees may be appropriate.

6

Law

6.1 INTRODUCTION

Legal frameworks are central to a consideration of the formation and implementation of public policy, including public policy in relation to government decision makers. McDonald and Sedgwick note in relation to health law, for example, that:

> Health law declares the values upon which the health system is based, shapes social processes to achieve public ends and provides a structure for the complex interactions that occur within a modern health system. Health law regulates decision-makers in health systems by establishing who has the power to participate in decisions and in what circumstances, establishing processes through which decisions are made, and creating mechanisms for decision-makers to be held publicly accountable.[1]

The legal frameworks governing data linkage and data-based research, in the jurisdictions considered in this book, are made up of several distinct but interrelated bodies of law. This includes constitutional arrangements; various causes of action under the common law such as breach of confidentiality; legislation regulating the handling and protection of data; and legislation authorising governments to collect, use, and share data. Each of these bodies of law developed with different objectives and from different sources but they all attempt to balance the various interests involved when governments collect and use citizens' data, including using and sharing it for research. Many of the restrictions on collection, use, and disclosure of data are intended to protect the privacy interests of individuals. Those who work with data must comply with all these bodies of law.

Although they are conceptually distinct, one body of law often has an impact on another, for example by way of an exception, and they must be reconciled with each other. Together, they contain the current legal norms concerning the collection, use, and disclosure of personal information.

Each of these bodies of law provides some protection for individual privacy; however, that protection is always limited. First, the legal rules only apply to 'personal' data. This is variously defined but all the definitions adopt the concept of reasonable identifiability, that is, that data is personal when it is reasonably possible to identify the individual from the data. Second, the model of protection offered largely centres on a model of individual control of their own data and is dependent on the ability of individuals to undertake the management of their data. Third, the restrictions on the use and sharing of data are qualified by a raft of exceptions that address the balance between individuals' interests in their data and wider public interests in the use of information. In seeking to find this balance, law and policy makers draw on the human rights norms and ethical principles discussed in the preceding chapters.

[1] F McDonald and D Sedgwick, 'The Legal Framework of the Australian Health System' in B White, F McDonald, and L Willmott (eds), *Health Law in Australia* (Thomson Reuters, 2nd ed, 2014) 69, 70–1.

This chapter describes the general operation of each of the relevant bodies of law and considers the way in which it impacts on research using linked data. Examples from Australia, Canada, and the United Kingdom (UK) are used to illustrate how the use of linked data for research is regulated. The chapter also explores ways in which the use of data for research is unjustifiably restricted by complex, overlapping, and poorly designed regulation and makes recommendations for reform to better balance the relevant interests of individuals, groups, and the community.

6.2 CONSTITUTIONAL LAW

Constitutional laws provide the broad framework for national regulatory regimes. Constitutional laws have the highest legal status within countries and all other laws and rules in a jurisdiction must be consistent with them. They are important in the context of decision making for data linkage because they establish the rules that regulate the institutions of government and the relationships between them – including between federal and state or provincial governments – and the relationship between government and citizens. Constitutional arrangements make clear which level of government is responsible for each area of law and policy such as the provision of health services or the collection, sharing, and linkage of personal information in each jurisdiction. In all jurisdictions under consideration, this involves a significant level of intergovernmental cooperation and coordination.

The UK, Canada, and Australia are all constitutional monarchies and parliamentary democracies based on written rules and unwritten but foundational 'conventions' of constitutional practice. For example, by convention UK government ministers, including the prime minister, must have a seat in Parliament in order to hold office.[2] This Westminster system of responsible government – which was adopted, with some amendments, into the Australian and Canadian contexts – ensures that government ministers, and the agencies they lead, are responsible to the parliament and, ultimately, to the public.

As discussed in Chapter 3, representative, democratic arrangements like this can provide broad political legitimacy for law and decision making in relation to the collection and linkage of data for health research. They do not, however, guarantee that a social licence will exist for specific laws and policies developed by a government. The failure of the National Health Service (NHS) England initiative care.data,[3] for example, has been attributed to a failure to win the public's trust and doctors' support,[4] and has been characterised as a loss of social

[2] R Blackburn, 'Britain's Unwritten Constitution', British Library: Magna Carta (Web Page, 13 March 2015) <www.bl.uk/magna-carta/articles/britains-unwritten-constitution#>.

[3] This was a UK National Health Service initiative to take data from general practice records and upload them to the National Health and Social Care Information Centre (HSCIC) database on the basis of an opt-out model. The scheme had a number of aims including to facilitate health research.

[4] F Godlee, 'What Can We Salvage from care.data?' (2016) 354 *BMJ* i3907.

licence.[5] On this basis, more needs to be done to gain and maintain community support for specific data initiatives than simply relying on democratic legitimacy.

Each of the three jurisdictions also has some form of constitutional power sharing arrangements in place. In the UK, this has been achieved by devolving certain powers to national and local governments through legislation. Canada and Australia are constitutional federations where power is shared between the federal and state or provincial governments. In both jurisdictions, constitutional power has also been devolved to a number of territories. The UK, Australia, and Canada have related but divergent constitutional arrangements and so will be discussed separately, focusing on the implications for law and decision making in relation to research using linked data.

6.2.1 *The United Kingdom*

For historical reasons, and unlike most modern states, the UK does not have a codified written constitution, although there are laws that create and regulate some aspects of the constitutional arrangements, for example the devolution of power to the national legislatures: the Scottish Parliament,[6] the Welsh Parliament,[7] and the Northern Ireland Assembly.[8] The legislation establishing these institutional arrangements specifies certain matters as reserved to the UK Westminster Parliament – including data protection – and, where matters are not reserved, they are devolved to each national legislature. The UK Parliament can still legislate in the devolved areas, but based on constitutional convention, it will not normally do so without a legislative consent motion passed by the relevant national body.[9]

Data protection legislation, for example, is made by the UK Westminster Parliament and applies throughout the UK to personal data held by both private and public sector organisations at Westminster and national levels. This avoids, to some extent, the issues of overlap and inconsistency evident in Australia and Canada and discussed further in the following sections.

While some areas of health have been reserved to the UK Parliament – for example, genetics and the funding of scientific research by Research Councils – devolved matters include the provision of health services. This means that many administrative data collections are held by the NHS systems in England, Scotland, Wales, and Northern Ireland. Greer has noted that all 'four UK health systems have lively health research communities that often use data from sites in those different

5 P Carter, G Laurie, and M Dixon-Woods, 'The Social Licence for Research: Why care.data Ran into Trouble' (2015) 41(5) *Journal of Medical Ethics* 404.

6 *Scotland Act 1998* (UK).

7 *Government of Wales Act 1998* (UK).

8 *Northern Ireland Act 1998* (UK).

9 C Sear and P Bowers, 'The "Sewel Convention"' (Standard Note No SN/PC/2084, UK Parliament, 25 November 2005).

systems'.[10] Other data collections, such as the UK Census data, are collected and held centrally by the UK Data Service.[11]

6.2.2 Canada

Unlike the UK, Canada does have a codified, written constitution made up of three elements: the *Constitution Act 1867*,[12] the *Constitution Act 1982*,[13] and the *Canadian Charter of Rights and Freedoms* ('*Canadian Charter*').[14] These constitutional documents define the powers of the executive, legislative, and judicial branches of government at both the federal and the provincial level. As discussed in Chapter 4, Canada is the only one of the three jurisdictions under consideration to have in place a constitutional charter of rights. Canada's three northern territories do not have legislative powers in their own right,[15] but the federal parliament has devolved legislative power in a range of areas to the territorial legislatures.

The *Constitution Act 1867* provides that the provincial legislatures have exclusive power in specified areas – including taxation within the province, the establishment and management of hospitals (other than marine hospitals) and other healthcare establishments, and the regulation of health and other professions – and the federal parliament has exclusive power in specified areas of national interest such as census and statistics, quarantine, and marine hospitals. The federal parliament also has power in residual areas not assigned exclusively to either jurisdiction under the power to legislate for the 'peace, order and good government of Canada'.[16] The federal and provincial legislatures both have power in some listed areas with provisions for resolving any inconsistency.

Not every important area of law and policy is explicitly listed in the Canadian constitutional arrangements and, despite the provisions relating to residual power, these may not fall exclusively within the power of the federal government. The Canadian Supreme Court has found that the broad area of health, for example, which is not specifically listed in the *Constitution Act 1867*, is an area of concurrent or shared jurisdiction and that both levels of government may legislate in the area depending on the focus of the legislation.[17] Federal legislation in the health context can be supported by, for example, the express federal power in relation to taxation[18] and the power to

[10] S Greer, 'Devolution and Health in the UK: Policy and its Lessons Since 1998' (2016) 118 *British Medical Bulletin* 17, 18.

[11] UK Data Service, 'Health and Health Behaviour', *Economic and Social Research Council* (Web Page) <www.ukdataservice.ac.uk/get-data/themes/health.aspx>.

[12] *Constitution Act 1867* (Imp), 30 & 31 Vict, c 3 ('*Constitution Act 1867*').

[13] *Canada Act 1982* (UK) c 11, sch B ('*Constitution Act 1982*').

[14] Ibid cl 11 sch B pt I.

[15] The Northwest Territories, Yukon, and Nunavut.

[16] *Constitution Act 1867* (n 12) s 91.

[17] *Carter v Canada (Attorney General)* [2015] SCC 5 [53]; *RJR MacDonald Inc v Canada (Attorney General)* [1995] 3 SCR 199 [32]; *Schneider v The Queen* [1982] 2 SCR 112, 142.

[18] *Constitution Act 1867* (n 12) s 91(3).

make payments out of consolidated revenue.[19] Together, these powers are referred to as the federal spending power.

While the provision of health care and the regulation of health insurance are areas within provincial jurisdiction,[20] the federal parliament – relying on the federal spending power – has the power to pass legislation such as the *Canada Health Act 1985*,[21] which concerns federal funding for provincial public health insurance schemes and the criteria that provincial laws must satisfy to receive full funding. These federal powers have also been used to legislate in relation to health research and the collection and use of health information.[22]

Because of these constitutional arrangements, administrative health data is primarily collected at the provincial level in the course of the provision of healthcare services. This includes data relating to public health insurance, which is administered at the provincial level, although partially funded and regulated by the federal government. There is, however, a level of standardisation and centralisation of the data, which is reported to federal institutions such as the Canadian Institute for Health Information (CIHI).[23] Gaudreault-Desbiens and Poirier have noted that in all federations intergovernmental cooperation is a practical necessity and that Canada is no exception to this despite the 'dualist' nature of the Canadian Constitution where constitutional power seems to be clearly divided between the federal government and the provinces.[24]

The constitutional arrangements in relation to data protection in Canada are also complex, with the federal government legislating based on its constitutional powers in relation to the federal public sector and its power to regulate trade and commerce. The provincial governments have also passed data protection legislation in relation to the provincial public sectors and the provision of healthcare services. This has resulted in multiple and, in some cases, overlapping levels of data protection regulation.

6.2.3 *Australia*

Australia, like Canada, has a codified, written constitution which defines the powers of the executive, legislative, and judicial branches of government at the federal

19 Ibid s 102.

20 Power to legislate in relation to public health insurance is not explicitly mentioned in the *Constitution Act 1867* (n 12) but was presumed to attach to the provincial power in relation to hospitals and other healthcare services: see D Martin et al, 'Canada's Universal Health-Care System: Achieving its Potential' (2018) 391 *Lancet* 1718, 1719.

21 *Canada Health Act*, RSC 1985, c C-6.

22 C Flood, W Lahey, and B Thomas, 'Federalism and Health Care in Canada: A Troubled Romance?' in P Oliver, P Macklem, and N Des Rosiers (eds), *The Oxford Handbook of the Canadian Constitution* (Oxford University Press, 2017) 449, 459; *Canadian Institutes of Health Research Act*, SC 2000, c 6.

23 K Lucyk et al, 'Administrative Health Data in Canada: Lessons from History' (2015) 15(69) *BMC Medical Informatics and Decision Making* 4.

24 J Gaudreault-Desbiens and J Poirier, 'From Dualism to Cooperative Federalism and Back? Evolving and Competing Conceptions of Canadian Federalism' in P Oliver, P Macklem, and N Des Rosiers (eds), *The Oxford Handbook of the Canadian Constitution* (Oxford University Press, 2017) 391.

level and largely preserves the broad constitutional powers of the states.[25] Like the UK and Canada, Australia's constitutional system includes a range of constitutional conventions that help to ensure responsible government.

Australia is also a federation in which the power to legislate is shared under the *Australian Constitution* between the federal and state parliaments. The federal legislature has the power to legislate in specified areas of national interest – for example, taxation, external affairs, quarantine, census and statistics, as well as pharmaceutical, sickness and hospital benefits, and medical and dental services.[26] There are a limited number of areas in which the federal legislature has exclusive power, for example in relation to the federal public service.[27] In contrast to the constitutional arrangements in Canada, the states in Australia have concurrent power in most areas and residual power in relation to areas not covered by the *Australian Constitution*. However, where a state law is inconsistent with a valid federal law, the federal law prevails to the extent of the inconsistency.[28] Like Canada, Australia's internal territories do not have legislative powers in their own right,[29] but the federal parliament has devolved legislative power in a range of areas to the territorial legislatures.

The result of these arrangements is that the state parliaments have general power to regulate health services. On the other hand, the federal parliament has explicit power in relation to taxation; the power to make conditional grants to the states and territories;[30] as well as pharmaceutical, sickness and hospital benefits, and medical and dental services. These powers provide the legal foundations for Australia's national public health insurance scheme. On this basis, legislative power in relation to health is shared between the federal and state governments, requiring a high level of cooperative federalism and intergovernmental programmes and policies. Although much administrative health data is collected at the state level – for example, public hospital admission and discharge data – some data collections are held at the national level – for example, those related to public health insurance: the Medicare and Pharmaceutical Benefits data collections.

6.3 COMMON LAW

In broad terms, there are three main sources of the law: constitutional law; statute law – such as the data protection legislation and authorising statutes – which is made by parliaments; and the common law, made by the courts. The common law,

25 *Commonwealth of Australia Constitution Act 1900* (Imp) 63 & 64 Vict c 12, s 9 ('*Australian Constitution*').
26 Ibid s 51(xxiiiA).
27 Ibid s 52.
28 Ibid s 109.
29 The Australian Capital Territory (ACT) and the Northern Territory (NT).
30 *Australian Constitution* (n 25) s 96.

like statute law, must be consistent with constitutional law and may be incorporated, amended, or overridden by statute. This reflects the primacy of the legislative branch of government, the parliament, in liberal democracies.

In the absence of statute law, the common law has developed several causes of action that protect private information and can limit the use of data for research. If the use or disclosure of private information for data linkage and research is not clearly authorised by statute, then it may be unlawful under the common law. For example, if the statutory authorisation is confined to 'medical research', then the sharing of data for other kinds of research will be governed by the common law. While most jurisdictions now have legislation dealing with the research use of data, it does not always cover all research and all data and it is not always clear that it provides immunity to common law actions. In these circumstances, or where there is doubt about the interpretation of the legislation, then the common law must also be considered.

The law in this area is dynamic, and the courts have responded to developing technology and new concerns about privacy; however, the common law can only respond to the cases that come to the courts and change can be slow. It can be criticised for failing to keep up.

The jurisdictions considered in this book all share common legal foundations and the issues faced are largely the same, but there is now a divergence between them in the way the common law has developed to meet these challenges. All jurisdictions have a common law action for breach of confidentiality, but in the UK the action for breach of confidence has developed to create an action for misuse of private information and in Canada two separate privacy torts have also been recognised by the courts – wrongful publication of private information and wrongful intrusions into private affairs and spaces. Each of these common law actions, and the possible implications for research using linked data, are considered in what follows.

6.3.1 *Breach of Confidence*

The duty of confidentiality, discussed here, was developed by courts applying principles of equity to ensure good faith in relationships recognised as confidential. Where information is confided by one person to another on the understanding that it is confidential, then the law will enforce that understanding. Duties of confidentiality may also be imposed by contract or statute and these duties will also be enforced by the courts.

The equitable duty of confidentiality can have a similar function to data protection legislation in protecting privacy, but the origins and essence of the duty are quite distinct. The equitable action for breach of confidence is based on public policy and the public interest in ensuring that people can confide information with the assurance their confidence will not be broken. The origin of the duty of confidence lies in maintaining confidential relationships.

The public interest in the confidentiality of the patient–carer relationship is clearly apparent. It is vital that patients trust their healthcare provider to maintain their confidence so that they confide the intimate information necessary for their health care,[31] thus ensuring the efficacy and efficiency of healthcare services.[32] Where the information is about personal matters, there is an additional underlying policy focus on protecting privacy.[33]

The traditional action for breach of confidence has three elements:

- the information has the quality of confidence;
- the information has been communicated in circumstances of confidence; and
- there has been unauthorised use of the information.[34]

6.3.1.1 Confidential Information

Almost all information confided in the context of health care will be regarded as confidential and will attract a duty of confidence. It has the quality of confidential information because it is information that is inaccessible to the public,[35] and it is intimate in nature.[36] This is clearly the case for information in clinical records and is equally so where health information is collected in administrative data collections, such as admission data, or diagnostic and treatment data. Identifiers separated from other content for linkage, such as name and address, should still be regarded as confidential information, even where they are publicly available, because the source of the data, for example a disease registry, can convey confidential health information. The disclosure of linkage variables to a linkage unit may, therefore, involve a breach of confidentiality if it is not authorised in some way.

Most linked data for research is shared without the identifiers such as name, address, and birth date. Therefore, the question arises as to whether individual-level information that has been de-identified in this way is still subject to a duty of confidentiality. The Court of Appeal (England and Wales) considered this question in R v. *Department of Health Ex parte Source Informatics Ltd* and held that there was no breach of confidentiality when Source Informatics Ltd bought patient prescription information from pharmacists and sold it on to pharmaceutical companies for marketing.[37] The information included the name of the

31 Z v *Finland* (1999) 45 BMLR 107, 124.

32 X v Y [1988] 2 All ER 648, 653; *Royal Women's Hospital* v *Medical Practitioners Board of Victoria* [2006] VSCA 85, [58].

33 T Aplin et al, *Gurry on Breach of Confidence* (Oxford University Press, 2nd ed, 2012) 194.

34 *Coco* v *AN Clark (Engineers) Ltd* [1969] RPC 41 (HC), 47 (Sir Robert Megarry J) ('*Coco* v *AN Clark*').

35 *Attorney General* v *Guardian Newspapers (No 2)* [1990] 1 AC 109, 215 (Bingham LJ) ('*AG* v *Guardian Newspapers [No 2]*'). Cf *Campbell* v *Mirror Group Newspapers Ltd* [2004] 2 AC 457, [157] (Baroness Hale) ('*Campbell* v *Mirror Group*').

36 *Stephens* v *Avery* [1988] 2 All ER 477.

37 R v *Department of Health Ex parte Source Informatics Ltd* [2001] QB 424.

prescribing doctor, the date of prescription, the product prescribed, and the quantity prescribed. The patient's name was removed. The court held that the patient's 'only legitimate interest is in the protection of his privacy' and that since privacy was adequately protected there was no breach of confidentiality.[38] The court rejected the argument that a breach of confidence should be recognised because the patient's autonomy was infringed. This aspect of the decision may no longer be accepted in light of subsequent decisions in the UK extending the action for breach of confidentiality based explicitly on the protection of autonomy and dignity and criticism that the case oversimplified the dignity interests involved.[39]

The decision in *R* v. *Department of Health Ex parte Source Informatics Ltd* is based on an assumption that patients' anonymity can be guaranteed. Source Informatics Ltd was confident that this could be achieved. This assumption may have been reasonable in 1999 when this case was heard; however, expanding technical capabilities enabling re-identification cast doubt on the applicability of this reasoning in the future.

6.3.1.2 Confidential Circumstances

There is a general expectation that information given by a patient to a healthcare provider is communicated and collected in circumstances of confidence.[40] The ethical obligation of confidence in health care has been recognised from the Hippocratic Oath through to all contemporary codes of professional ethics for health professionals[41] and is equally well recognised in law.[42]

The contemporary provision of health care is no longer confined to the intimacy of a direct personal relationship between patient and doctor. More often, it is provided by a series of employees of the public health system or of a corporate healthcare practice. Health records are compiled by a variety of professionals during various episodes of care at multiple geographic sites over the life of the patient. The healthcare organisation is subject to a duty of confidence and the duty extends to all those in the treating team as well as the administrative staff of the organisation who need to access the information. Where information is disclosed to other health professionals for referral, testing, and diagnosis or continuing care, the duty of confidentiality extends to the new recipients since they have notice of its confidentiality.[43]

38 Ibid 440 [35] (Simon Brown LJ).

39 *Campbell* v *Mirror Group* (n 35) [51] (Lord Hoffman); B Kaplan, 'Selling Health Data: De-identification, Privacy, and Speech' (2015) 24(3) *Cambridge Quarterly of Healthcare Ethics* 256.

40 *Coco* v *AN Clark* (n 34) 47–8 (Megarry J).

41 See, eg, UK General Medical Council, 'Confidentiality: Good Practice in Handling Patient Information', *Ethical Guidance for Doctors* (Web Page, 25 May 2018) <www.gmc-uk.org/ethical-guidance/ethical-guidance-for-doctors/confidentiality>.

42 *Hunter* v *Mann* [1974] QB 767; AG v *Guardian Newspapers [No 2]* (n 35) 255 (Lord Keith).

43 AG v *Guardian Newspapers [No 2]* (n 35) 281.

Health data managers, data linkers, and researchers who receive health information have a duty of confidentiality to the organisation that releases the data to them; however, there is no professional healthcare relationship with the patient on which to base a duty of confidentiality. The absence of a pre-existing relationship will no longer be critical in the UK with the development of the action for misuse of private information, discussed in Section 6.3.2.[44] In those jurisdictions in which the common law has not developed beyond the traditional action for breach of confidentiality, such as Australia, the courts have indicated that a duty of confidentiality will also extend to those who have notice that the information is confidential.[45]

All those involved in research using linked data are aware of the confidential nature of the information and the confidential circumstances under which it is collected, and therefore they are also under a duty of confidentiality to the patient. This duty will be recognised under the common law, and it may also be included in contractual terms in a data release agreement or in statutory provisions authorising the release of data for research.

6.3.1.3 Unauthorised Use

There will be a breach of confidence if the information is used or disclosed in an unauthorised way.[46] The permitted uses depend on the nature of the relationship, the expectations in that relationship, and the purpose for which the information was confided.[47] In the context of a healthcare relationship, the purpose is the clinical care of the patient. Confidential information can only be used for the health care of the patient and can only be disclosed to employees of the organisation who are involved in delivering care to the patient. Any other access, use, or disclosure by employees of the organisation will be a breach of confidence unless it is authorised in some other way, for example where there is consent or statutory authority.

Health data managers, data linkers, and researchers who receive confidential information may only use it for authorised purposes. For example, where there is consent for the use and disclosure of information for research, then it can only be used for research within the scope of that consent. Where there is statutory authorisation, then the use is confined by the scope of the statutory authority.

[44] Ibid 281 (Lord Goff); A v B *(a company)* [2002] 2 All ER 545, 553 (Woolf CJ); *Campbell* v *Mirror Group* (n 35) [14] (Lord Nicholls), [44] (Lord Hoffman), [85] (Lord Hope), [134] (Baroness Hope).

[45] *Lenah Game Meats* v *Australian Broadcasting Commission* (2001) 185 ALR 1, 11 [34]–[35] (Gleeson CJ); *AMI Australia Holdings Pty Ltd* v *Fairfax Media Publications Pty Ltd* (2011) Aust Torts Rep 82-077, [28], [135] (Brereton J).

[46] *Coco* v *AN Clark* (n 34) 47–8 (Megarry J).

[47] *Smith Kline & French* v *Community Services* (1991) 28 FCR 291, 303.

6.3.1.4 Consent and Implied Consent

A patient may give express consent to the use and disclosure of their health information for purposes other than their health care, such as the linkage of their data and its use for research. The consent must be voluntary, adequately informed, and given by a person who is sufficiently competent. The scope of the consent must cover the relevant use or disclosure of the confidential information.

Seeking consent is often problematic in data-intensive research because the linkage and extraction of data are remote in time and place from the original collection of data in the healthcare facility.[48] There is usually no direct relationship between the patient and the data custodian, the data linkage unit, or the researcher, and the cohorts can be very large. Specific consent for linkage and research can be sought at the time health care is provided if a prospective research project with a limited cohort has been defined. More often, research using linked data involves large retrospective studies of historic data. Blanket unspecified consent to use health information for research could be sought at the time of health care. This is sometimes done as part of general admission procedures; however, there is doubt as to whether this can be regarded as sufficiently voluntary or informed to be a valid consent to the use of information.[49]

Implied consent is inferred where it is reasonable to assume that the patient understood and agreed that the information would be used or disclosed in a particular way. It extends to the use of the information for record keeping and administrative purposes necessary for the delivery of health care. It may include audits conducted by staff within the health facility; however, it is unlikely to include the disclosure of information for audit to third parties not employed by the health facility. It would not currently extend to disclosure for research purposes. Implied consent cannot be relied on if a patient has explicitly refused, opted-out, or objected to the proposed use.

The general level of awareness in the community of the ways in which health information is used will determine the scope of implied consent. Privacy statements about the use of information given to patients may have an impact on this level of awareness, but it should not be assumed that patients are generally aware of the information in such privacy statements or that general community assumptions about use of information accurately reflect those statements.

Where there is a valid and express patient consent for the use of health information for a research project, then the use and disclosure of the information within the terms of the consent will not breach the duty of confidentiality. Reliance on extended or unspecified consent, or on implied consent, leaves the person disclosing the information vulnerable to an action for breach of confidence because of uncertainty about the validity and scope of the consent.

[48] See Chapter 2 'Individual, Collective, and Public Interests'.

[49] T Caulfield and N Ries, 'Consent, Privacy and Confidentiality in Longitudinal, Population Health Research: The Canadian Legal Context' (2004) 11 *Health Law Journal* 1.

6.3.1.5 Statutory Authority

The duty of confidence is not breached where the use or disclosure of the information is authorised or required by statute. Statutory provisions authorising the use and release of information for research generally, and for data linkage in particular, may be in data protection legislation or the authorising legislation directed at government data custodians. Both options are discussed in detail in Section 6.5.

Authorising provisions contain a variety of conditions under which the use and disclosure of information are authorised. These may be conditions minimising the impact on privacy, imposing public interest criteria, or specifying approval processes. The authorising provisions may also be limited to certain kinds of research. Provided these conditions are satisfied, there will be no breach of confidentiality. Clear statutory authority provides the most secure footing for the lawful use and release of data for research. However, this protection will only apply to research purposes authorised in the legislation, for example 'medical research',[50] and use and disclosure of data for other kinds of research that are not authorised may still be subject to an action for breach of confidence.

6.3.1.6 Public Interest

A defence to an action for breach of confidentiality is recognised where the public interest in preserving confidentiality is outweighed by a competing public interest.[51] The defence developed as a justification for a disclosure that revealed an 'inequity' such as a crime or intended crime. The defence now extends beyond the disclosure of crime or misconduct and includes disclosure to prevent a serious and imminent threat to health or safety.[52] The defence is expanding but its reach is unclear and varies between jurisdictions. In the UK, the defence now requires a court to weigh competing public interests against the public interest in preserving confidentiality.[53] For example, in X v. Y, Rose J concluded that the public interest in a free press and informed public debate did not outweigh the public interest that 'AIDs sufferers should be able to resort to hospitals without fear of this being revealed'.[54] In contrast, Australian courts have been more conservative and have been reluctant to adopt the approach of considering this broader range of competing interests.

50 *Privacy Act 1988* (Cth) s 95 ('*Australian Privacy Act*').

51 *AG* v *Guardian Newspapers [No 2]* (n 35) 282. Australian courts have been reluctant to adopt a general approach of weighing competing public interests. See, eg, *Smith Kline & French Laboratories (Australia) Ltd* v *Secretary, Department of Community Services and Health* (1990) 22 FCR 73, 110 (Gummow J).

52 W v *Edgell* [1990] Ch 359.

53 *AG* v *Guardian Newspapers [No 2]* (n 35) 282; *Blum* v *ANZ Bank New Zealand Ltd* [2015] NZCA 335.

54 X v Y (n 32) 660 (Rose J).

There needs to be a strong public interest argument to outweigh the public interest in maintaining trust in the confidentiality of health care. The public interest in the conduct of research has not been considered by the courts in this context but where parliament has considered the public interest and provided express statutory authority in certain prescribed circumstances, then it is unlikely that the public interest would be considered an adequate defence at common law in other circumstances that went beyond those statutory confines.

6.3.2 *Misuse of Private Information*

In the UK, the action for breach of confidence has developed under the direct influence of human rights instruments and the public policy basis of the duty of confidentiality has expanded to include an explicit role in protecting privacy.[55]

As discussed in Chapter 4, the *Human Rights Act 1998* (UK) – which incorporates provisions of the European Convention on Human Rights (ECHR), including the right to privacy[56] – makes it unlawful for public authorities, including courts, to act in ways that are incompatible with ECHR rights.[57] The courts have, therefore, interpreted the action for breach of confidentiality in light of those rights and have drawn on decisions of the European Court of Human Rights in this process. These developments have led to the recognition of a distinct cause of action for the misuse of private information.[58]

This new approach has led to two significant changes. First, the new cause of action has expanded to protect private information more broadly and is not confined to a relationship of confidence. Second, it has led to a more explicit evaluation of competing rights and public interests.

6.3.2.1 Reasonable Expectation of Privacy

The action for misuse of private information places less emphasis on the nature of the relationship in establishing obligations and more emphasis on the private nature of the information. There no longer needs to be an obligation of confidence imposed by the context of the communication. The nature of the information can be enough. There may be a cause of action where one 'knows or ought to know that

[55] *Campbell* v *Mirror Group* (n 35) [51] (Lord Hoffman).

[56] *Convention for the Protection of Human Rights and Fundamental Freedoms*, opened for signature 4 November 1950, 213 UNTS 221 (entered into force 3 September 1953), as amended by *Protocol No 11 to the Convention for the Protection of Human Rights and Fundamental* Freedoms, opened for signature 11 May 1994, ETS No 155 (entered into force 1 November 1998) art 8.

[57] *Human Rights Act 1998* (UK) s 6.

[58] *Campbell* v *Mirror Group* (n 35) [13]–[17] (Lord Nicholls); *OBG Ltd* v *Allan, Douglas* v *Hello! Ltd (No 3), Mainstream Properties Ltd* v *Young* [2008] 1 AC 1, 72 [255] (Lord Nicholls).

the person can reasonably expect his privacy to be protected'.[59] Health information has been described as 'easy to identify as private'.[60]

In *Campbell* v. *Mirror Group Newspapers*, the House of Lords held that the publication of photos and information about the plaintiff's attendance at meetings of Narcotics Anonymous was private information that should be protected even though there was no recognisable relationship of confidence and the photos were taken in a public place, because it was information about Ms Campbell's therapy.[61]

6.3.2.2 Public Interest Defence for Misuse of Private Information

The public interest defence has been reconfigured in the new action for misuse of private information. The courts are no longer focused on balancing the public interest in confidentiality with other public interests but instead are evaluating the individual right to privacy against competing rights and interests. These developments have occurred primarily in cases involving the media and have required the courts to consider the balance between the right to privacy and the right to freedom of expression. In these cases, the courts evaluate the comparative importance of the competing rights and consider whether the intrusion on the right is proportionate.[62] This explicit balancing of a range of competing rights and interests broadens the public interest defence and opens it to application in the context of health research. In that specific context, courts will need to consider the content and structure of ECHR article 8, which allows a public authority to place limits on the individual right to privacy where such limits are in accordance with the law and necessary in a democratic society for the protection of health and the rights and freedoms of others. This formulation includes both the public interest in protecting the health of the community and the individual right to health.

Where parliament has considered this balance between the right to privacy, the rights and freedoms of others, and the public interest in the health of the community, and has enacted statutory authority for some research but not all research, it may be more difficult to argue a public interest defence for research not included in those provisions. It is important, therefore, that statutory authority for the use and disclosure of information for research is framed broadly and in accordance with the principles articulated in Section 6.5 in relation to authorising legislation. Otherwise, it may inadvertently exclude a defence of public interest in an action for misuse of private information.

59 *Campbell* v *Mirror Group* (n 35) [85] (Lord Hope).

60 *Australian Broadcasting Commission* v *Lenah Game Meats* (2001) 208 CLR 199, 11 [42] (Gleeson CJ) ('ABC v *Lenah Game Meats*').

61 *Campbell* v *Mirror Group* (n 35).

62 *Re S (A Child)* [2005] 1 AC 593.

6.3.3 *Privacy Torts*

In the UK, the action for misuse of private information is now sometimes described as a tort.[63] In Australia, the possibility of the action for breach of confidence developing into a tortious action to protect privacy was recognised by the High Court in *ABC* v. *Lenah Game Meats*,[64] but the Court has not subsequently considered a case requiring it to address the issue directly. There have been some steps in that direction in Victoria and Western Australia, with the award of damages for distress in actions for breach of confidentiality.[65]

In Canada, two separate privacy torts have been recognised by courts: wrongful publication of private information and wrongful intrusions into private affairs and spaces.[66] The first of these torts, the wrongful publication of private information, was recognised by the Ontario Superior Court of Justice in *Jane Doe 46533* v. *ND*, a revenge porn case.[67] Justice Stinson held that publication was wrongful where 'the matter publicized or the act of the publication (a) would be highly offensive to a reasonable person; and (b) is not of legitimate concern to the public'.[68]

The second tort, invasion of seclusion, could apply to the unauthorised use and disclosure of health information for linkage and research even where there is no wider disclosure of identifiable information to others. In *Jones* v. *Tsige*, the Ontario Court of Appeal held the defendant liable where she had repeatedly accessed the personal bank details of her partner's former wife through her workplace computer.[69] She had no legitimate reason for accessing the records. The elements of the cause of action were held to be (1) intentional conduct; (2) invasion of the plaintiff's private affairs and concerns without lawful justification; and (3) that a reasonable person would regard the invasion as highly offensive, causing distress, humiliation, or anguish.[70] These privacy torts will be relevant to research using linked data if the use or disclosure goes beyond statutory authority. The court would need to determine whether a reasonable person would find the publication or intrusion offensive or highly offensive.

While some jurisdictions have developed common law privacy torts, others have legislated to create statutory privacy torts.[71] In Australia, where the common law has

63 *Vidal-Hall* v *Google Inc* [2015] EWCA Civ 311, 165 NLJ 7648, [2015] All ER (D) 307.

64 *ABC* v *Lenah Game Meats* (n 60) [132] (Gummow and Hayne JJ), [313]–[335] (Callinan J).

65 *Giller* v *Procopets* (2008) 24 VR 1; *Wilson v Ferguson* [2015] WASC 15.

66 These torts reflect two of Prosser's categories of privacy torts: see W Prosser, 'Privacy' (1960) 48 *California Law Review* 383.

67 *Jane Doe 46533* v *ND* (2016) 128 OR (3d) 352 ('*Jane Doe 46533*'). See also *Hosking* v *Runting* [2004] NZCA 34.

68 *Jane Doe 46533* (n 67) [46] (Stinson J).

69 *Jones* v *Tsige* (2012) 108 OR (3d) 241 ('*Jones* v *Tsige*'). See also *C* v *Holland* [2012] NZHC 2155.

70 *Jones* v *Tsige* (n 69) 261 [71].

71 See, eg, *Privacy Act*, RSBC 1996, c 373 (British Columbia); *Privacy Act*, CCSM 1996, c P-125 (Manitoba); *Privacy Act*, RSS 1978, c P-24 (Saskatchewan); *Privacy Act*, RSNL 1990, c P-22 (Newfoundland and Labrador).

been slow to develop, federal and state law reform bodies have recommended the introduction of a statutory cause of action for breach of privacy.[72] To date, none of these recommendations have been implemented.

Although courts have attempted to respond to the challenges of contemporary technology, the common law has not kept pace with the rapid changes in data-based research. The common law is complicated by a variety of causes of actions that remain relevant to data linkage and the use of data for research, and there are no significant differences between jurisdictions. The elements of these actions and the available defences have not been explored in the context of research, so their application remains unclear. This uncertainty has a dampening effect on the conduct of research and requires a clear statutory response.

6.4 DATA PROTECTION LEGISLATION

As discussed in Chapter 4, the right to privacy in international human rights law protects a broad array of interests, including one's private life, family life, home, and correspondence.[73] The right to protect one's personal data is one element of this broader right to privacy. This element of the right has been incorporated into the domestic law of all three jurisdictions under consideration and is central to decision making in relation to research using linked data. Privacy risks in the data linkage context include the increased risk of identifiability of research participants as data sets are combined as well as other risks to the individual and to any collectives to which they belong. These risks are discussed in detail in Chapter 2. In this section, we consider whether existing data protection legislation is fit for purpose in terms of appropriately regulating the collection, use, and disclosure of personal data for research using linked data.

Data protection legislation in Australia, Canada, and the UK developed in response to concerns about the increasing use of computers by government and the private sector in the 1960s and 1970s. In an ongoing dialogue, data protection legislation continues to be amended and updated in response to emerging technologies. The legislation was explicitly intended to implement international instruments dealing with human rights, privacy, and data protection. Federal public sector data protection legislation in Australia,[74] for example, was developed in order to give effect to the Organisation for Economic Co-operation and Development (OECD)

72 Australian Law Reform Commission, *For Your Information: Australian Privacy Law and Practice* (Report No 108, May 2008) ('*ALRC Report No 108*'); Australian Law Reform Commission, *Serious Invasions of Privacy in the Digital Era* (Report No 123, September 2014); New South Wales Law Reform Commission, *Invasion of Privacy* (Report No 120, August 2009); Victorian Law Reform Commission, *Surveillance in Public Places* (Report No 18, August 2010).

73 See, eg, *International Covenant on Civil and Political Rights*, opened for signature 16 December 1966, 999 UNTS 171 (entered into force 23 March 1976) art 17; ECHR (n 56) art 8.

74 *Australian Privacy Act* (n 50).

Guidelines on the Protection of Privacy and Transborder Flows of Personal Data ('*OECD Guidelines* 1980')[75] – which incorporated the first internationally agreed set of privacy principles – as well as obligations under the *International Covenant on Civil and Political Rights* (UN ICCPR).[76] The Guidelines were intended to facilitate the transfer of personal data across national borders by setting minimum standards in relation to the privacy of personal data and encouraging consistency in domestic regulation of the handling of personal data.[77] This remains a necessary and valuable aspiration in the context of research using linked data.

The *OECD Guidelines* 1980 were also foundational to the development of the *Privacy Act 1985* (Can)[78] and the *Data Protection Act 1984* (UK), although the UK statute was specifically enacted to allow the UK to ratify the Council of Europe's *Convention for the Protection of Individuals with Regard to Automatic Processing of Personal Data*.[79]

Although data protection legislation is, in our view, a foundational and necessary element in the regulatory framework for research using linked data, there are a number of ways in which the current legislation across the three jurisdictions unjustifiably impedes, rather than supports, such research. These issues – continued reliance on the notice and choice paradigm, regulatory complexity, inconsistency, reliance on the false binary between identifiable and 'de-identified' personal data, and some requirements for the use of personal data without consent for research – are discussed further in this section.

6.4.1 *Notice and Consent Model*

As data protection legislation is rights-based – drawing on the individual right to privacy in international law – there is a strong focus on the individual and individual control of personal data. Data protection legislation is often characterised as emphasising the individual's right to notice of and consent to the collection, use, and disclosure of their personal data with a range of exceptions to this paradigm. Consent is not always legally required for the collection, use, and disclosure of personal data under data protection legislation but still tends to dominate the discourse in the context of research.

75 Council of the OECD, *Recommendation of the Council Concerning Guidelines on the Protection of Privacy and Transborder Flows of Personal Data* (23 September 1980). The Guidelines were updated in 2013 ('*OECD Guidelines* 2013').

76 UN ICCPR (n 73) art 17; *Australian Privacy Act* (n 50) Preamble.

77 *OECD Guidelines* 1980 (n 75) Explanatory Memorandum [25].

78 *Privacy Act 1985*, RSC 1985, c P-21 ('*Canadian Privacy Act*'). See A Savoie and M Thibodeau, 'Canada's Federal Privacy Laws' (Background Paper, Parliamentary Information and Research Service, Parliament of Canada, 17 November 2020).

79 *Convention for the Protection of Individuals with Regard to Automatic Processing of Personal Data*, opened for signature 28 January 1981, 25702 UNTS 65 (entered into force 1 October 1985); A Warren and J Dearnley, 'Data Protection Legislation in the United Kingdom' (2005) 8(2) *Information, Community and Society* 238, 250.

Solove refers to this approach as 'privacy self-management' and notes that this model 'takes refuge in consent'.[80] Laurie and Postan refer to the fetishisation of the consent form in the field of health research.[81] In addition, as Solove notes in relation to the use of data for research, the self-management paradigm does not take into account countervailing social values – we would include here the rights and freedoms of others, including the right to health, and the public interest in the protection of the health of the community – when it focuses exclusively on individual choice.[82]

In many situations, the notice and consent model does not, in reality, provide individuals with meaningful control or protection of their data. For example, it is questionable whether individuals can give voluntary and fully informed consent to the collection and use of their personal data for research based on information in privacy policies provided by health service providers and others at the time of service. Consent implies being fully informed but, as Solove and others have made clear, individuals rarely read privacy policies and so very often cannot be described as fully informed.[83] Individuals tend not to read them because they do not have time and they may not understand them when they do read them.[84]

Consent also implies choice. In the context of the provision of health or social services, there is often little real choice on whether to provide information. If individuals need a health service, then they will need to provide detailed personal information before they are provided with the service. It is not sufficient justification to say that data subjects all 'consented' to the use of their data for research by signing the – potentially unread or partially comprehended – privacy policy that was provided to them at the time they received a service. The UK *General Data Protection Regulation* (UK GDPR)[85] explicitly recognises this problem in relation to information provided to a public authority stating that:

80 D Solove, 'Introduction: Privacy Self-Management and the Consent Dilemma' (2013) 126(7) *Harvard Law Review* 1880.

81 G Laurie and E Postan, 'Rhetoric or Reality: What Is the Legal Status of the Consent Form in Health-Related Research' (2013) 21(3) *Medical Law Review* 371.

82 Solove (n 80) 1893.

83 Consumer Policy Research Centre, *Data and Technology Consumer Survey* (CPRC 2020) 18: 94 per cent of Australian consumers reported not reading all of the privacy policies that applied to them in the last twelve months and 33 per cent reported that they never read these documents.

84 K Kemp, '94% of Australians Do Not Read All Privacy Policies That Apply to Them – And That's Rational Behaviour', *The Conversation* (14 May 2018) <https://theconversation.com/94-of-australians-do-not-read-all-privacy-policies-that-apply-to-them-and-thats-rational-behaviour-96353>.

85 *Regulation (EU) 2016/679 of the European Parliament and of the Council of 27 April 2016 on the Protection of Natural Persons with Regard to the Processing of Personal Data and on the Free Movement of Such Data, and Repealing Directive 95/46/EC* (General Data Protection Regulation) [2016] OJ L 119/1 (EU GDPR), as it forms part of the law of England and Wales, Scotland and Northern Ireland by virtue of the *European Union (Withdrawal) Act 2018* (UK) s 3 and as amended by *The Data Protection, Privacy and Electronic Communications (Amendments etc) (EU Exit) Regulations 2019*, regs 2–3, sch 1 (UK GDPR).

> consent should not provide a valid legal ground for the processing of personal data in a specific case where there is a clear imbalance between the data subject and the controller, in particular, where the controller is a public authority and it is therefore unlikely that consent was freely given in all the circumstances of that specific situation.[86]

Finally, 'consent' on each separate interaction with a health service is unlikely to give any protection against the privacy risks associated with future aggregation of the data collected.

As discussed in Chapter 2, consent has an important role to play in research where researchers collect information directly from participants and participants can be fully informed and given a real choice about whether or not to participate in the research. Data protection legislation in all three jurisdictions provides that consent is a lawful basis for the collection and use of personal information for research in these circumstances. It also recognises that there are limits to the consent model by providing a range of exceptions including:

- where the use or disclosure is authorised by law; and
- research exceptions – where the data is to be used for research and certain conditions are met.

These options are discussed in detail in this chapter, including the need for clear statutory authorisation for the use of personal data for research.

6.4.2 *Regulatory Complexity*

It is well established that regulatory complexity leads to compliance issues because decision makers do not understand what is required or are deterred by the time and effort required to understand and comply.[87] There is a significant level of regulatory complexity in the data protection regimes in Canada and Australia due to the multiple levels of data protection legislation at the federal, state or provincial, and territorial level. For example, in Canada at the federal level there are two pieces of legislation: the *Privacy Act 1985* (Can)[88] – which regulates how the federal government handles personal information – and the *Personal Information Protection and Electronic Documents Act 2000* (Can) ('*PIPEDA* (Can)')[89] – which regulates how organisations handle personal information in the course of commercial activities

[86] UK GDPR (n 85) Preamble [43].

[87] C Parker and V Lehmann Nielsen, 'Compliance: 14 Questions' in P Drahos (ed), *Regulatory Theory: Foundations and Applications* (ANU Press, 2017) 217, 225–6; OECD, *Reducing the Risk of Policy Failure: Challenges for Regulatory Compliance* (OECD Publishing, 2000) 14.

[88] *Canadian Privacy Act* (n 78).

[89] *Personal Information Protection and Electronic Documents Act*, SC 2000, c 5 (Can).

across Canada.[90] *PIPEDA* (Can) applies to private hospitals and healthcare providers in private practice, such as doctors and dentists, who are engaged in commercial activity.[91]

There is also data protection legislation regulating the public sector in each province and territory. In addition, almost all the provinces and territories have separate health privacy legislation based on their constitutional or devolved power in relation to health services.[92] The health privacy legislation in New Brunswick, Newfoundland and Labrador, Nova Scotia, and Ontario has been deemed 'substantially similar' to *PIPEDA* (Can) in respect to commercial health service providers and so these organisations are exempt from the provisions of *PIPEDA* (Can). The handling of personal data, including health data, by public sector agencies, public sector health service providers, and public universities is covered by provincial or territorial data protection legislation unless the organisation is involved in a commercial transaction.[93] Despite the number of data protection statutes across Canada, there are still gaps in coverage, for example in relation to charities and other non-profit organisations.

In Australia, the situation is also complex. There is data protection legislation at the federal level,[94] which regulates the handling of personal information by the federal public sector and by much of the private sector across Australia. There is also legislation at the state and territory level, which regulates the handling of personal information by the state and territory public sectors in all states and territories except Western Australia and South Australia. In South Australia, there are binding administrative privacy principles in place which regulate the handling of personal information by the state public sector.[95] In Western Australia, there is also a binding policy framework that regulates the handling of personal information by the state public sector and requires compliance with the Australian Privacy Principles (APPs) – as set out in the federal *Privacy Act 1988* (Cth) – and discussed further in Section 6.4.3.[96] There is also separate health privacy legislation in three jurisdictions:

90 It is limited to commercial activities because *PIPEDA* (Can) (n 89) is based on the federal government's constitutional power in relation to 'the regulation of trade and commerce'. See *Constitution Act 1867* (n 12) s 91(2).

91 On 17 November 2020, the Canadian government introduced Bill C-11, which proposes a new Consumer Privacy Protection Act to replace *PIPEDA* (Can) (n 89) to regulate privacy in the privacy sector.

92 See, eg, *Freedom of Information and Protection of Privacy Act*, RSM 1997, c F-175; *Personal Health Information Act*, RSM 1997, c P-33.5 ('*Manitoba Personal Health Information Act*'). Nunavut is the only jurisdiction that does not have separate health privacy legislation.

93 See further Office of the Privacy Commissioner of Canada, 'Provincial and Territorial Privacy Laws and Oversight', *Government of Canada* (Web Page, 11 June 2020) <www.priv.gc.ca/en/about-the-opc/what-we-do/provincial-and-territorial-collaboration/provincial-and-territorial-privacy-laws-and-oversight/>.

94 *Australian Privacy Act* (n 50).

95 Government of South Australia, 'Information Privacy Principles (IPPS) Instruction' (Cabinet Administrative Instruction No 1 of 1989, 4 May 2020).

96 Western Australian Government, 'Policy Framework and Standards: Information Sharing Between Government Agencies' (Policy Framework, November 2017) 4 [1.4].

New South Wales (NSW), Victoria, and the Australian Capital Territory (ACT).[97] The *Privacy Act 1988* (Cth) allows state and territory privacy legislation to operate to the extent that it is not inconsistent with the federal legislation.[98]

The situation is more straightforward in the UK as the *Data Protection Act 2018* and the UK GDPR apply throughout the UK to both private and public sector organisations and to all personal data including health data. There is, however, a higher level of regulatory complexity in England and Wales by virtue of the *Health Service (Control of Patient Information) Regulations 2002* (UK), which regulate the use of personal health information for research and are discussed further in Section 6.4.3.

6.4.3 *Inconsistency*

Privacy legislation in all three jurisdictions is principles-based, rather than rules-based, drawing on the principles set out in international instruments such as the *OECD Guidelines* 1980 and 2013 and the EU GDPR. This means, in general terms, that the legislation relies on high-level principles rather than detailed rules for the handling of personal data. As Sethi notes, however, the distinction between principles and rules is not entirely clear and there are areas of grey.[99]

Principles-based regulation has the potential to create a level of consistency across international, national, and subnational borders – particularly where jurisdictions are drawing on the same set of international principles – and, as a result, data protection legislation is often aligned in significant ways. It is also the case, however, that the principles set out in international instruments are broadly phrased and that countries are left a level of discretion in how they are reflected in domestic law. When these broad principles are implemented in legislation, they are often phrased in ways that are similar but not the same across jurisdictions and even within a jurisdiction where there are multiple pieces of privacy legislation in place, for example privacy legislation and health privacy legislation. The principles may also come to look more like rules as they move from international instrument to domestic legislation.

In its 2008 report, the Australian Law Reform Commission (ALRC) recommended that, in the Australian context, the most effective method of dealing with this inconsistency was the adoption of an identical set of principles across Australia, the Unified Privacy Principles.[100] In addition, the ALRC recommended that state and territory health privacy legislation should not apply to the private sector to limit

[97] *Health Records and Information Privacy Act 2002* (NSW) ('NSW *Health Records and Information Privacy Act*'); *Health Records Act 2001* (Vic); *Health Records (Privacy and Access) Act 1997* (ACT).

[98] *Australian Privacy Act* (n 50) s 3.

[99] N Sethi, 'Reimagining Regulatory Approaches: On the Essential Role of Principles in Health Research Regulation' (2015) 12(2) *SCRIPT-ed* 91.

[100] ALRC *Report No 108* (n 72), Recommendations 3–4, 18–2.

overlapping regulation.[101] The OECD has also called on governments to 'develop national privacy strategies that reflect a co-ordinated approach across governmental bodies'.[102] The Australian government did develop a unified set of APPs[103] – now enshrined in the *Privacy Act 1988* (Cth) – but these have not been picked up by the states and territories, except in the ACT and, at the policy level, in Western Australia. The Australian government has not legislated to limit the application of state and territory health privacy legislation to the public sector.

While privacy principles in Australia and Canada have their origins in the *OECD Guidelines 1980*, the UK privacy principles derive most directly from the EU GDPR. This introduces a level of inconsistency between national regimes that has the potential to impede international data sharing. The OECD reported that, in responding to the *2019 OECD Privacy Guidelines Questionnaire*, countries identified uncertainty caused by evolving regulatory developments as a major challenge to sharing data and the need for greater interoperability to reap the benefits of trans-border data flows.[104] The need to share data across borders is clearly demonstrated in relation to research to address global health problems such as COVID-19. Aiming to achieve some level of international consistency and interoperability is necessary to address international public health issues but it has not, to date, received sufficient global attention.

6.4.4 *Personal Data*

6.4.4.1 What Is Personal Data?

Data protection legislation in all three jurisdictions applies to 'personal information' or 'personal data', which is generally defined as information that relates to an identified or identifiable individual. Whether data is identifiable is context-specific and is assessed on a case-by-case basis. In the data linkage context, the question of whether data is identifiable is complex and, as discussed in Chapter 2, the risk of identifiability increases as more data is linked.

The Office of the Australian Information Commissioner (OAIC) has noted that an individual can be identifiable where information is able to be linked with other information that could ultimately identify the individual and suggests that, where there is uncertainty, it is preferable to 'err on the side of caution by treating the information as personal information'.[105] The Office of the Privacy Commissioner of Canada (OPCC) has also noted that the definition of personal information must be

101 Ibid Recommendation 3–1.
102 *OECD Guidelines 2013* (n 75) pt 5 art 19(a).
103 *Privacy Amendment (Enhancing Privacy Protection) Act 2012* (Cth).
104 OECD, *OECD Digital Economy Outlook 2020* (OECD Publishing, 2020) 164.
105 OAIC, 'What Is Personal Information?' (APP Guidelines, Australian Government, 5 May 2017) 3–8.

given a 'broad and expansive interpretation' and that where there is a 'serious possibility that an individual could be identified through the use of that information, alone or in combination with other information' then the information is personal information.[106]

6.4.4.2 What Is Not Personal Data?

While it may sometimes be possible to completely de-identify data – so that the data cannot be re-identified – this is increasingly difficult given developments in information technology and comes at a cost to utility, including utility for research. The process of de-identification involves taking steps to remove or alter personal identifiers and other techniques to obscure, aggregate, or alter data to reduce the risk of re-identification. As each step is taken to decrease the privacy risks associated with a data set, the utility of the data set for research may also decrease. The UK Medical Research Council has stated that 'obtaining total anonymity of personal-level information may be impossible' and that 'almost no person-level information, rich enough to be useful for research, could be considered inherently anonymous'.[107] The risks of relying on 'de-identification' have been demonstrated when so called 'anonymised' data collections have been released publicly only to have researchers demonstrate that they could successfully identify individuals by combining the information in the 'anonymised' data collection with data from other sources. It is now thought necessary to create legal defences for people who re-identify information for the express purpose of testing others' de-identification mechanisms in the public interest.[108]

The UK GDPR provides for a category of pseudonymisation, which is defined as:

> the processing of personal data in such a manner that the personal data can no longer be attributed to a specific data subject without the use of additional information, provided that such additional information is kept separately and is subject to technical and or organisational measures to ensure that the personal data are not attributed to an identified or identifiable natural person.[109]

This is a useful category in relation to processing personal data for research, indicating, as it does, that privacy risks can be mitigated in particular contexts, such as research using linked data, by separating personal data from its identifiers. Pseudonymised information is still, however, personal data in the relevant legal sense if it is reasonably likely that the information could be re-identified. In *ALRC Report No 108*, the ALRC noted that stakeholders, particularly those involved in

[106] OPCC, 'Personal Information' (PIPEDA Interpretation Bulletins, Government of Canada, October 2013).

[107] Medical Research Council, 'Identifiability, Anonymisation and Pseudonymisation' (Guidance Note No 5, September 2019).

[108] See, eg, *Data Protection Act 2018* (UK) s 172 ('*UK Data Protection Act*').

[109] UK GDPR (n 85) art 4(5).

research, found it difficult to determine when information was sufficiently de-identified for the purposes of the *Privacy Act 1988* (Cth).[110]

In our view, this legal binary of identifiable and de-identified personal data is no longer fit for purpose in the face of emerging information technology. In addition, as discussed in Chapter 2, the individual may still have relevant interests in 'de-identified' information that need to be considered. A better approach would be to accept that most, perhaps all, data used for data linkage research is identifiable and to treat it as such. The use of identifiable personal data for research is allowed under data protection legislation in all three jurisdictions, where it is not possible to conduct the research using 'de-identified' data. In our view, as data is rarely 'de-identified' in the relevant sense, the focus should move to the controls and safeguards necessary in a particular research context to mitigate the risks of using individual-level data in research. More broadly, it is our view that data protection legislation, as it is currently drafted, does not provide adequate protection for personal data because it relies on the distinction between identified and 'de-identified' data and does not protect 'de-identified' data. It is timely to consider whether a new approach is needed so that data protection legislation also extends protection to all individual-level data.

6.4.5 *Using Data for Research without Consent*

Data protection legislation in all three jurisdictions recognises the public interest in using collections of personal data for research as well as the problems associated with obtaining consent and provides for the use of personal data for research without consent. Where the data is used and disclosed in accordance with these provisions, the use or disclosure will not be a breach of the data protection legislation.

It is important to note, however, that this does not necessarily amount to a use or disclosure 'authorised by law' in all jurisdictions. Where the research provisions are framed as an exception to a duty arising under the data protection legislation, then compliance with data protection legislation may not be sufficient to protect the user from an action for breach of confidentiality in equity or under the common law and may not protect the data controller from action for breach of confidentiality provisions in authorising statutes.

In addition, constitutional charters and legislative bills of rights such as the *Human Rights Act 1998* (UK) and the *Canadian Charter of Rights and Freedoms* provide avenues of complaint and review in relation to a breach of privacy that are distinct from those provided under data protection legislation. This means that, even where there has not been a breach of the data protection legislation, it may still be possible to bring an action for breach of privacy under one of these instruments. For all these reasons, we argue that authorising statutes must very clearly

110 ALRC *Report No 108* (n 72) [6.64].

authorise the use of personal data for research without consent, ensuring that this legal authority is consistent with human rights norms and that the legal authority expressly sets aside other causes of action in equity, the common law, and under legislation for breach of confidentiality.

The relevant research exceptions in data protection legislation are framed in similar but not identical terms in Australia and Canada but are quite different in the UK as they reflect the approach taken in the European Union. Each jurisdiction is discussed separately in what follows.

6.4.5.1 Australia

There is data protection legislation at the federal level and in most states and territories in Australia, excluding Western Australia and South Australia. There is also health data protection legislation in three jurisdictions. Each of these statutes includes an exception for the use of personal data, or personal health data, without consent for research under certain conditions. Australian data protection legislation allows for the use of personal data for activities ranging from 'medical research'[111] to the much broader 'research, or the compilation or analysis of statistics'.[112]

There are significant similarities between the various data protection statutes and the conditions imposed on the use of personal and health data for research. The most common conditions imposed on the use of health data for research are that:

- it is necessary to use identifiable personal data to carry out the research;
- it is impracticable to gain consent;
- reasonable steps are taken to de-identify the information and/or the information is not subsequently published in a form that identifies an individual;
- the research is in the public interest; and
- the research is conducted in accordance with guidelines issued by, at the federal level, the National Health and Medical Research Council (NHMRC) or a state or territory statutory officer. For example, in Victoria the guidelines under the *Health Records Act 2001* (Vic) are issued by the Health Complaints Commissioner.[113] These guidelines all require that research using personal data without consent is approved by an ethics committee.

Government data custodians are thus tasked with assessing a number of issues, including whether the research is in the public interest; however, there is little to no guidance provided on what this means in the legislation. Despite the shared aims and significant overlap in the research exception provisions, there is also inconsistency

[111] *Australian Privacy Act* (n 50) s 95.

[112] NSW *Health Records and Information Privacy Act* (n 97) sch 1 cl 11(f).

[113] Office of the Health Services Commissioner (Victoria), 'Statutory Guidelines on Research Issued for the Purposes of the Health Privacy Principles 1.1(e)(iii) & 2.2(g)(iii)' (Statutory Guidelines, February 2002).

in terms of expression and conditions imposed across the jurisdictions. This is one cause of difficulty with cross-jurisdictional and multi-jurisdictional sharing.

6.4.5.2 Canada

There is data protection legislation in every jurisdiction in Canada – at the federal level and in each province and territory – and health data protection legislation in every province and territory except Quebec and Nunavut. Each of these statutes includes an exception for the use of personal data, or personal health data, without consent for research under certain conditions. This discussion will focus on the health data protection legislation across the provinces and territories – which is most relevant to use of administrative health data for research. Canadian health data protection legislation allows for 'research into health issues',[114] 'health research',[115] or, more broadly, 'research'.[116]

There are significant similarities between the various health data protection statutes and the conditions imposed on the use of administrative health data for research. The most common conditions imposed are that:

- it is necessary to use individually identifiable health data to carry out the research;
- gaining consent is unreasonable, impracticable, or not feasible;
- the researcher must use the data only for the purpose of the proposed research;
- the researcher must not subsequently publish individually identifiable data;
- there are sufficient safeguards in place to protect security, privacy, and confidentiality; and
- the research meets some form of public interest test.

Most of the health data protection statutes require that these issues are assessed by an ethics committee[117] and/or by some other decision maker such as a data stewardship committee[118] or a health information privacy committee.[119] Individual

[114] *E-Health (Personal Health Information Access and Protection of Privacy) Act*, SBC 2008, c 38, s 4(h) ('*BC E-Health (Personal Health Information Access and Protection of Privacy) Act*').

[115] *Manitoba Personal Health Information Act* (n 92) s 24.

[116] *Personal Health Information Privacy and Access Act*, SNB 2009, c P-7.05, s 1 ('*New Brunswick Personal Health Information Privacy and Access Act*').

[117] *Health Information Act*, RSA 2000, c H-5, s 50(1); ibid s 43(2); *Personal Health Information Act*, SNL 2008, c P-7.01, s 44; *Health Information Act*, SNWT 2014, c 2, s 70; *Personal Health Information Act*, SNS 2010, c 41, s 56(a)(iii); *Personal Health Information Protection Act*, SO 2004, c 3, sch A s 44(1)(a)(iii); *Health Information Act*, RSPEI 1988, c H-1.41, s 22(5); *Health Information Protection Act*, SS 1999, c H-0.021, s 29(2)(c) ('*Saskatchewan Health Information Protection Act*'); *Health Information Privacy and Management Act*, SY 2013, c 16, s 68(2).

[118] *BC E-Health (Personal Health Information Access and Protection of Privacy) Act* (n 114) s 11(1).

[119] *Manitoba Personal Health Information Act* (n 92) s 24(2)(a). At the time of writing, the data protection legislation in Quebec is under revision to more closely align Quebec's laws with those of other jurisdictions. For this reason, the current discussion does not focus on Quebec except to note that the current decision maker is the Commission d'accès à l'information.

government data custodians are also sometimes tasked with assessing whether a research proposal meets some of these conditions before releasing personal health data to researchers.[120] Where legislation does not expressly require the assessment and approval of an ethics committee, such assessment and approval may still be required under the terms of the *Tri-Council Policy Statement: Ethical Conduct for Research Involving Humans* (the '*Tri-Council Statement*'),[121] as compliance with the *Tri-Council Statement* is a condition attached to research funding and administration.

Despite the shared aims and significant overlap in the research exception provisions, there is also significant inconsistency across Canadian jurisdictions. This is one cause of difficulty with cross-jurisdictional and multi-jurisdictional sharing.

6.4.5.3 The United Kingdom

UK GDPR. The provisions of the UK GDPR provide that processing of personal data is lawful in an exclusive list of circumstances that include with consent of the data subject or where it is 'necessary for the performance of a task carried out in the public interest or in the exercise of official authority vested in the controller'.[122] The discussion in this section focuses on the use of personal data without consent as this is most relevant for research using linked administrative data.

The basis for processing without consent must be laid down in UK law.[123] The law must set out the lawful purposes for processing and a range of matters, including the general conditions governing lawful processing; the relevant data subjects and the types of data involved; the purposes for which personal data may be disclosed; and to whom the data may be disclosed. Finally, any such law must 'meet an objective of public interest and be proportionate to the legitimate aim pursued'.[124]

More restrictive provisions apply to the processing of sensitive data – including genetic, biometric, and health data – which may only be processed without consent in specific circumstances, including for scientific research or statistical purposes based on UK law and in accordance with article 89(1).[125] The relevant UK law must:

120 See, eg, *Saskatchewan Health Information Protection Act* (n 117) s 29(2).

121 Canadian Institutes of Health Research, Natural Sciences and Engineering Research Council of Canada, and Social Sciences and Humanities Research Council, *Tri-Council Policy Statement Ethical Conduct for Research Involving Humans* (Document No TCPS2 2018, December 2018).

122 UK GDPR (n 85) art 6(1)(e).

123 Ibid art 6(3)(b).

124 Ibid art 6(3).

125 Ibid art 9.

- be proportionate to the legitimate aim pursued;
- respect the essence of the right to data protection; and
- provide for suitable and specific measures to safeguard the fundamental rights and interests of the data subject.[126]

Article 89 deals specifically with processing personal data for scientific research or statistical purposes. Data protection rights may be limited where those rights would render impossible or seriously impair the scientific research or statistical purposes and the limitations are necessary to achieve those purposes. Otherwise, the processing of the sensitive data is explicitly prohibited.[127] The provision also provides that any such processing must be subject to appropriate safeguards to protect the rights and freedoms of the data subject. These safeguards:

- must ensure technical and organisational measures are in place to ensure respect for the principle of data minimisation; and
- may include the use of pseudonymised or de-identified data where possible.[128]

DATA PROTECTION ACT 2018 (UK). The UK GDPR provides the broad framework for the conduct of research without consent – reflecting international human rights law requirements of legitimate aim, legality, necessity, and proportionality discussed in Chapter 4 – allowing for limitations on data protection rights to be set out in UK law where necessary. The *Data Protection Act 2018* (UK) (the '*UK Data Protection Act*') implements the UK GDPR and provides that next level of regulation.

The *UK Data Protection Act* reflects the UK GDPR legal basis for the processing of personal data where necessary for the performance of a task carried out in the public interest or in the exercise of a data controller's official authority. The Act provides that this includes processing that is necessary for 'the exercise of a function conferred on a person by an enactment or rule of law'.[129]

The *UK Data Protection Act* also makes provision for processing sensitive personal data, including health data, where it is necessary for scientific research; carried out in accordance with article 89(1) of the UK GDPR, supplemented by section 19 of the Act; and in the public interest.[130] Section 19 of the *UK Data Protection Act* contains further safeguards, including that the processing must not be likely to cause substantial damage or distress to the data subject.

In Scotland, research using linked data is carried out based on this legislative framework. Data controllers must clearly identify a legal basis for processing data

[126] Ibid art 9(j).
[127] Ibid art 9(1). There is also scope for relying on the exemption provided in art 85 of the UK GDPR (n 85) for processing carried out for the purpose of academic expression. However, it is unlikely that art 85 would allow processing that did not involve art 89 safeguards.
[128] Ibid art 8, 9(1).
[129] *UK Data Protection Act* (n 108) s 8(c).
[130] Ibid ss 10(2), sch 1 pt 1 s 4.

for research – this will usually be that it is necessary for the performance of a task carried out in the public interest – and ensure that the processing complies with the *UK Data Protection Act*. Data controllers must also have a legal power to share data, whether express or implied. We would say that, while the simplicity of this approach is laudable, it does not make sufficiently clear that processing of personal data for research consistent with these provisions sets aside any common law or statutory duty of confidentiality. We would suggest a provision in authorising legislation that makes clear that compliance with data protection legislation does protect data controllers and users from legal liability.

OTHER LEGISLATIVE PROVISIONS. By way of contrast, in England and Wales the *National Health Service Act 2006* (UK) provides a further level of regulation, specifying that the Secretary of State for Health may make regulations about the use of confidential patient information for a number of purposes, including medical research.[131] The *Health Service (Control of Patient Information) Regulations 2002* (UK) ('*UK Control of Patient Information Regulations*') go on to make provision for processing personal data for medical research in the data linkage context without consent and provide that anything done by a person in accordance with the regulations 'shall be taken to be lawfully done despite any obligation of confidence owed by that person in respect of it'.[132] This is an example of an authorising provision that clearly sets aside obligations of confidence, although it is limited in its scope and complex in its drafting. The regulations apply to a limited range of processing for 'medical research', including processing for the purpose of linking information from more than one source.[133] This is the most commonly used legal route for processing personal data for research using linked data without consent.[134]

Any such processing for medical research must be approved by the Health Research Authority (HRA).[135] The HRA must not give its approval unless a research ethics committee has first approved the medical research concerned.[136] The HRA makes decisions on the basis of advice from the Confidentiality Advisory Group (CAG).

These provisions have come under criticism for several reasons, despite the fact that they provide clear legal authority for the processing of data for linkage and protect data controllers and users from breach of duties of confidentiality. Mourby and colleagues note, for example, that the provisions are limited to 'medical research'; it is unclear whether and how administrative health data can be linked with

[131] *National Health Service Act 2006* (UK) s 251 ('*UK National Health Service Act*').
[132] *Health Service (Control of Patient Information) Regulations 2002* (UK) reg 4.
[133] Ibid sch.
[134] M Mourby et al, 'Health Data Linkage for Public Interest Research in the UK: Key Obstacles and Solutions' (2019) 4(1) *International Journal of Population Data Science* 6.
[135] *UK Control of Patient Information Regulations* (n 132) reg 5(1)(a).
[136] Ibid reg 5(2).

non-health data; and that the involvement of CAG can lead to significant delays.[137] The regulations are also restrictive in that they do not appear to permit the sharing of identifiable data with researchers for analysis. In other jurisdictions, identifiable data can be provided to researchers where it is necessary for a project – for example, full birth dates may be necessary for research on outcomes for neonates – and the sharing arrangements meet stringent conditions. Research requiring the release of this kind of identifiable data does not appear to be possible in England and Wales under the *UK Control of Patient Information Regulations*.

NATIONAL DATA OPT-OUT. In 2017, the UK Department of Health – as it was then called – announced a range of reforms to the way that personal data is shared for research.[138] Despite recognising that 'sharing data has immense potential to improve the health and social care system, as well as improving outcomes for individuals',[139] the reforms included providing a mechanism for individuals to opt out of sharing personal data beyond their direct care. The *NHS Constitution for England* already includes a right for individuals to request that their confidential information not be used beyond their own care and treatment;[140] however, the new scheme provides a clearer mechanism for individuals to do so. The scheme is underpinned by policy set by the Department of Health and Social Care (DHSC).[141]

Under the scheme, which came into operation in England on 25 May 2018, it is possible for individuals to decide that their personal data should not be used for 'planning to improve health and care services' or 'research to find a cure for serious illnesses'.[142] There are also opt-out arrangements in place in relation to disease registries.[143] The opt-out approach was adopted on the basis that it would help to ensure public trust in the using and sharing of information for public benefit. It was intended to align with authorisation for sharing personal health data under the equitable and common law duties of confidentiality.

Although the scheme is referred to as a 'national data opt-out', the policy only applies to information that originates in the health and adult care system in England.[144] It does not apply to personal data collected in Scotland, Wales,

[137] M Mourby et al (n 134).

[138] Department of Health Data Sharing and Cyber Security Team, 'Your Data: Better Security, Better Choice, Better Care' (Government Response to the National Data Guardian for Health and Care's Review of Data Security, Consent and Opt-Outs and the Care Quality Commission's Review 'Safe Data, Safe Care', Government of the United Kingdom, 12 July 2017).

[139] Ibid 23.

[140] Department of Health and Social Care, 'NHS Constitution for England' (Guidance, Government of the United Kingdom, 1 January 2021).

[141] NHS Digital, 'National Data Opt-Out Operational Policy Guidance Document' (Policy Guidance Version 4.0, National Health Service, 21 February 2020).

[142] Ibid 15.

[143] Ibid 28.

[144] Ibid 13.

or Northern Ireland but it does apply to information collected in England to be shared across national and international borders. There are other, more limited, opt-out schemes in operation across the UK. For example, it is possible to opt out of the collection and use of personal data by the Scottish Primary Care Information Resource (SPIRE) – which collects data from GP practice records for specific statistical and research purposes. However, this does not apply to general administrative data collected by the Scottish government when, for example, an individual uses an NHS service in Scotland. The Scottish government *Charter of Patient Rights and Responsibilities* notes that individuals have a right to tell NHS staff if they do not want their personal data shared in a particular way; however, this right is not absolute, and NHS Scotland can use personal data without consent in some circumstances.

In its statement of policy, *How the NHS Handles Your Personal Health Information*, NHS Scotland makes clear that it uses and shares information for a range of lawful reasons, including for research and statistical purposes, and, in relation to sensitive information such as health information, that the legal basis for this use is that it is necessary 'for reasons of substantial public interest for aims that are proportionate and respect people's rights, for example, research' or 'for scientific research and statistical purposes that are proportionate and respect people's rights'.[145] This formulation is drawn from the UK GDPR.[146]

NHS Digital has published statistics on the national data opt-out 'to help organisations to understand the impact of the opt-out on their data'.[147] These statistics show that there were 1,616,720 opt-outs in place as at 1 October 2020, which represented an opt-out rate of 2.67 overall and an opt-out rate of 2.9 for all females and 2.4 for all males with opt-out rates of up to 4.2 in females aged 70 to 79 years.[148]

Opt-out arrangements introduce bias into data collections as well as another layer of regulatory and practical complexity to the arrangements for sharing personal data for research. Piel and colleagues have noted that this could potentially have dramatic consequences for population-wide public health research – which requires access to the best available and most complete health data – as well as slowing down urgent research into environmental health hazards and disease clusters and the time taken to respond to such hazards.[149] Researchers are investigating

145 Scottish Government, 'How the NHS Handles Your Personal Health Information', *NHS Inform* (Web Page, 1 December 2020) <www.nhsinform.scot/care-support-and-rights/health-rights/confidentiality-and-data-protection/how-the-nhs-handles-your-personal-health-information>.

146 UK GDPR (n 85).

147 NHS Digital, 'National Data Opt-Out' (Web Page, 29 October 2020) <https://digital.nhs.uk/data-and-information/publications/statistical/national-data-opt-out/october-2020>.

148 NHS Digital, 'National Data Opt-Out October 2020: Age and Gender CSV' (Web Page, 1 October 2020) <https://files.digital.nhs.uk/67/CCA589/NDOP_age_gen_Oct_2020.csv>.

149 F Piel et al, 'The Challenge of Opt-Outs from NHS Data: A Small-Area Perspective' (2018) 40(4) *Journal of Public Health* e594, e599.

the impact that the opt-out is likely to have on the reliability of data available for research.[150]

We are of the view that opt-out mechanisms of this kind do not provide an appropriate balance between the relevant rights and interests. They pay insufficient attention to the responsibilities of individuals to respect the rights and freedoms of others, including the right to health, and to the legitimate limitations placed on the right to privacy in international law, discussed in Chapter 4. They do not give sufficient weight to the collective and group interests at stake in the context of public health.

Recognising that an opt-out mechanism is just one way of building trust in the community, NHS Digital – the statutory safe haven for collecting, storing, and analysing health and care information – also publishes a register which sets out what data has been released, why, and to whom, as well as the intended benefits. This mechanism relies on transparency to build trust and, in our view, is a more appropriate way to build and maintain the social licence necessary to support the use of individual-level data without consent for research.

6.5 AUTHORISING LEGISLATION FOR DATA COLLECTIONS IN GOVERNMENT AGENCIES

Many of the most valuable data collections used in research are held by government agencies. This includes administrative data collected while providing services such as health care, education, and social services. In countries where most health care is publicly provided, the collection by governments of data on hospital admissions, births and deaths, pharmaceutical prescriptions, and general practitioner services is a comprehensive resource for understanding: the health of the community; disease and its treatment; and for evaluating healthcare delivery. Disease registers such as cancer registries and infectious disease notifications are also typically held by government agencies.

Since government agencies must act within their statutory powers, they are only able to collect, use, and share information if they are authorised to do so. The statutes containing these powers are referred to here as authorising legislation. Authorising legislation has not always kept pace with developments in technology and changing norms about data use. Although work has been done to update the legislation in most jurisdictions in recent years, not all the authorising statutes achieve these purposes effectively. Historically, the enactment of authorising statues occurred in an ad hoc manner. Many health data collections had their own

150 K Lewis and P Hardelid, 'National Data Opt Out Programme: Consequences for Maternal and Child Health Research in England' (2019) 73(Supp 1) *Journal of Epidemiology and Community Health* A61.

individual authorising statutes or special provisions, for example cancer registries or birth records. They were established with a particular purpose in mind, for example collections of birth mortality data were established to support the investigation of early childhood deaths and their provisions reflect those purposes. The data collected was focused on the specific purpose and the permitted uses were often very limited and sometimes poorly defined. Research use was not always envisaged when the data collections were established. Different data collections had different access criteria and different approval processes, resulting in complexity and uncertainty about the lawful use of data.

The development of data linkage and analytics has transformed the value of the historic data, and data collections are now seen as valuable parts of the whole picture that can be drawn together by data linkage. Governments are increasingly aware of the value of the data they hold and an obligation to maximise the beneficial use of the data.[151] At the same time, community concerns have been growing about the way governments are collecting and using data about citizens, with calls for greater transparency and accountability. These changes have necessitated a new approach to legislation authorising governments to collect and use data. The necessary powers to use and release data are now more likely to be contained in one statute that applies to all data collections held by a particular agency or across the whole of government. The benefits of this are more uniformity and more clarity.

The landscape of research using linked data is changing so rapidly that legislation needs to be very flexible. Legislation that is too detailed and prescriptive will rapidly become outdated and either too restrictive or irrelevant. In this context, the role of legislation should be to provide general authority and to empower transparent and accountable decision making on the access and use of information.

These statutes should:

- provide authority to collect and store the data;
- provide authority to use it and disclose it for approved purposes;
- establish transparent, accountable, and efficient decision making; and
- impose robust risk-based security and confidentiality obligations.

[151] Office for National Statistics, 'Delivering Better Statistics for Better Decisions' (Web Page, 1 March 2016) <www.ons.gov.uk/news/news/deliveringbetterstatisticsforbetterdecisions>; Department for Digital, Culture, Media and Sport, 'National Data Strategy Policy Paper' (Policy Paper, Government of the United Kingdom, 9 December 2020); Australian Government, 'Public Data Policy Statement' (Policy Statement, 7 December 2015) <https://pmc.gov.au/sites/default/files/publications/aust_govt_public_data_policy_statement_1.pdf>; Australian Government Productivity Commission, *Data Availability and Use* (Productivity Commission Inquiry Report No 82, 31 March 2017); Council of Canadian Academics, *Accessing Health and Health-Related Data in Canada: The Expert Panel on Timely Access to Health and Social Data for Health Research and Health System Innovation* (Report, 2015).

6.5.1 *Restrictions on the Collection, Use, and Release of Data by Governments*

There are two sources of restriction on the collection, use, and release of data that apply to government agencies in addition to the limits imposed by data protection legislation and the common law. First, where government bodies are given a power to collect information for a particular purpose, then they must not disclose it for any other purpose. This is true whatever the nature of the information. This implied duty not to disclose information for unauthorised purposes has been described by Justice Brennan of the High Court of Australia as 'closely analogous to the duty imposed by equity'.[152]

Second, many authorising statutes impose an express duty of confidentiality on government employees who collect and manage data collections.[153] This statutory duty sometimes extends to those who subsequently receive the information, such as researchers.[154] A breach of such statutory duties of confidentiality is usually a criminal offence.[155] The duty is generally confined to personal information and will not be breached if the use or disclosure of the data is authorised by statute.

6.5.2 *Statutory Authorisation for the Use and Release of Data for Research*

The most reliable basis for the lawful use and sharing of data for research by government agencies is express statutory authority. The authorising provisions may include research as one of the primary purposes of the collection of the data or it may expressly authorise the use and sharing for research.

Research is sometimes included as an exception to restrictive provisions such as confidentiality provisions. This type of provision can be relied on to provide statutory authority only where the statute expressly states that the exception provides immunity from liability under all bodies of law.[156] It is not enough if the provisions provide an exception only to the duties imposed by that statute.[157] It must provide complete immunity from both civil and criminal liability, including that arising under other statutes and the common law.[158]

Authorising provisions may be in primary legislation (statutes) or secondary legislation such as regulations. Where they are found in secondary legislation, their authority is sourced from the primary statute. The primary statute can be:

[152] *Johns v Australian Securities Commission* (1993) 178 CLR 408, 424.

[153] See, eg, *Health Protection and Promotion Act*, RSO 1990, c H-7, s 39; *Public Health Act*, SBC 2008, c 28, s 91; *Public Health Act 2010* (NSW) s 130 ('*NSW Public Health Act*').

[154] See, eg, *Health Insurance Act 1973* (Cth) s 130(4).

[155] See, eg, ibid s 130(1); NSW *Public Health Act* (n 153) s 130.

[156] See, eg, UK *Control of Patient Information Regulations* (n 132), s 4.

[157] See, eg, NSW *Health Records and Information Privacy Act* (n 97) s 18.

[158] See, eg, *Health Services Act 2016* (WA) s 220(3) ('WA *Health Services Act*').

- The statute that authorises the collection of the data. The authorising provisions may apply to a specific data collection or they may apply to all data collected under the authority of the same statute.[159]
- A statute that provides authority for the sharing of all data, or all health data, held by a single agency.[160]
- A statute that provides authority for the use and sharing of data, or all health data, for all government agencies in that jurisdiction.[161]
- General data protection or privacy statutes that authorise the use and sharing of data.[162]

Whichever model is adopted, there will be similar issues relating to the scope of the authority to use and release data for research, such as the kind of data included and the purposes covered. The statutory authority provisions for research are sometimes confined to particular types of research such as medical research or health research and this gives rise to definitional issues.

Definitional problems can also arise as to the nature of 'research' and what it includes. Other activities that use linked data – such as quality assurance activities and health service monitoring – are usually the subject of separate provisions. There is some doubt as to whether 'research' includes the construction of research infrastructure such as enduring data linkage maps or linked data repositories. These facilities may be created so that they can be used for future research, but they may not be seen as research in themselves. To avoid doubt, the legislation should deal separately and explicitly with the use and sharing of data for data linkage.[163] If enduring linkage systems are to be established, then the statutory authority should extend to the collection, storage, and use of linkage variables for the creation of new links and for the ongoing maintenance of linkages.

One of the difficulties faced by data custodians and applicants for data is the proliferation of statutes authorising and regulating the use and sharing of data for research. Different data collections have different requirements and approval procedures, and a data collection may be governed by a number of overlapping statutes. If there is no stated order of precedence between them, then the data can only be released if they are all satisfied. This level of complication unnecessarily impedes the beneficial use of data and does not support well-balanced decisions about the use of data.

In New Brunswick in Canada, for example, amendments were made to the privacy statutes to facilitate the release of data to the Institute for Research, Data and Training, New Brunswick's only administrative data centre.[164] Amendments to

[159] See, eg, *Improving Cancer Outcomes Act 2014* (Vic) ss 4, 14.

[160] See, eg, *WA Health Services Act 2016* (n 158) ss 215–6.

[161] See, eg, *UK National Health Service Act* (n 131) s 251; *UK Control of Patient Information Regulations* (n 132).

[162] See, eg, *Manitoba Personal Health Information Act* (n 92) s 24.

[163] See, eg, *UK Control of Patient Information Regulations* (n 132) sch.

[164] *New Brunswick Personal Health Information Privacy and Access Act* (n 116); *Right to Information and Protection of Privacy Act*, SNB 2009, c R-10.6

twenty other statutes were included to avoid conflict between the statutes and to ensure authority to release data from other public bodies.[165] Further amendments were made in 2019 to broaden the coverage to include data from additional public bodies.[166]

The procedures for sharing data generally require that the application is reviewed by an ethics or privacy committee.[167] This is an important part of the review process which enables a range of community perspectives to be considered and is one mechanism for involving the community in the decision making. As discussed in Chapter 3, community involvement has been identified as an important factor in establishing social licence. These committees usually operate as advisory committees advising the decision maker. The ultimate decision to release data lies with the data custodian; however, the review committees often have a power of veto because their approval is a prerequisite to the sharing of data.[168] The role of these committees and the relationship between their role and that of the data custodian need to be clearly articulated.[169] In some cases, review by multiple committees is required. The differences between the roles of these different committees are not always clear and they appear to play substantially similar roles. If their role overlaps and they are in fact considering the same matters, then this multiple review appears to be unnecessary.

6.6 CROSS-JURISDICTIONAL SHARING

The COVID-19 pandemic has highlighted the need for and the benefits of sharing data across jurisdictional borders, including international borders. However, decision makers are often, understandably, even more cautious about sharing data with other jurisdictions than within their own jurisdiction.

The complexity and inconsistency of data protection legislation are significant barriers to the cross-jurisdictional sharing and linkage of administrative data in the hands of public sector agencies and health service providers. In Australia, for example, an individual's health data is distributed across federal, state, and territory government departments and private health providers, each subject to different data protection legislation and policies. In its 2017 report, the Australian Productivity Commission recommended 'streamlining access to identifiable data within and between Australian governments, and for the limited range of other trusted users with which such data is shared'.[170]

[165] *Act Respecting Research*, SNB 2017, c 29.
[166] *Act Respecting Research*, SNB 2019, c 18.
[167] See, eg, *Manitoba Personal Health Information Act* (n 92) s 24(2).
[168] *UK Control of Patient Information Regulations* (n 132) s 5.
[169] F Flack, C Adams, and J Allen, 'Authorising the Release of Data without Consent for Health Research: The Role of Data Custodians and HRECs in Australia' (2019) 26(3) *Journal of Law & Medicine* 655.
[170] Australian Government Productivity Commission (n 151) 27.

In response, the Australia government introduced the Data Availability and Transparency Bill 2020, to authorise and regulate access to federal government data for specific purposes, including research, and to establish the position of the National Data Commissioner. The Bill explicitly authorises data custodians to share federal public sector data with accredited users where the sharing is consistent with stated data sharing principles and a data sharing agreement.[171] Positive aspects of the Bill include that sharing is allowed for the broadly framed 'research and development'[172] and that the authorisation to share has effect despite other laws of the Commonwealth, states, and territories that restrict or prohibit the collection, use, and disclosure of information.[173] This immunity does not extend, however, to sharing that contravenes or infringes a common law duty[174] – which presumably includes the common law duty of confidentiality. The data sharing scheme proposed in the Bill will not necessarily assist with cross-jurisdictional access to information for linkage and research as the Bill is limited in its coverage to federal data. Finally, the Bill preserves other legal avenues for sharing data,[175] and this has the potential to give rise to complexity as data custodians will be required to choose among parallel provisions, with different legal requirements, that authorise the sharing of data for research.

Similar issues arise in Canada in relation to cross-jurisdictional sharing of administrative data for research. It has been noted that, as a result, the 'sharing of patient-level health data across Canadian provinces is uncommon'.[176] The sharing and use of population health data in Canada is complex due to existing regulations, legislation, and community concerns about privacy and data security, and it has been suggested that 'national discussions with governments and regulators related to privacy legislation' are needed.[177]

As a result of this complexity, a myriad of intergovernmental institutional arrangements, networks, and agreements have been developed to facilitate the sharing and use of personal data for research, including across jurisdictional boundaries. Some examples include:

- the Population Health Research Network in Australia (PHRN) – an Australian government initiative, funded by federal, state, and territory governments as well as academic institutions;

[171] *Data Availability and Transparency Bill 2020* (Cth) cl 13(1).

[172] Ibid cl 15(10)(c).

[173] Ibid cl 23.

[174] Ibid cl 17(3).

[175] Ibid cl 22.

[176] R Urquhart et al, 'A Framework to Facilitate Interprovincial Sharing of Secondary Health Data in Canada' (2018) 3(4) *International Journal of Population Data Science*.

[177] Health Data Research Network Canada, 'Population Health Digital Research Infrastructure: Building Up and Out from a Collaborative Network' (White Paper Submission to the New Digital Research Infrastructure Organisation, 9 December 2020) 6.

- the Health Data Research Network Canada (HDRN) – an initiative of the Canadian Institutes of Health Research (CIHR), Canada's federal funding agency for health research; and
- Health Data Research (UK) – an initiative led by the Medical Research Council (UK) in association with a range of other agencies and organisations.

While cross-jurisdictional sharing is a problem within federal states, the problems are amplified when sharing across international borders.[178] In December 2020, the European Commission – responsible for developing European Union strategy and policy – published a proposed Data Governance Act for consultation.[179] The draft legislation is designed to facilitate data sharing across the European Union and between sectors by, for example, introducing conditions under which public sector bodies may allow the reuse of personal data while safeguarding the protection of rights and interests. The draft legislation supports the use of 'privacy-friendly' techniques such as anonymisation, pseudonymisation, suppression, and randomisation as well as the use of secure processing environments put in place and supervised by the public sector.[180]

The United Nations (UN) Human Rights Council has noted a growing global consensus on the minimum standards, or principles, that should govern the processing of personal data.[181] There have been attempts to articulate these minimum standards, or principles, in a range of international instruments discussed in Chapter 4. There is not, however, a detailed and consistent global approach to the sharing of personal data for research except to the extent that such use is designated an exception to the minimum standards. These instruments do not provide sufficient guidance to drive global consistency in relation to this more specific issue.

6.7 CONCLUSION

All three jurisdictions considered in this chapter have complex legal regimes that govern research using linked data. The legal framework includes constitutional arrangements; various causes of action under the common law; legislation regulating the handling and protection of data; and legislation authorising governments to collect, use, and share data. Data custodians, data linkers, and researchers using the data must comply with all these bodies of law and understand the interaction

[178] All European Academies, European Academies Science Advisory Council, and Federation of European Academies of Medicine, *International Sharing of Health Data for Research* (The ALLEA, EASAC, and FEAM Joint Initiative on Resolving the Barriers of Transferring Public Sector Data Outside the EU/EEA, April 2021).

[179] *Proposal for a Regulation of the European Parliament and of the Council on European Data Governance (Data Governance Act)* (2020/0340 (COD), 25 November 2020).

[180] Ibid art 6.

[181] UN High Commissioner for Human Rights, *The Right to Privacy in the Digital Age*, UN HRC, 39th sess, Agenda Items 2 and 3, UN Doc A/HRC/39/29 (3 August 2018) 9 [28].

between them. There has been significant and ongoing legislative activity in all jurisdictions attempting to better regulate the use of administrative data for linkage and research but, in many jurisdictions, problems of complexity, inconsistency, and restricted scope continue to impede research.

Complexity can give rise to uncertainty and, as the Australian Productivity Commission noted in its 2017 report *Data Availability and Use,* uncertainty can have a chilling effect on the sharing and release of data, including sharing and release for research. The Commission expressed the view that such 'risk aversion is not desirable where it results in the public interest being poorly served'.[182] Our own empirical research with data custodians across Australia in 2017 confirmed that regulatory complexity was leading to a culture of risk aversion in relation to releasing information for research,[183] confirming the findings of earlier research and reports in the UK.[184] The ALRC found that fragmentation and inconsistency in privacy regulation can also give rise to unjustified compliance burdens and costs as well as other impediments to the conduct of research.[185]

While complexity in terms of layers of regulation poses one barrier to the use and disclosure of personal data for research, the more pressing issue is inconsistency in relation to the principles regulating the use and disclosure of personal data for research. In our view, the level of inconsistency that exists in data protection regulation within jurisdictions and across intranational and international borders poses an unjustifiable barrier to the sharing of data within jurisdictions and across national and international borders. It should be possible to develop internationally agreed privacy principles – including consistent provisions for the use and disclosure of personal data for research – and for these to be consistently reflected in data protection legislation in every state, province, and territory.

Such regulatory reform will, however, require a level of leadership at national and international level that is not yet in evidence, as well as a significant dedication of resources to underwrite the necessary consultation and negotiation. At the time of writing, the regulatory inconsistency and uncertainty are absorbing enormous resources as all the stakeholders – including researchers, their institutions, data linkers, and data custodians – struggle to understand and work with the regulatory complexity and inconsistency.[186] This is an unconscionable waste of resources that is ongoing and, in addition, impedes and prevents important public health research.

182 Australian Government Productivity Commission (n 151) 11.

183 C Adams, J Allen, and F Flack, 'Data Custodians and the Decision-Making Process: Releasing Data for Research' (2018) 26 *Journal of Law & Medicine* 433, 451.

184 House of Lords Science and Technology Committee, *Genomic Medicine* (Report, 2008–09) [6.15], quoted in N Sethi and G Laurie, 'Delivering Proportionate Governance in an Era of eHealth: Making Linkage and Privacy Work Together' (2013) 13(2–3) *Medical Law International* 168, 173.

185 *ALRC Report No 108* (n 72) 2023 [60.34].

186 G Laurie et al, 'Charting Regulatory Stewardship in Health Research' (2018) 27 *Cambridge Quarterly of Healthcare Ethics* 333.

There have been efforts made at the regional and international organisational level – for example, by the OECD and the European Union – to move in a more consistent direction. In addition, the EU GDPR model of assessing adequacy is one way to approach cross-border transfers by allowing a central expert agency to assess the adequacy of the level of protection provided in other jurisdictions.[187] Where an adequacy assessment of this kind is made outside the EU, we would suggest that the assessment be done by an appropriately skilled agency or officer – for example, a privacy commissioner – on a jurisdictional basis rather than requiring researchers or data custodians to assess adequacy on a case-by-case basis. While these efforts are helpful, a global framework is needed to ensure that research using linked data can address global concerns such as the COVID-19 pandemic. This points to the need for further action at the global level by the UN. The process leading to the production of the 2018 UN report *The Right to Privacy in the Digital Age* may provide a basis for continuing cooperation and coordination towards a consistent global approach to these issues.[188]

Narrow definitions of research pose another unjustified barrier to research allowed under statutory provisions. The statutory definition of research across the jurisdictions varies widely from the broad term 'research' to much narrower formulations such as 'medical research'. This is problematic as research is increasingly multidisciplinary and the boundaries between different categories of research are blurred. Human well-being is dependent on the interrelationship of health with multiple other factors including housing, crime, education, and the built environment, and research cannot be neatly categorised. The research use of data held by governments should not be limited to specific disciplines and should be available for any research that can demonstrate that it meets criteria such as the potential for significant public benefits.[189]

The common law continues to operate in the gaps between the legislative regimes where statutory authority is absent. In our view, the balance between the competing interests in confidentiality and privacy and in research is better managed through legislation that provides clear statutory authority in appropriate circumstances. This should not be left in the hands of the courts of common law because they are ill-equipped to provide the rapid and uniform change required to support the clear public interest in the use of data for research. In our view, the linkage and use of data for research should be regulated by statute and the operation of the common law excluded.

The focus on consent or anonymisation is not appropriate in the context of research using linked data as they can rarely be effectively achieved and do not provide real protection for individual interests. Consent remains important where there is a direct relationship between participants and researchers, but in all other contexts the focus should be on an authorisation and approval model. This model

187 EU GDPR (n 85) art 103.

188 UN High Commissioner for Human Rights (n 181).

189 ALRC, *ALRC Report No 108* (n 72) 2164 [65.40]; Flack, Adams, and Allen (n 169).

should apply to all individual-level data, not just personal information as defined in data protection legislation. This is because the binary between identifiable and de-identified information is no longer sustainable and the ethical concerns about the use of individual-level data apply whether or not the information is identifiable.

6.7.1 *Authorisation*

Clear statutory authority for the use and disclosure of data for research is needed to provide the lawful basis for the sharing of all individual-level data for linkage and research. This authorisation should not be located in data protection legislation, as data protection legislation is limited in its coverage to identifiable personal information. The authorisation and approval framework should extend to all individual-level data. For government-held data, the authorising legislation should specify the decision maker, for example the minister or the chief executive. Decision making should be centralised as much as possible to ensure efficiency and consistency. The statutory authority to allow the use and disclosure of data for specific projects must be exercised in accordance with a statutory approval process, discussed in Section 6.7.2.

It is important that statutory authority for the sharing of individual-level data for research is framed broadly and in accordance with the following principles:

- There should be one uniform source of statutory authority for the use and sharing of data for linkage and for research for all data and all agencies in a jurisdiction.
- The legislation should provide clear authority for the use and sharing of all data held by agencies in specified circumstances.
- The legislation should specify the decision maker who can authorise the sharing of data for linkage and research.
- The legislation should provide clear immunity from liability under any other statute and the common law for the use or disclosure of information authorised by the provisions.
- The authorised purposes for the use and sharing of data should include:
  - research (and should not be limited to, for example, 'medical research' or 'health research'); and
  - the creation of research infrastructure.
- The legislation should not limit the recipients of the data to particular persons or institutions.
- The legislation should deal separately and explicitly with the use and sharing of information for data linkage.
- The legislation should permit data linkage facilities to collect, store, and use the information for the maintenance of linkages and creation of approved new linkages.

6.7.2 *Approval*

Once the authorising legislation establishes a clear legal basis on which data 'may' be released, then a decision maker will be required to make decisions to link data and to release data for specific projects and in particular circumstances. To facilitate this, each jurisdiction needs a uniform approval process for all data and all agencies in the jurisdiction. In Chapter 7, we explore and evaluate the approval processes currently in use in the three jurisdictions under consideration. Chapter 8 will make recommendations to improve these processes to meet the following criteria. The statutory approval process should be consistent with human rights and ethical principles; provide proper protection for privacy; and enable the balancing of individual, collective, and public interests. The decision-making process should be transparent, accountable, and efficient. The approval regime should also support social licence.

PART III

Practice and Process of Decision Making

Our aim in this book is to improve decision making in the context of the use of linked administrative data for research. Better decision making involves asking the right questions, developing appropriate criteria, and ensuring that the most appropriate and qualified person or committee makes each decision. In addition, decision-making processes should comply with accepted norms of good decision making – transparency, accountability, rationality, efficiency, and fairness. By improving decision making, we aim to ensure that better decisions are made and that decision-making practice and process help to develop and support the social licence required to support research using linked data.

Part I considers the context in which decisions about research using linked data are made. The fundamental interests and values engaged in linking and sharing data for research and the interrelationship between the interests of individuals and communities are discussed. The importance of these values and the individual, collective, and public interests in play are reflected in qualitative studies of community views. The conditions under which the use of individual-level data for research without consent are acceptable include substantive conditions – beneficial outcomes, non-discriminatory outcomes, acceptable uses, and privacy protection – and procedural conditions – trustworthiness, transparency, accountability, and community consultation and collaboration. If these conditions are embedded in decision making, they will help to build and sustain the social licence for data linkage and data sharing.

Part II examines the three regulatory frameworks governing research using linked data: human rights, ethics, and the law. These intersecting frameworks must all be

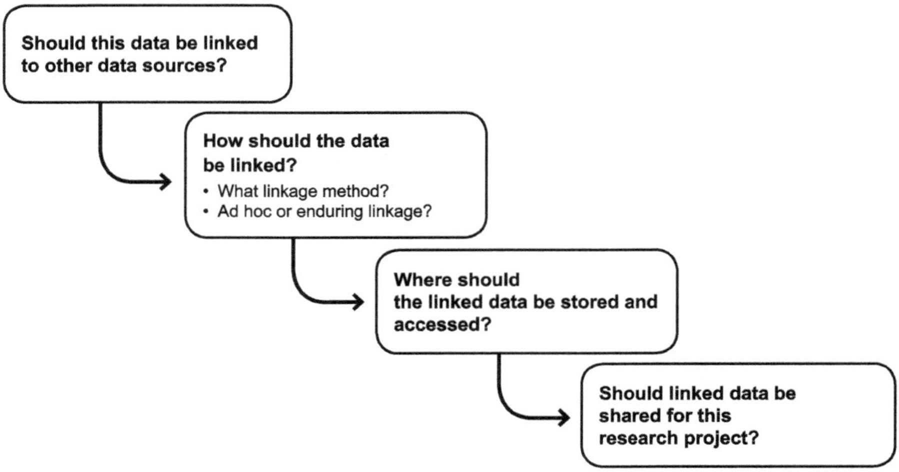

FIGURE III.1 The decisions to be made about linking and sharing data for research

taken into consideration in decision making. This makes implementation in practice complicated and potentially burdensome for decision makers and researchers. The human rights framework makes it clear that all rights – including the rights to privacy, health, and to enjoy the benefits of scientific progress – are equally important and should be given weight in the decision-making process. The legal and ethics frameworks, however, currently give priority to the right to privacy. These frameworks are also flawed by unjustified and outdated reliance on paradigms based on consent and anonymisation, both of which are under challenge in the context of research using linked data.

Part III of this book explores the real-world application of these three frameworks. It considers the decision-making processes that are currently being used and how they might be improved. It focuses on the relevant decision-making criteria and considerations, who makes the decisions, and how the decisions are made.

The decisions that must be made about linking and sharing data are described in Figure III.1. The decisions include decisions about the creation of data linkage infrastructure – the linkage of new data collections, the method of linkage, the storage and access arrangements for linked data – and decisions about the provision of linked data for individual research projects.

Chapter 7 investigates how decisions about linking data for research are currently being made. A hypothetical research project is used to examine the decision-making processes in three jurisdictions and to draw attention to the similarities and differences between them. The analysis highlights some common problems, including complex legal frameworks, multiplicity of review, and lack of transparency.

Chapter 8 demonstrates how a decision-making framework of clear and transparent criteria can be developed that includes an evaluation of all the relevant interests, values, and rights. The chapter sets out the relevant decision-making criteria and some of the considerations that must or may be examined to establish each criterion. The chapter also establishes who is best placed, with the relevant skills, expertise, and access to information, to make decisions against each of the criteria. It seems straightforward to state that ethics committees should make decisions about ethical issues and data custodians should make decisions about governance issues, but this is not what is happening in practice in all jurisdictions. It is also important, for reasons of transparency and accountability, that the final decision to release government administrative data for research should be made by a government data custodian. In streamlining the 'who' and the 'what' of decision making, we also address the issues of legislative complexity and multiplicity of review that were highlighted by our case studies in Chapter 7.

Chapter 8 goes on to provide guidance on the decision-making process and the norms that should frame all good decision making, including decisions about research using linked data. This discussion aims to ensure that decision making by data custodians and by ethics committees results in the best possible decisions based on all the relevant considerations and principles of fairness, transparency, and accountability. Chapter 8 demonstrates that it is possible to have decision-making practices and processes that establish and sustain social licence for the enterprise of research using linked data.

7

Existing Practice and Processes

7.1 INTRODUCTION

Part I of this book described the context in which decisions are made about the use of linked data for research without consent. Part II described the regulatory frameworks that apply to those decisions. In this chapter, the implementation of these frameworks at the national and subnational level is investigated.

The mechanisms used to regulate research and ensure the ethical conduct of researchers draw on international human rights and ethics frameworks. They are implemented through domestic law, including the common law, primary legislation – Acts – and secondary legislation – such as regulations and orders. The legislation includes data protection legislation and authorising legislation dealing with government data collections. The implementation of decision-making processes is often set out in organisational policies. In addition, decision makers may be guided by statutory or organisational guidelines. Each of these forms of regulation needs to be considered to understand how decisions about research using linked data without consent are made.

While there is commonality of approach in the countries considered in this book, there are significant differences in the type of decision makers, the review requirements, and the criteria for the release of data for research.

In this chapter, we compare the approaches to decision making about the release of data for research in three different jurisdictions. Without a better understanding of the similarities and differences, methods of streamlining review and decision making are unlikely to occur. It is also important to understand the range of national decision-making practice and process to facilitate international cooperation moving forward. There are strengths and weaknesses and lessons to be learned from the different approaches in each jurisdiction.

We use a hypothetical research study to demonstrate how international principles and frameworks for human rights and ethics are implemented at the national level and how they interact with domestic law. We illustrate a range of approaches by considering how the decision whether to release data would be made for cohorts in three subnational jurisdictions, Western Australia, Scotland, and Manitoba. The analysis of the case study considers the following aspects of the decision-making process:

- Who are the decision makers?
- What are the domestic laws, policies, and guidelines governing the release of data without consent for this project?
- Is ethics review required and what guidelines are considered?

The analysis then considers the extent to which the decision-making processes in each jurisdiction reflect the following aspects of good governance:

- efficiency – proportionality, timeliness, and minimisation of duplication;
- transparency;
- accountability; and
- community participation.

7.2 WESTERN AUSTRALIA

In Australia, the hypothetical study will be considered using a Western Australian (WA) population cohort. The data collections required are:

CASE STUDY

A mandatory childhood vaccination law is introduced in 2015. The law requires preschool and school-age children to have specified childhood vaccinations. The law requires that parents must provide proof of vaccinations to gain admission to all preschools, day-care centres, and schools. Parents who do not vaccinate their children face administrative fines.

The aim of this research project is to evaluate vaccine compliance before and after the introduction of the new legislation. The data required will be birth registration data, perinatal records, and vaccination records. Full date of birth will be required to adequately measure compliance with the vaccine schedule. For example, in Australia the first vaccine in the schedule is Hepatitis B. Best results are achieved if the vaccine is administered within twenty-four hours of birth and it must occur within seven days. If researchers only know month/year or year of birth, it is not possible to measure compliance with this vaccination. Information about location and ethnicity will also be required, where available, as the results of the study will be used to inform vaccine promotion and compliance campaigns.

Individuals would be reasonably identifiable from the variables required for the study so the data would be categorised as personal information. It is proposed that the data will be used without consent.

There has been a high-profile and polarised debate in the community about the new law and the topic of vaccination in general. There have also been a few very public, violent incidents outside schools related to the debate. Knowledge of the vaccination status of an individual, family, group, or community could result in stigmatisation, discrimination, and legal consequences.

- WA Registry of Births, Deaths and Marriages;[1]
- WA Midwives Notification System;[2] and
- Australian Immunisation Register.[3]

These data collections are held in two different jurisdictions. The birth registration and midwives' data are held by different instrumentalities of the WA state government. The Australian Immunisation Register is held by the Australian federal government.

The three data collections necessary for this research project are not all routinely linked together. Linkage would be conducted in two stages by different linkage units. First, identifiable data from the Registry of Births, Deaths and Marriages would be

1 *Births, Deaths and Marriages Registration Act 1998* (WA) ('*WA Births, Deaths and Marriages Registration Act*').

2 *Health (Miscellaneous Provisions) Act 1911* (WA) s 335; *Health (Notifications by Midwives) Regulations 1994* (WA) reg 4.

3 *Australian Immunisation Register Act 2015* (Cth) ('*Australian Immunisation Register Act*').

linked to identifiable data from the Midwives Notification Scheme by the data linkage unit in the WA Department of Health to obtain the most reliable birth data and select the study cohort. The identifiers (name, address, date of birth, sex) along with a project-specific person identifier would then need to be transferred to the Australian Institute of Health and Welfare (AIHW), which would conduct the linkage to the Australian Immunisation Register. Each of the data custodians would then extract the records necessary for the study, remove the names and addresses, and replace them with the project-specific identifier. This process is dictated by what is sometimes called the 'separation principle' and is designed to minimise the risks of identification.[4] This data would then be transferred to a secure remote analysis environment such as the Secure Unified Research Environment (SURE) for the researchers to conduct the analysis.[5]

The linkage of the data requires the collection, use, and disclosure of personal information. The data provided to the researchers for analysis would also be categorised as personal information since it includes the full birth date, location, and ethnicity.

7.2.1 *Decision Makers*

Each of the data collections involved has a separate statutory data custodian with authority to release the data. All three will be required to authorise the release of the data:

- WA Registry of Births, Deaths and Marriages – WA Registrar of Births Deaths and Marriages.[6]
- WA Midwives Notification System – WA Department of Health CEO.[7]
- Australian Immunisation Register – Australian Government Minister for Health.[8]

The AIHW Human Research Ethics Committee also has a statutory decision-making role and has the power to approve the release of information from the AIHW.[9]

7.2.2 *Domestic Laws, Policies, and Guidelines Governing the Release of Data for Linkage and Research*

The births data from the Registrar of the WA Registry of Births, Deaths and Marriages can be provided if there is 'an adequate reason for wanting the information'. The Registrar has a broad discretion and can impose any conditions considered

4 C Kelman, A Bass, and C Holman, 'Research Use of Linked Health Data: A Best Practice Protocol' (2002) 26(3) *Australian New Zealand Journal of Public Health* 251.

5 Sax Institute, 'Design and Functionality', *Our Work* (Web Page) <www.saxinstitute.org.au/our-work/sure/design-and-functionality/>.

6 *WA Births, Deaths and Marriages Registration Act* (n 1) ss 54.

7 *Health Services Act 2016* (WA) ss 216 ('*WA Health Services Act*').

8 *Australian Immunisation Register Act* (n 3) ss 22(3).

9 *Australian Institute of Health and Welfare Act 1987* (Cth) s 29(2)(c) ('*AIHW Act*').

appropriate.[10] The data custodian of the WA Midwives Notification System can provide personal information for 'health related research'.[11] Consent is generally required but it may be waived if:

- the information is reasonably necessary for the purpose;
- the purpose cannot be achieved by providing information that is not personal information;
- it is impracticable to obtain consent; and
- the research is approved by an ethics committee.[12]

If an ethics committee approved the case study project, then the remaining conditions would be satisfied.

The *Health Services Act 2016* (WA) takes precedence over the common law duty of confidentiality and specifically provides that authorised disclosures under the Act are not a breach of the duty of confidentiality.[13] WA does not have dedicated data protection legislation; however, the *Information Sharing between Government Agencies* policy requires Western Australian government agencies to comply with the Australian Privacy Principles (APPs) of the federal *Privacy Act 1988*.[14]

The immunisation data is collected under the federal *Australian Immunisation Register Act 2015*. The purposes of the Register include 'research relating to vaccinations'.[15] The minister can authorise the use and disclosure of personal information for a specified purpose subject to a public interest test.[16] The public interest is not defined and the matters to be considered are not specified in the statute or subsidiary legislation so it is difficult to predict whether the release of data is likely to be approved; however, the project does appear to fall clearly within the purposes of the register.[17] Consent for the use and release of information is not required but the Act does permit individuals to opt out to prevent the use of their information for research and other purposes.[18]

The functions of the AIHW include facilitating researchers' access to health-related information.[19] The AIHW provides linkage services and it holds and administers the Australian Immunisation Register. Personal information can be released to researchers, subject to the approval of the AIHW ethics committee.[20]

10 WA *Births, Deaths and Marriages Registration Act* (n 1) s 54.
11 WA *Health Services Act* (n 7) s 216(d).
12 *Health Services (Information) Regulations 2017* (WA) rr 3(2)–(3) ('WA *Health Services (Information) Regulations*').
13 WA *Health Services Act* (n 7) s 220(3)(d).
14 WA Government, *Policy Framework and Standards: Information Sharing Between Government Agencies* (Policy Framework, November 2017).
15 *Australian Immunisation Register Act* (n 3) s 10.
16 Ibid s 22(3).
17 Ibid s 10.
18 Ibid s 11(2).
19 *AIHW Act* (n 9) s 5(h).
20 Ibid s 29(2)(c).

The federal data protection legislation, the *Privacy Act 1988*, applies to all Australian government entities, including the Department of Health and the AIHW. The APPs in the Act impose obligations relating to the collection, use, disclosure, and management of personal information, as well as the protection of privacy. Australian government agencies that collect, use, or disclose personal information for medical research, including epidemiological research, will not be in breach of the APPs provided they comply with the statutory guidelines.[21] While consent is generally required for research purposes, personal information can be collected, used, and disclosed without consent provided the research is approved by an ethics committee under the statutory guidelines.

7.2.3 *Ethics Review*

The legislation governing the use of the data requires ethics committee approval as a condition of release.[22] Ethics committee approval is required for the use and disclosure of data from the Department of Health (WA) without consent.[23] Where the research project involves data linkage, then it must be reviewed by the Department of Health specialist ethics committee.[24]

The release of the data from the Australian Immunisation Register without consent is governed by the federal *Privacy Act 1988* and the 'Guidelines under Section 95 of the Privacy Act 1988' ('Section 95 Guidelines'). These guidelines require that an agency must satisfy itself that the research has been approved by an ethics committee.[25] The approval of any ethics committee registered with the National Health and Medical Research Council (NHMRC) will meet this requirement.

The federal *AIHW Act 1987* requires review by the AIHW ethics committee before any 'information concerning another person' can be disclosed or accessed for research.[26] This includes the linkage of data by the AIHW. The research project must, therefore, be approved by two specialist ethics committees: the Department of Health (WA) ethics committee and the AIHW ethics committee. If Aboriginal and Torres Strait Islander ethnicity is a focus of the study, a further specialised ethics review process may be required and specialised guidelines would need to be considered.[27]

21 *Privacy Act 1988* (Cth) s 95 ('*Australian Privacy Act*'); National Health and Medical Research Council, 'Guidelines under s 95 of the *Privacy Act 1988*' (Australian Government, November 2014).

22 Ibid; *WA Health Services Act* (n 7) s 216; *WA Health Services (Information) Regulations* (n 12) rr 3(2)–(3); *AIHW Act* (n 9) s 29(2)(c); *Australian Institute of Health and Welfare (Ethics Committee) Regulations 2018* (Cth) ('*AIHW (Ethics Committee) Regulations*').

23 *WA Health Services Act* (n 7) s 216; *WA Health Services (Information) Regulations* (n 12) rr 3(2)–(3).

24 Department of Health, 'WA Health Research Governance Policy and Procedures' (Government of Western Australia, OD No 0411/02, November 2012) 49 [3.3.2].

25 National Health and Medical Research Council, 'Section 95 Guidelines' (n 21) Guideline 1.2.

26 *AIHW Act* (n 9) s 29(2)(c).

27 NHMRC, 'Ethical Conduct in Research with Aboriginal and Torres Strait Islander Peoples and Communities: Guidelines for Researchers and Stakeholders' (Australian Government, August 2018).

All human research ethics committees in Australia must be registered by the NHMRC and are required to apply the *National Statement on Ethical Conduct in Human Research* (the '*National Statement*').[28] The *National Statement* briefly references the *World Medical Association Declaration of Helsinki – Ethical Principles for Medical Research Involving Human Subjects* ('*Declaration of Helsinki*') in the Preamble but does not specifically cite any of the other international ethics guidelines.[29] However, the *National Statement* is organised around the four core values (research merit and integrity, justice, beneficence, and respect) that form the basis for all the international guidelines discussed in Chapter 5. The *National Statement* specifies criteria that must be satisfied before an ethics committee can approve a waiver of consent.[30] The ethics committees reviewing this project are also required to apply the Section 95 Guidelines when they consider a waiver of consent.

The authors have previously analysed the matters that all Australian ethics committees must consider when reviewing applications for waivers of consent, taking into account the *National Statement* core values and waiver criteria and the applicable legislation.[31] For this hypothetical example, both committees would consider the following:

- Ethical principles – research merit and integrity, justice, respect, and beneficence.
- The justification for waiver of consent including:
  - the impracticality of seeking consent;
  - the risk of undermining trust by not seeking consent; and
  - the necessity of using personal information.
- Public interest.
- Whether the waiver is prohibited by law.
- Protection of privacy and confidentiality.

The assessment of beneficence would include risks and benefits to participants and non-participants and should include any social harms, including damage to social networks and stigmatisation that would be relevant to this example. This would also be relevant to the consideration of justice. Given the large numbers of participants required and the need for full population coverage to avoid bias, the ethics committees are likely to agree that it is impractical to gain informed consent. The risk of undermining trust would be evaluated by considering the sensitivity of

28 NHMRC, Australian Research Council, and Universities Australia, 'National Statement on Ethical Conduct in Human Research, 2007 (Updated 2018)' (Australian Government, 2018).

29 *World Medical Association Declaration of Helsinki – Ethical Principles for Medical Research Involving Human Subjects*, 64th WMA General Assembly (October 2013).

30 Ibid 21–2 [2.3.10].

31 F Flack, C Adams, and J Allen, 'Authorising the Release of Data without Consent for Health Research: The Role of Data Custodians and HRECs in Australia' (2019) 26(3) *Journal of Law & Medicine* 655.

the information and community expectations about the use of the data. It is necessary to use personal information, but approval would be limited to the data variables necessary to conduct the study.

Two differently worded public interest tests must be met:

> The benefits from the research justify any risks of harm associated with not seeking consent.[32]
>
> If the public interest in the proposed research does not outweigh, to a substantial degree, the public interest in the protection of privacy, then the research should not be carried out.[33]

As the public health benefits of immunisation are substantial, the ethics committees would be likely to approve this application provided they were convinced that the study results would be used to improve the delivery of immunisation and that publication of the study results would not result in a backlash which might affect vaccination rates or cause other collective harms to groups in the community. Appropriate measures to protect the participants' privacy and confidentiality would need to be in place.

7.2.4 *Good Decision Making*

7.2.4.1 Efficiency

There is significant duplication in the approval processes described in sections 7.2.1, 7.2.2, and 7.2.3. The separate approval required from the data custodian of each collection is probably unavoidable where the data is held in multiple jurisdictions, but duplication can be minimised within a jurisdiction by centralising the decision-making authority. There is duplication in ethics review because of the special statutory role of the AIHW ethics committee and the WA Health policy of requiring review by its own specialist committee.

There is also overlap in the waiver criteria considered by the data custodians and the ethics committees.[34] In WA, for the midwives' data, both the data custodian and the ethics committee must be satisfied that the data is necessary for the project and that consent is impracticable. For the immunisation data, both the minister and the ethics committee must consider the public interest.

The need for proportionality in ethics review is recognised in the *National Statement*, which provides for non-ethics committee levels of review for low-risk projects; however, projects requesting a waiver of consent for the use of personal information must always be reviewed by a full ethics committee.[35]

32 *National Statement* (n 28) 21 [2.3.10(b)].
33 NHMRC, 'Section 95 Guidelines' (n 21) Guideline 3.2(b).
34 Flack, Adams, and Allen (n 31).
35 *National Statement* (n 28) 21 [2.3.9].

There are no provisions in the relevant statutes requiring the timely resolution of data requests. The WA Health *Information Access, Use and Disclosure Policy 2019* includes a very general statement recognising the need for timely decision making but it merely requires that access applications are assessed 'at a reasonable review date at the discretion of the authorising authority'.[36]

The authors' previous study of Australian data custodians' perspectives indicates that review and approval timelines vary widely depending on the complexity of the data request, the quality of the application, and the engagement of applicants with the iterative process of refinement.[37]

7.2.4.2 Transparency

The APPs require government agencies to manage data in an open and transparent way. They must have a privacy policy that is reasonably available and includes information about the purposes for which the information is used and disclosed and how an individual can access and correct their information.[38] While all government departments comply with these requirements, the effectiveness of privacy policies with respect to the secondary collection and use of administrative data is questionable. People are often unaware that their information is collected by government departments when the primary collection occurs during the provision of services such as health care.

The *National Statement* requires that institutions publish 'summary descriptions of all its research projects for which consent has been waived'.[39] Both the WA Department of Health and the AIHW publish lists of summary descriptions of approved data linkage projects on their ethics committee web pages.[40] These lists include all approved projects and do not distinguish the projects where consent has been waived, but they do provide relevant information.

All ethics committees are required to report to the NHMRC annually on the details of all research projects involving a waiver of consent for the use of personal information under the federal *Privacy Act 1988*.[41] This information is summarised in the annual activity report to the Australian Health Ethics Committee.[42]

36 Department of Health, 'Information Access, Use and Disclosure Policy' (Government of Western Australia, MP No 0015/16, October 2019) 2–3 [3.1.1].

37 C Adams, J Allen, and F Flack, 'Data Custodians and the Decision-Making Process: Releasing Data for Research' (2018) 26(2) *Journal of Law & Medicine* 433.

38 *Australian Privacy Act* (n 21) s 95, sch 1 APP 1.

39 *National Statement* (n 28) 22 [2.3.12].

40 AIHW, 'Approved AIHW Linkage Projects', *Australian Government* (Web Page) <www.aihw.gov.au/our-services/data-linkage/approved-aihw-linkage-projects>; Department of Health, 'Project Summaries for Approved Proposals', *Government of Western Australia* (Web Page) <ww2.health.wa.gov.au/Articles/A_E/Department-of-Health-Human-Research-Ethics-Committee>.

41 NHMRC, 'Section 95 Guidelines' (n 21) Guidelines 4–5.

42 NHMRC, 'Human Research Ethics Committees' (Web Page) <www.nhmrc.gov.au/research-policy/ethics/human-research-ethics-committees>.

Information about the decision-making criteria is not readily available to the public. In this case study, the statutory criteria applied by the data custodian for the WA data can be found in the statutory regulations, but this may not be transparent to the general public. The only statutory criterion for the immunisation data is 'the public interest'. The way in which the public interest should be evaluated is not elaborated.

The application process for linked data in WA is publicly available on the data linkage unit website.[43] Extensive support is provided to applicants by Research Data Services so that they understand the process. The application is an iterative process between the applicant and the data custodian whereby the applicant is given feedback and advice and the application is refined. While there is no formal requirement or process to give reasons for the rejection of an application this iterative process effectively provides this information and allows for explanation, negotiation, and refinement. Outright rejection of an application is rare.[44]

The application process for the Australian Immunisation Register is less transparent. Very little information is provided publicly, and it may not be obvious to applicants that they should apply through the Data Integration Services Centre at the AIHW when the data custodian is Services Australia.

7.2.4.3 Accountability

Each of the statutes that authorise the collection and use of the relevant data contain accountability provisions that create offences for unauthorised use and disclosure of the data by employees of the agencies.[45] In the federal legislation, the offence extends to researchers who misuse the information they receive. The Section 95 Guidelines also provide for complaints to be made to the Australian Information Commissioner.[46]

7.2.4.4 Community Participation

The *National Statement* provides for community participation in the ethical review of projects. It specifies the minimum membership of registered ethics committees (eight people) and requires the inclusion of two members of the general community, described as 'lay members' who are intended to represent general community views. These members must have no affiliation with the institution and must not be currently engaged in medical, scientific, legal, or academic work.[47] The regulations governing the AIHW ethics committee also require that membership includes at least two people 'able to represent general community attitudes'.[48]

43 Data Linkage WA, 'Applying for Linked Data' (Web Page) <www.datalinkage-wa.org.au/>.

44 Ibid; Adams, Allen, and Flack (n 37).

45 *Australian Immunisation Register Act* (n 3) s 23; *AIHW Act* (n 9) s 29; *WA Health Services Act* (n 7) s 219; *WA Births, Deaths and Marriages Registration Act* (n 1) s 63.

46 NHMRC, 'Section 95 Guidelines' (n 21) Guideline 6.1(b).

47 *National Statement* (n 28) 87 [5.1.29]–[5.1.32].

48 *AIHW (Ethics Committee) Regulations* (n 22) s 7(i).

In Australia, ethics committees are increasingly requiring evidence of community consultation as part of ethics review. This is regarded as particularly important where a waiver of consent is sought, since community support is relevant to two of the *National Statement* waiver criteria. It is evidence that:

- the risk of not seeking consent is low;[49] and
- 'there is no likely reason for thinking that participants would not have consented if they had been asked'.[50]

If the project focused on Indigenous status, then there would be increased expectations for community consultation and issues of data sovereignty would need to be considered.

Practical support for community involvement is provided by the WA Consumer and Community Involvement Program in partnership with research institutions, universities, and WA state government departments.[51] The WA data linkage unit explicitly supports community involvement and applicants for data linkage are expected to document the level of consumer and community involvement when they make their application.[52] The AIHW has no specific requirements for community involvement other than what is prescribed in the *National Statement*.

7.3 SCOTLAND

In Scotland, the case study will require data from the following data collections:

- birth variables from the National Health Service (NHS) Central Register; and
- immunisation variables from the Scottish Immunisation and Recall System.

The NHS Central Register at National Records of Scotland and the Scottish Immunisation and Recall System at Public Health Scotland are routinely linked. Linkage services are provided by the National Records Scotland Indexing Team or National Services Scotland (NSS) Indexing Team. The data for the study would be extracted by the Electronic Data Research and Innovation Service (eDRIS) of Public Health Scotland and transferred to the NSS National Safe Haven (Safe Haven) for the research team to access. The Safe Haven is a physical data laboratory where authorised users can access the data.

Linkage variables including names, addresses, and universal identifying codes, such as Community Health Index (CHI) numbers, would not be included in the data extract provided to researchers. They would, however, be retained by the linkage unit for verification. The data could therefore be re-identifiable and would be classified

49 *National Statement* (n 28) 21 [2.3.10(b)].

50 Ibid 21 [2.3.10(d)].

51 Consumer and Community Involvement Program, 'About Us', *Western Australian Health Translation Network* (Web Page) <https://cciprogram.org/about-us/>.

52 Data Linkage WA, 'Consumer Representation', *Privacy and Ethics* (Web Page) <www.datalinkage-wa.org.au/privacy-and-ethics/consumer-representation/>.

as pseudonymised data under the United Kingdom (UK) *General Data Protection Regulation* (UK GDPR) and the UK *Data Protection Act 2018* (*'UK Data Protection Act'*).[53] The identifiability of the extracted data could be minimised by replacing birth dates with derived variables, such as age at events, and postcodes could be aggregated.

7.3.1 *Decision Makers*

Research governance for Scotland's national health data is centralised and is conducted by the Public Benefit and Privacy Panel for Health and Social Care (PBPP), which is a privacy committee. It has delegated authority from the Registrar General of National Records of Scotland to review and approve requests for data from the NHS Central Register (NHSCR). Its remit also includes requests for data from national data sets such as the Immunisation and Recall System.[54]

The PBPP take a proportionate approach to the review of applications for data. The level of scrutiny escalates depending on the complexity and risks in each application from Tier 1 (governance review only) to Tier 2 out of committee and finally Tier 2 sitting committee. Tier 1 panels include three information governance practitioners and a panel manager. Decisions can be made by a quorum of three. There are fifteen members on the sitting committee, including four public and two researcher representatives. The remaining members are drawn from Scottish government agencies and health services. Out-of-session decisions can be made by a quorum of five. Eight members are required to form a quorum for the full committee.[55] The decision of a Tier 2 panel is final.[56]

7.3.2 *Domestic Law, Policies, and Guidelines Governing the Release of Data for Linkage and Research*

The Register General is authorised to provide birth information, collected under the *Registration of Births, Deaths and Marriages (Scotland) Act 1965* to any other public body, including Public Health Scotland.[57] Births information provided to

53 *Regulation (EU) 2016/679 of the European Parliament and of the Council of 27 April 2016 on the Protection of Natural Persons with Regard to the Processing of Personal data and on the Free Movement of such Data, and Repealing Directive 95/46/EC* (General Data Protection Regulation) [2016] OJ L 119/1 (EU GDPR), art 4 as it forms part of the law of England and Wales, Scotland, and Northern Ireland by virtue of the *European Union (Withdrawal) Act 2018* (UK) s 3 and as amended by *The Data Protection, Privacy and Electronic Communications (Amendments etc) (EU Exit) Regulations 2019*, regs 2–3, sch 1 (UK GDPR); *Data Protection Act 2018* (UK) s 5.

54 PBPP, 'Terms of Reference and Constitution' (National Health Service Scotland, ver. 2.3, June 2020) annex A ('PBPP Terms of Reference and Constitution').

55 Ibid 8–11.

56 Ibid 30.

57 *Registration of Births, Deaths and Marriages (Scotland) Act 1965* (UK) ss 13, 14, 16A; *Local Electoral Administration and Registration Services (Scotland) Act 2006* (Scot) s 56 ('*Local Electoral Administration and Registration Services (Scotland) Act*').

the Registrar General is also included in the NHS Central Register.[58] The Registrar General is authorised to provide information from the NHS Central Register to prescribed persons including a 'researcher conducting a medical research project'.[59] The general functions of Public Health Scotland include 'the collection, dissemination and analysis of epidemiological data', 'the provision of information services' in support of other functions, and assisting with research.[60] No decision-making criteria are specified for the exercise of these statutory powers to release data for research.

In practice, the powers to release information are delegated to the PBPP. Its focus is privacy, specifically weighing the public benefit against individual privacy risks. Its powers are exercised according to *Public Benefit and Privacy Panel for Health and Social Care – Panel Guiding Principles and Proportionate Governance Criteria* ('PBPP principles'), the Caldicott principles, and the data protection principles.[61]

The PBPP principles include seven principles that relate to privacy and data security (privacy, consent, transparency of use, anonymisation, privacy impact, safeguards, and security). The panel is also required to consider the public interest and the scientific merit of the project. Although neither the principles nor the governance criteria include specific criteria for assessing a request for a waiver of consent, Principle 4 recognises that in some circumstances the requirement for consent can be waived if the researcher provides a justification:

> There is a general expectation that wherever practicable individual's consent will be obtained to process their data … But it is recognised that in some circumstances it is not possible or appropriate to obtain consent. In such circumstances, a clear explanation and justification should be given.[62]

It is likely that this case study would be approved applying these principles. The data will be linked and pseudonymised before the researchers access the data in the NSS Safe Haven. Therefore, the privacy and confidentiality requirements are likely to be met. It would meet the research merit and integrity requirements, assuming the science is sound and conducted by an experienced research team from a Scottish university. Since the case study is about vaccination, a significant contributor to improved public health, it is also likely to meet the public benefit test:

> Before approving access to data, the PBPP must be satisfied that the public interest will be furthered by the proposal at hand, that there is both a demonstrable social need for such processing and a reasonable likelihood that it will result in tangible benefits for society.[63]

58 *Local Electoral Administration and Registration Services (Scotland) Act* (n 57) s 57.
59 Ibid; *The National Health Service Central Register (Scotland) Regulations 2006* (Scot) s 4, sch 2.
60 *The Public Health Scotland Order 2019* (Scot) art 4.
61 PBPP, 'PBPP Terms of Reference and Constitution' (n 54) app B (Panel Guiding Principles and Proportionate Governance Criteria).
62 Ibid Principle 4.
63 Ibid Principle 2.

The Caldicott principles are as follows.

1. Justify the purpose(s) for using confidential information.
2. Use confidential information only when it is necessary.
3. Use the minimum necessary confidential information.
4. Access to confidential information should be on a strict need-to-know basis.
5. Everyone with access to confidential information should be aware of their responsibilities.
6. Comply with the law.
7. The duty to share information for individual care is as important as the duty to protect patient confidentiality.
8. Inform patients and service users about how their confidential information is used.[64]

These principles are focused on protection of individual privacy and cover much of the same ground as the PBPP principles.

The disclosure of personal information must also comply with the *UK Data Protection Act* and the UK GDPR.[65] The PBPP would need to be satisfied that there was a lawful basis for processing the data under the UK GDPR. The lawful basis for processing the data for the case study would be 'the performance of a task carried out in the public interest or in the exercise of official authority vested in the controller'.[66] The relevant data is 'data concerning health' so it is 'special category data' that must also come within one of the exceptions in article 9 of the UK GDPR. In this case, there are several exceptions that may apply, the most relevant exception being for scientific research or statistical purposes.[67]

Processing under this exception must be in accordance with article 89(1) of the UK GDPR and the *UK Data Protection Act*, which both impose additional conditions.[68] These conditions are that processing without consent must be:

- necessary for research purposes;[69]
- in the public interest;[70]

64 UK Caldicott Guardian Council, 'The Eight Caldicott Principles' (Web Page, December 2020) <www.ukcgc.uk/manual/principles>.

65 *UK Data Protection Act* (n 53); UK GDPR (n 53); *European Union (Withdrawal) Act 2018* (UK) ss 2–3; *The Data Protection, Privacy and Electronic Communications (Amendments etc) (EU Exit) Regulations 2019* (UK) ss 3, 4; *The Data Protection, Privacy and Electronic Communications (Amendments etc) (EU Exit) Regulations 2019* (UK) schs 1, 2.

66 UK GDPR (n 53) art 6(1)(e).

67 Ibid art 9(2)(j).

68 *UK Data Protection Act* (n 53) ss 10, 19(2).

69 Ibid pt. 1 sch 1 s 4(a).

70 Ibid pt. 1 sch 1 s 4(c).

- subject to safeguards that ensure that technical and organisational measures are in place in particular in order to ensure respect for the principle of data minimisation including minimising identifiability; and[71]
- not likely to cause substantial damage or substantial distress to a data subject.[72]

It is likely that the PBPP will also be satisfied that these requirements are met and that the release of the data is lawful under the *UK Data Protection Act* and the UK GDPR.

For projects covered by a generic (infrastructure) ethics approval, this is the only review of the proposed research. The PBPP is not required to consider any risks other than risks to individual privacy. There is no specific requirement to consider the social and cultural context in which the study would occur. The risks and benefits to groups and communities, including groups that may be created by the analysis, are not required to be considered in the review.

7.3.3 *Ethics Review*

In the UK, there is no uniform requirement for ethics review of all research involving humans and no uniform guiding principles used in ethics review. Ethical review will depend on the policies and rules of the specific sector responsible for the research. Ethics review of research that involves users of the NHS or adult social care comes under the auspices of the United Kingdom NHS Health Research Authority and is governed by Governance Arrangements for Research Ethics Committees (GAfREC).[73] The policies governing ethics review of research conducted in or by universities vary between universities and ethics review is often devolved to individual schools or colleges within the university. There are no uniform requirements or guiding ethical principles applied to their ethical review.

In Scotland, there is no legislative requirement for ethics review if a waiver of consent is requested. If the project required identifiable NHS data, then ethics review would be required under the GAfREC.[74] An online decision-making tool is available to assist researchers to decide when ethics review is required.[75] If researchers are given the full date of birth in the data extract for the case study, the data would be considered potentially identifying and must be reviewed by an ethics committee.

The project may be covered by generic approval and hence may not be required to undergo ethics review. The Electronic Data Research and Innovation Service at

[71] UK GDPR (n 53) art 89(1).

[72] *UK Data Protection Act* (n 53) s 19(2).

[73] Health Research Authority, 'Governance Arrangements for Research Ethics Committees: 2020 Edition' (National Health Service, London, 26 March 2020) ('GAfREC: 2020 Edition').

[74] Ibid 9 [2.3.5(d)]; Health Research Authority, 'Standard Operating Procedures for Research Ethics Committees' (National Health Service, London, March 2021) s 11.2 ('Standard Operating Procedures for Research Ethics Committees').

[75] Health Research Authority, 'Do I Need NHS REC Approval?', *National Health Service* (Web Page) <www.hra-decisiontools.org.uk/ethics/>.

Public Health Scotland has received a generic ethics approval from East of Scotland NHS Research Ethics Service to allow external researchers (like the research team in the example) access to data without project-specific ethics approval and without consent but they 'must not receive data in identifiable form or be able to identify subjects through linkage with other databases'.[76] If the birth dates and geographic locations are replaced with derived variables, then the data extract for the case study may not be regarded as identifiable. If the research meets the following additional requirements, then an ethics review of the project is not required. The project:

- is in the field of Health or Social care research;
- does not involve any contact with research participants/subjects;
- has undergone scientific peer review;
- data is held in and accessed via the national safe haven; and
- will be carried out by UK-based researchers only.[77]

The case study meets all these requirements.

Where NHS ethics committee review is required, then the work of the committee is governed by the UK Policy Framework for Health and Social Care, GAfREC, and the Standard Operating Procedures for Research Ethics Committees.[78] These documents refer to the World Medical Association's *Declaration of Helsinki* as a source but do not require ethics committees to consider these principles in their review and do not provide any other detailed guidance on the ethical principles that should be considered.[79] There are broad level principles for good practice in the conduct of research in the UK Policy Framework for Health and Social Care.[80]

The 'Ethical Review Form' provided by the Health Research Authority indicates the ethical categories that reviewers are expected to consider.[81] These reflect the core values described in Chapter 5 and include:

- social or scientific value – scientific design and conduct of the study (including involvement of patients, service users, and the public in the design, management, and undertaking of the research);
- recruitment arrangements and access to health information, as well as fair research participant selection;

[76] Health Research Authority, 'Standard Operating Procedures for Research Ethics Committees' (n 74) ss 11.23–11.25.

[77] Public Health Scotland, 'Frequently Asked Questions' (Web Page) <www.isdscotland.org/Products-and-Services/eDRIS/FAQ-eDRIS/index.asp#d4>.

[78] Health Research Authority, 'UK Policy Framework for Health and Social Care Research' (National Health Service, London, May 2020) ('UK Policy Framework for Health and Social Care Research'); Health Research Authority, 'GAfREC: 2020 Edition' (n 73); Health Research Authority, 'Standard Operating Procedures for Research Ethics Committees' (n 74).

[79] *Declaration of Helsinki* (n 29).

[80] Health Research Authority, 'UK Policy Framework for Health and Social Care Research' (n 78) 8.

[81] Health Research Authority, 'Ethical Review Form', *Guidance and Policy for REC Members* (Web Page, 12 May 2020) <www.hra.nhs.uk/about-us/committees-and-services/res-and-recs/research-ethics-committee-members-area/guidance-and-policy-for-rec-members/>.

- favourable risk–benefit ratio – anticipated benefits and risks for research participants (present and future);
- care and protection of research participants – respect for potential and enrolled research participants' welfare and dignity;
- informed consent process and the adequacy and completeness of research participant information;
- suitability of the applicant and supporting staff;
- independent review; and
- Suitability of supporting information.

The possibility of waiver of consent is not acknowledged in this document. There is no guidance on how to evaluate the risks of undermining trust if no consent is sought.

This case study could potentially have significant impacts both positive and negative well beyond the individual participants in the study and children receiving future vaccinations. The ethics committee does not appear to be required to consider risks and benefits to people who will not or do not want to receive vaccinations in the future. There is no requirement to consider beneficence in the context of the Scottish population as a whole or subgroups of the population whether existing, for example, cultural groups or groups that may be created by the research. This may in part be mitigated by the references to including involvement of patients, service users, and the public in the design, management, and undertaking of the research.

7.3.4 *Good Decision Making*

7.3.4.1 Efficiency

There has been significant focus on efficiency and timeliness of approvals for the release of data for research in Scotland. Efficiency is achieved through centralisation of approvals by delegating decision making to the PBPP. The PBPP adopts a proportionate approach to review and triages applications to different levels of review. Only a small number of applications are reviewed by the full committee, with the majority being dealt with by small Tier 1 panels where the expected turn around is twenty to thirty working days.[82]

The PBPP appears to combine review of governance matters, such as the legality of the release of data, with review of some ethical matters, such as the balance between privacy and public benefit. Where ethics review is required, then there will be some duplication between the matters considered by the ethics committee and the PBPP; however, the PBPP only considers ethical issues related to privacy of the participants. Where there is no ethics review, then there will be no consideration of the wider ethical issues such as justice.

82 PBPP, 'PBPP Terms of Reference and Constitution' (n 54) cl 36–40.

7.3.4.2 Transparency

Public Health Scotland provides information about the use of personal information in the Privacy Notice published on its website in accordance with obligations under the UK GDPR.[83] The PBPP publishes lists of the applicants, project titles, and approval outcomes on its website. It appears to be the intention to publish lay summaries in the future, but these are not available at the time of writing. End of Project Summaries and Benefit Summaries are also published on the website when they are available.[84] The Guiding Principles used by the PBPP in decision making are readily available to both members of the public and applicants.[85] Extensive advice is given to applicants about the application process on the PBPP website.[86] Client support is also provided by eDRIS.[87]

7.3.4.3 Accountability

The Data Processing Act provides for offences for misuse of personal data and enforcement by the Information Commissioner.[88]

7.3.4.4 Community Participation

There is limited community participation in PBPP decisions to release data. Although the full Tier 2 panel of the PBPP includes four public members, the majority of approvals are given by Tier 1 panels that consist only of information professionals. There is no description of what is meant by a 'public' member in the Terms of Reference of the PBPP, but at the time of writing three out of four of the public, or lay, members are current or retired academics. The 'Lay Representative Person Specification' indicates that essential attributes include the ability to 'rapidly assimilate and understand large amounts of information about high-level medical and social project proposals and strategic developments' and familiarity

83 Public Health Scotland, 'Privacy Notice' (Web Page, 1 April 2020) <https://publichealthscotland.scot/our-privacy-notice/organisational-background/>; UK GDPR (n 53) arts 12–14.

84 PBPP, 'Meetings, Reports: Application Outcomes', *National Health Service Scotland* (Web Page, 2021) <www.informationgovernance.scot.nhs.uk/pbpphsc/application-outcomes/>; PBPP, 'End of Project Report Summaries', *National Health Service Scotland* (Web Page, April 2021) <www.informationgovernance.scot.nhs.uk/pbpphsc/wp-content/uploads/sites/2/2021/04/End-of-Project-Reporting-summaries.pdf>.

85 PBPP, 'Guiding Principles and Policy for Decision Making', *National Health Service Scotland* (Web Page) <www.informationgovernance.scot.nhs.uk/pbpphsc/wp-content/uploads/sites/2/2020/12/Guiding-Principles-v2.0.docx>.

86 PBPP, 'Information for Applicants' (Web Page) <www.informationgovernance.scot.nhs.uk/pbpphsc/home/for-applicants/>.

87 Public Health Scotland, 'Your Research Proposal: What Next?' (Web Page, 2020) <www.isdscotland.org/Products-and-Services/eDRIS/Research-Proposal/>.

88 *UK Data Protection Act* (n 53) pt 6.

'with the current legislative and advisory environment regarding personal data, especially health and social care data'.[89] People who meet these requirements are people with specialist knowledge rather than ordinary members of the public.

Community views are considered in the review conducted by the PBPP. Applicants are asked to indicate 'whether any members of the public or lay representatives have been involved in the design of the proposal' and to include 'details of any public engagement or consultation activity which has been undertaken in the course of designing the proposal'.[90] Panel members are required to consider 'the value of lay consultation in providing additional assurance in respect of public or patient benefit, and of indicating any potential public or patient concern which might arise from the proposal'.[91]

If the project is reviewed by an ethics committee, then the membership of the committee will include at least a third of members who are lay members and are 'not employed in health or care professions or whose primary professional interest is not health or care related research'.[92] An ethics committee would consider the 'involvement of patients, service users and the public, in the design, management, and undertaking of the research'.[93]

INVOLVE, which was funded by the National Institute for Health Research, has in the past provided support for community involvement in NHS, public health, and social care research.[94] It has now been superseded by the National Institute for Health Research Centre for Engagement and Dissemination.

7.4 MANITOBA

In Manitoba, Canada, the study will be conducted using data held at the Manitoba Centre for Health Policy (MCHP). Data is required from the following collections:

- Manitoba Immunization Registry – Panorama.
- Hospital Abstracts.
- Midwifery Summary Reports.

89 PBPP, 'Lay Representative Person Specifications 2020', *National Health Service Scotland* (Web Page) <www.informationgovernance.scot.nhs.uk/pbpphsc/vacancies/>.

90 PBPP, 'Public Benefit and Privacy Panel for Health and Social Care Application Form', *National Health Service Scotland*, s 3.1.15 (Web Page) <www.informationgovernance.scot.nhs.uk/pbpphsc/wp-content/uploads/sites/2/2021/05/HSC-PBPP-Application-form-v4.0.docx>.

91 PBPP, 'Guidance for Tier 1 Panel Participants', Question 6 (Web Page) <www.informationgovernance.scot.nhs.uk/pbpphsc/>.

92 Health Research Authority, 'GAfREC: 2020 Edition' (n 73) 20 [4.2.7].

93 Health Research Authority, 'Ethical Review Form', *Guidance and Policy for REC Members* (Web Page, 12 May 2020) <www.hra.nhs.uk/about-us/committees-and-services/res-and-recs/research-ethics-committee-members-area/guidance-and-policy-for-rec-members/>.

94 INVOLVE, 'Welcome to INVOLVE', *National Institute for Health Research* (Web Page) <www.invo.org.uk/>.

The MCHP holds and routinely links data from these collections provided by Manitoba Health.[95] The collections are provincial so the study will be limited to people who are both born and immunised in Manitoba. If birth dates and small geographic area codes are included in the data extract, then the information released to the researchers would be personal health information as defined by the Manitoba *Personal Health Information Act*.[96]

7.4.1 *Decision Makers*

Research projects must be approved by the University of Manitoba Health Research Ethics Board and the Manitoba Health Information Privacy Committee.[97]

7.4.2 *Domestic Law, Policies, and Guidelines Governing the Release of Data for Linkage and Research*

The data in these collections is part of the health surveillance system established under the *Public Health Act 2006* for a variety of purposes, including facilitating public health research and planning. Information can be collected, used, linked, and disclosed by the minister, or a person authorised by the minister, for these purposes.[98]

Both the Minister for Manitoba Health and Seniors Care, and the University of Manitoba must also comply with the *Personal Health Information Act* when they use or disclose personal health information.[99] Personal health information for research can be released without consent with the approval of either the Health Information Privacy Committee, where the information is held by a government 'trustee', or an institutional research review committee, where it is held by a non-government 'trustee'. In either case, the committee must be satisfied that:

(a) the research is of sufficient importance to outweigh the intrusion into privacy …;
(b) the research purpose cannot reasonably be accomplished unless the personal health information is provided in a form that identifies or may identify individuals;

[95] *Personal Health Information Act*, SM 1997, c 51, ss 22(2)(f), 24.1 ('*Personal Health Information Act Manitoba*'). The MCHP is a prescribed health research organisation under *Personal Health Information Regulation*, Man Reg 245/97, s 8.5(1) ('*Personal Health Information Regulation Manitoba*').

[96] *Personal Health Information Act Manitoba* (n 95) s 1.

[97] Rady Faculty of Health Sciences, 'MCHP Data Access Process – Step 5 – Privacy, Ethics and Data Provider Approvals/Permissions', *University of Manitoba* (Web Page, 6 July 2020) <https://umanitoba.ca/faculties/health_sciences/medicine/units/chs/departmental_units/mchp/resources/access/Step5-ApprovalsandPermissions.html>; *Personal Health Information Act Manitoba* (n 95) ss 22(2)(f), 24(2), 59(1).

[98] *Public Health Act*, SM 2006, c 14, s 82. For collection of immunisation data, see *Public Health Immunization Regulations*, Man Reg 36/2009, s 5.

[99] *Personal Health Information Act Manitoba* (n 95) ss 1, 20(1), 21(e), 22(2)(f).

(c) it is unreasonable or impractical … to obtain consent from the individuals … ; and
(d) the research proposal contains
  (i) reasonable safeguards to protect the confidentiality and security of the personal health information, and
  (ii) procedures to destroy or remove, at the earliest opportunity … information that … allows individuals to be readily identified.[100]

7.4.3 *Ethics Review*

It is a requirement of the University of Manitoba that the University of Manitoba Health Research Ethics Board reviews all applications for access to linked data. Therefore, ethics committee approval is a precondition to release of the information. If the indigenous ethnicity of those within the cohort is examined, then additional specialist ethical review may be required.

The ethics committee will apply the *Tri-Council Policy Statement: Ethical Conduct for Research Involving Humans* (the '*Tri-Council Statement*').[101] The *Tri-Council Statement* is the ethical guidance document that applies to all institutions which administer or receive funding from the three federal research agencies in Canada. It specifies the minimum membership of ethics committees (five people) and that they should include both men and women. At least two members should have relevant research expertise, one member should be knowledgeable in ethics, one member should be knowledgeable in the relevant law, and at least one member should be a community member with no affiliation to the institution.

The *Tri-Council Statement* does not explicitly reference any of the international ethics guidelines; however, it is organised around three core principles that originate from the four core values that form the basis of all the international guidelines discussed in Chapter 5. The three core principles are:

- respect for persons – encompassing respect for intrinsic human value and respect for autonomy;
- concern for welfare – including the elements of beneficence; and
- justice – the obligation to treat people fairly and equitably.

Although research merit and integrity are not explicitly stated as core values, the ethics committee must be satisfied that appropriate peer review has been undertaken or conduct it themselves.[102]

[100] *Personal Health Information Act Manitoba* (n 95) s 24(3).
[101] Canadian Institutes of Health Research, Natural Sciences and Engineering Research Council of Canada, and Social Sciences and Humanities Research Council, *Tri-Council Policy Statement Ethical Conduct for Research Involving Humans* (Document No TCPS2 2018, December 2018).
[102] Ibid art 2.7.

The *Tri-Council Statement* addresses data linkage research expressly. It notes the risk of re-identification as a result of linkage and requires the ethics committee to be satisfied that the data linkage is essential and that appropriate security measures are in place.[103]

There are five general criteria for waiving consent and an additional six criteria an ethics committee must consider when assessing a request for a waiver of consent for secondary use of identifiable information with some overlap between the two categories.[104] Two criteria relate to the risks to participants – the project must pose no more than minimal risk to participants and the absence of consent must be unlikely to adversely affect the welfare of participants.[105] These map on to the Council for International Organizations of Medical Sciences (CIOMS) criterion that 'the research poses no more than minimal risks to participants'.[106] The criteria do not address the risk to public trust in the confidentiality of data if consent is waived. Two criteria relate to the practicability of seeking consent and the practicability of carrying out the research if the prior consent of participants is required.[107]

The general principles in the *Tri-Council Statement* require that all research must be evaluated against the core principle of concern for welfare. This includes the requirement that '[r]esearchers must also consider the risks and potential benefits of their research and the knowledge it might generate for the welfare of society as a whole'.[108] This consideration would include an assessment of the social value of the research. The *Tri-Council Statement* directs attention to the welfare of particular groups but states that this 'consideration does not imply, however, that the welfare of a group should be given priority over the welfare of individuals'.[109] This is consistent with the approach taken in the *Declaration of Helsinki* and the United Nations Educational, Scientific and Cultural Organization (UNESCO) *Universal Declaration on Bioethics and Human Rights*.[110]

The remaining criteria cover the necessity of using identifiable information, the use of adequate measures to protect privacy and confidentiality, compliance with any known preferences of the participants, plans for debriefing, and governance issues.

In assessing concern for welfare in the case study, the ethics committee would need to consider the risks and benefits both to the individual participants and to

[103] Ibid art 5.7.

[104] Ibid arts 3.7A, 5.5A.

[105] Ibid arts 3.7A(a)–(b), 5.5A(b).

[106] CIOMS, *International Ethical Guidelines for Health-Related Research Involving Humans* (Geneva, 4th ed, 2016) Guideline 10.

[107] *Tri-Council Statement* (n 101) arts 3.7A(c), 5.5A(e).

[108] Ibid 8.

[109] Ibid.

[110] *Declaration of Helsinki* (n 29); *Universal Declaration on Bioethics and Human Rights*, 33rd UNESCO General Conference (October 2005).

groups and communities. Although the privacy risks to participants are minimal, there is a real possibility of stigmatisation and discrimination as a result of this project. This could affect both the individual participants and the wider groups to which they belong. The ethics committee would weigh this against the significant benefits of improving compliance with Manitoba's vaccine schedule.

7.4.4 *Good Decision Making*

7.4.4.1 Efficiency

There is duplication between the role of the Health Information Privacy Committee and the ethics committee in approving the release of personal health information without consent. Both committees must consider the necessity of using identifiable information, the impracticability of seeking consent, the security of the data, and the safeguards to protect privacy.

The *Tri-Council Statement* directs ethics committees to adopt a proportionate approach to review and to triage review to a level of scrutiny appropriate to the level of risk.[111] Where the ethics committee has a statutory role in approving the release of data, delegated decision making would not be adequate. Projects using identifiable data such as birth dates would require review by the full committee.[112]

7.4.4.2 Transparency

The Manitoba Centre for Health Policy publishes a Privacy Code that provides information about the handling and protection of information held by the Centre.[113] The Centre's annual reports include examples of research conducted by researchers at the Centre and a list of active research projects is available on the Centre's website. No publicly available information was located that provided a comprehensive list of data projects approved by the Health Information Privacy Committee or the University of Manitoba Health Research Ethics Board.

The decision makers have clear decision-making criteria in the legislation and the *Tri-Council Statement*. These documents are publicly available online. The application procedures are clearly documented by the Manitoba Centre for Health Policy, which provides support for research applicants.[114]

111 *Tri-Council Statement* (n 101) arts 2.9, 6.12.

112 Bannatyne Campus Research Ethics Boards, 'Categories and Procedures for Review of New Research Protocols' (University of Manitoba, July 2015).

113 Manitoba Centre for Health Policy, 'Privacy Code: Manitoba Centre for Health Policy' (University of Manitoba, June 2016).

114 Rady Faculty of Health Sciences, 'MCHP Data Access Process (DAP)', *University of Manitoba* (Web Page, 11 March 2020) <https://umanitoba.ca/faculties/health_sciences/medicine/units/chs/departmental_units/mchp/resources/access.html>.

7.4.4.3 Accountability

The *Personal Health Information Act* empowers the Ombudsman to receive and investigate complaints about privacy.[115] If the complaint is well founded, the outcomes are limited to recommendations to cease or modify a practice or destroy a collection of personal health information.[116] The Manitoba Centre for Health Policy has clear lines of responsibility for the data in its custody and procedures for complaints about compliance with its privacy principles.[117]

7.4.4.4 Community Participation

The committees that make the decisions about the release of data both include community members. The Health Information Privacy Committee must include one-quarter of members appointed as 'public representatives who are not health professionals or persons who conduct health research or employees of the government'.[118] Of the remaining members, six are appointed to represent professional bodies, healthcare providers, and the University of Manitoba.[119] The *Tri-Council Statement* requires that ethics committees have at least one community member with no affiliation to the institution.[120] At the time of writing, the relevant University of Manitoba Research Ethics Board had two community members.[121]

The Health Information Privacy Committee is not required to consider whether there has been any community consultation or participation in the project. Neither the statutory criteria nor the information required in the application for approval mentions community involvement.[122]

The *Tri-Council Statement* directs attention to consultation with the relevant community in relation to the risks of the research, noting that '[e]ngagement during the design process with groups whose welfare may be affected by the research can help to clarify the potential impact of the research and indicate where any negative impact on welfare can be minimized'.[123]

115 *Personal Health Information Act Manitoba* (n 95) pt 5.
116 Ibid s 47(3).
117 Manitoba Centre for Health Policy (n 113) Principles 1, 10.
118 *Personal Health Information Act Manitoba* (n 95) s 59(2).
119 *Personal Health Information Regulation Manitoba* (n 95) s 8.3(2).
120 *Tri-Council Statement* (n 101) art 6.4.
121 Office of Research Ethics and Compliance, 'Board Membership', *University of Manitoba* (Web Page, 2020) <www.umanitoba.ca/research/orec/ethics_medicine/board.html>.
122 *Personal Health Information Act Manitoba* (n 94) s 24(3); *Personal Health Information Regulation Manitoba* (n 95) s 8.2(1).
123 *Tri-Council Statement* (n 101) 8.

7.5 DISCUSSION

The comparison of three jurisdictions – WA, Scotland, and Manitoba – reveals generally similar approaches to decision making on the release of data; however, there are some significant differences. All three jurisdictions have a formal application and approval process based on statutory requirements. The number and type of decision makers vary in each jurisdiction. In WA, the decision makers are the data custodians of each data collection included in the study. As data from three different data collections with different data custodians is required to conduct the study and there is no centralised statutory authority to authorise the data sharing, there are three decision makers. Projects must also be approved by two ethics committees. This is in part because of the cross-jurisdictional responsibility for the data, but it contributes to a relatively inefficient decision-making process.

In Scotland and Manitoba, the decision makers are committees. In Manitoba, a privacy committee (Health Information Privacy Committee) and the University of Manitoba Ethics Committee are the decision makers and there is some overlap in their roles. In Scotland, there is only one decision maker, the PBPP, a privacy committee. It takes a proportionate approach to the review of applications where the scrutiny escalates with increasing risk and complexity. This approach is the most efficient of the jurisdictions examined. On the other hand, the review and approval processes are confined to privacy concerns and many projects do not receive ethical review that considers broader ethical issues beyond individual privacy.

There are four decision-making criteria required to waive consent that are common to each of the three jurisdictions. The exact wording varies but the four criteria can be summarised as:

- low risk – participation in the research should be of low or minimal risk to the participants;
- necessity – the data requested must be necessary for the conduct of the research;
- impracticality – it must be impracticable to obtain consent from the individuals to whom the data relates; and
- privacy and confidentiality – there must be appropriate measures to protect the privacy and confidentiality of the research participants.

Two of these criteria align with the three waiver criteria in the international CIOMS guidelines, low risk and impracticality.[124] The third CIOMS criteria – 'the research has important social value' – is a form of public interest test.

Both WA and Scotland include a public interest test, but there is no explicit requirement to assess public interest in Manitoba. There are, however, elements

[124] CIOMS (n 106) Guideline 10.

of a public interest test in the criteria 'the research is of sufficient importance to outweigh the intrusion into privacy'.[125] Interestingly, only Australia has criteria that assess the risk of undermining community trust in the health system or government by waiving the need for consent. Both the *National Statement* and the statutory guidelines require that ethics committees must be satisfied that the benefits of the research outweigh the risks of undermining public trust.[126] Given the central role of trust in the maintenance of social licence, it is important that this is considered.

For all jurisdictions, there was at least some overlap between the issues considered by the ethics committee and the data custodians or privacy committee. This is another thing that may contribute to inefficiencies in the decision-making process.

Information about the approval processes and decision-making criteria are publicly available on the relevant organisations' websites. All the jurisdictions also provide at least some public information about the research that is approved. However, this is not always very detailed – sometimes just a project title – or written in a language accessible to the general community. Clear information about specific roles and responsibilities as well as complaints processes are not available in all jurisdictions. There are opportunities for improved transparency in all the jurisdictions considered.

In each jurisdiction, there are complaints processes and offences for unauthorised use and disclosure of the data. The Manitoba Centre for Health Policy clearly documents lines of responsibility; however, elsewhere accountability could be demonstrated by more transparency around the roles and responsibilities of the officers involved in these processes.

Community involvement in decision making about data sharing as well as involvement in individual research projects is critical in building and maintaining the social licence for the use of data without consent. All three jurisdictions require lay members on ethics committees and privacy committees to assist in decision making, although the definitions of lay members vary between jurisdictions. For example, the lay members of the PBPP in Scotland could be better described as members with specialist expertise rather than ordinary members of the public. None of the jurisdictions has specific criteria about community involvement to consider when waiving the requirement for consent; however, WA and Scotland ask for information about community involvement in research in their application forms, and the *Tri-Council Statement* in Canada does encourage community engagement in the design of research projects.

[125] *Personal Health Information Act Manitoba* (n 95) s 24(3).

[126] *National Statement* (n 28) 21 [2.3.10(b)], [2.3.10(d)]; NHMRC, 'Section 95 Guidelines' (n 21) Guideline 3.2(b).

7.6 CONCLUSION

In summary, our conclusions in this chapter are:

1. There are significant similarities in the decision-making processes in the three jurisdictions, WA, Scotland, and Manitoba. These include:
   - formal application processes;
   - a statutory basis for decision making;
   - criteria for waiving consent including low risk, impracticality, necessity, and protection of privacy and confidentiality; and
   - at least some community participation in decision making and research.
2. The main areas where decision making could be improved are:
   - efficiency – the number of decision makers and duplication of the issues considered by different decision makers may reduce the efficiency of these processes;
   - transparency and accountability – the decision-making criteria and processes including roles and responsibilities, complaints procedures, and information about approved research should be transparent to both researchers and the general public, and information about approved research in lay language should be more accessible; and
   - community involvement – involvement of genuinely lay members of the public in decision making as well as more specific requirements for community consultation and community involvement in research projects would assist in improving the social licence for the use of data without consent.

8

Better Practice and Processes

8.1 INTRODUCTION

In this book, we have described the competing rights and interests, and benefits and risks in sharing linked data for research as well as the three main decision-making frameworks: human rights, ethics, and law. Chapter 7 sets out examples of how these frameworks are applied in the real world and demonstrate the complex processes used to make decisions about whether to link and share data. These existing decision-making practices and processes are not keeping pace with the data tsunami and technological progress that enables data analysis at a scale that was not envisaged even twenty years ago. Improvements are required to meet the needs and expectations of researchers, data custodians, and the community.

Researchers want access to as much linked data as possible to answer difficult questions about health and health systems and to develop better preventions, treatments, and services. They are frustrated with the complicated application and approval processes and the time it takes for decisions to be made about data sharing.[1]

Government data custodians are struggling to deal with the increasing demand for data and the complexity of the requests.[2] They require guidance and training on how to make the decision to share data as well as additional resources to meet the extra workload required.[3]

Community attitudes to the sharing of health data for research are generally positive but are qualified. The community has concerns about the security of the data and the use of data resulting in stigmatisation and discrimination, as well as specific concerns about sharing with private companies.[4] However, there is support for sharing health data for research where there is clear public interest, the data is shared securely, and the risks of re-identification are minimised.[5]

As described in Chapter 3, maintenance of a social licence for research based on linked data requires decision makers to demonstrate trustworthiness and the decision-making process to demonstrate transparency and accountability and include public consultation and involvement. The inclusion of these elements in decision-making processes will help to develop and support social licence in a dynamic way that will be responsive to the changing technological landscape.

1 N Dattani et al, 'Accessing Electronic Administrative Health Data for Research Takes Time' (2013) 98(5) *Archives of Disease in Childhood* 391; R Gilbert, H Goldstein, and H Hemingway, 'The Market in Healthcare Data' (2015) 351 *BMJ* h5897; D Palamuthusingam et al, 'Health Data Linkage Research in Australia Remains Challenging' (2019) 49(4) *Internal Medicine Journal* 539.

2 C Adams, J Allen, and F Flack, 'Data Custodians and the Decision-Making Process: Releasing Data for Research' (2018) 26(2) *Journal of Law & Medicine* 433.

3 Ibid; J Teng and K Mcgrail, 'Cultural and Institutional Barriers among Data Stewards Regarding Data Access for Research' (2018) 3(4) *International Journal of Population Data Science* 363.

4 M Aitken et al, 'Public Responses to the Sharing and Linkage of Health Data for Research Purposes: A Systematic Review and Thematic Synthesis of Qualitative Studies' (2016) 17(1) *BMC Medical Ethics* 73; N Garrison et al, 'A Systematic Literature Review of Individuals' Perspectives on Broad Consent and Data Sharing in the United States' (2016) 18(7) *Genetics in Medicine* 663; S Davidson et al, *Public Acceptability of Cross-Sectoral Data Linkage: Deliberative Research Findings* (Report, Scottish Government Social Research, 2012); J Street et al, 'Sharing Administrative Health Data with Private Industry: A Report on Two Citizens' Juries' (2021) *Health Expectations* <https://doi.org/10.1111/hex.13268>.

5 Aitken et al (n 4); Davidson et al (n 4); A Braunak-Mayer et al, *Exploring the Public Interest in and Social Licence for the Use of Linked Administrative Data in Therapeutic Development through a Scoping Review, Survey of Community Attitudes, and Hypothetical Case Studies* (Report Summary, Australian Centre for Health Engagement, Evidence and Values, 2016) <www.phrn.org.au/media/81832/report-summary.pdf>.

In this book, we have identified a range of challenges that must be overcome to improve the decision-making processes and the decisions made about the sharing of linked health data for research in ways that ensure all the relevant interests are taken into account and the decision-making processes are not unduly burdensome on the applicants or decision makers.

Many researchers consider the existing application and approval processes to be too burdensome and that, as a result, the benefits of research are limited or delayed, or harm may be caused by the research not being conducted.[6] If decisions about data applications are made efficiently, then the results of research will be available sooner and theoretically this should result in more timely improvements to health and health care. In addition, if researchers spent less time writing data applications, they could do more research, which would also result in more timely improvements to health care. The processes to decide whether or not to share data should be designed to encourage scientific progress while recognising that the benefits of conducting as much research as possible as quickly as possible must be weighed against the risks of spending insufficient time reflecting on the potential impact and consequences of each research project.[7]

Some researchers take the view that the most efficient solution to this problem would be to give researchers unfettered access to linked health data to conduct whatever research they see fit. However, this assumes they have no interests other than the public interest and are the best judges of the consequences and outcomes of their research.

As described in Chapters 5 and 6, the current legal and ethical frameworks for making these decisions are complex and overlapping, particularly regarding linking and sharing data across jurisdictions. These complex frameworks are resource-intensive for both the organisations who manage them and the researchers who submit applications for approval. The regulation of data use is just one aspect of research regulation and some researchers, such as those doing clinical trials, must also navigate a range of additional requirements.[8] This can lead to confusion and frustration, which result in unnecessary duplication and poor decision making.[9]

6 J Allen et al, 'Privacy Protectionism and Health Information: Is There Any Redress for Harms to Health?' (2013) 21(2) *Journal of Law & Medicine* 473; R Mitchell et al, 'Data Linkage Capabilities in Australia: Practical Issues Identified by a Population Health Research Network "Proof of Concept Project"' (2015) 39(4) *Australian and New Zealand Journal of Public Health* 319; K Jones et al, 'The Other Side of the Coin: Harm Due to the Non-Use of Health-Related Data' (2017) 97 *International Journal of Medical Informatics* 9.

7 V Xafis et al, 'An Ethics Framework for Big Data in Health and Research' (2019) 11(3) *Asian Bioethics Review* 227.

8 I Fletcher et al, 'Co-Production and Managing Uncertainty in Health Research Regulation: A Delphi Study' (2020) 28(2) *Health Care Analysis* 99.

9 F Flack, C Adams, and J Allen, 'Authorising the Release of Data without Consent for Health Research: The Role of Data Custodians and HRECs in Australia' (2019) 26(3) *Journal of Law & Medicine* 655.

The assumption for many years has been that the only risk or concern regarding the use of individual-level health data was the risk of individual re-identification. The approach to this problem has been to rely on consent or anonymisation. This approach is embedded in the legislation of all the countries referenced in this book and has resulted in increasingly demanding consent protocols and a focus on technical solutions to preventing re-identification rather than a broader consideration of competing interests and risks and benefits. It is no longer fit for purpose. This is because seeking consent is often impracticable given the volume of data, number of people, and unknown future uses of linked data. It also fails to provide real protection for individual autonomy. Anonymisation is no longer as effective as it was once considered because re-identification is easier due to the volume of data and technological advances. Anonymisation also decreases the utility of the data for research. In addition, re-identification is not the only risk or interest that should be considered when making decisions about data linkage. There can be harms associated with the implementation of the results of research that are not related to individual re-identification and that affect others beyond those whose data is used. While the right to privacy, for example, is important in this context it is also necessary to consider other rights, such as the right to health, in order to ensure more balanced decision making.

In this final chapter, we discuss the problems with existing approaches to decision making. We consider the frameworks for decision making and outline our view of the relevant decision-making criteria and considerations. We consider those who are tasked with decision making and propose a more efficient allocation of decision making that best reflects the expertise and responsibilities of decision makers. Lastly, we discuss the decision-making process and identify the qualities of good decision making.

8.2 DECISION-MAKING FRAMEWORK

Approval for research using linked data without consent involves decisions about which data sets should be linked and which projects should have access to linked data. The decision makers are making decisions on behalf of the individuals whose data is included and on behalf of the whole community. It is important that decision makers are clear as to the matters they should consider in exercising their discretion. Decision makers who are uncertain about what is expected of them are likely to be risk-averse and to make defensive decisions. Clear decision-making criteria are essential to ensure consistency, fairness, transparency, and accountability. Decisions need to be explicable and reviewable, and this is only possible if the approval criteria are clearly articulated.

In Part II, we discussed the approval criteria found in the legal and ethical frameworks governing the sharing of data for research using linked data without consent. In Chapter 7, we illustrated the approval processes in three subnational jurisdictions that incorporate some or all of these approval criteria. Although there is a variety of approaches and criteria between jurisdictions, there is much commonality. All jurisdictions have criteria directed at protecting individual privacy, such as minimising the identifiability of data used, and requiring that the use of identifiable data be necessary. Most require that seeking consent is impracticable, unreasonable, or not feasible.

These criteria reflect their context. The criteria in data protection legislation are focused on protecting individual privacy interests. The default position is that individuals have a right to control their information through notice and consent. Research exceptions in data protection legislation that permit a waiver of consent recognise that the right to privacy may be limited and must be balanced against broader community interests, but these are framed as an exception to this norm. Similarly, the principles in ethics guidelines used by ethics committees are largely focused on protecting the participants in the research and weighing their interests against the benefits of research.

Sitting alongside these criteria directed at individual privacy there is usually some kind of public interest requirement in either the legislation or the ethics guidelines. These public interest tests are framed in various ways in the relevant legislation and ethical guidelines. Some are framed as threshold tests – the project must be 'in the public interest'.[10] Some are framed as a comparison between public interest and individual privacy – 'the potential benefits of the research project clearly outweigh the potential risk to the privacy of the subject individual'.[11] Some require comparison between the public interest in the research and the public interest in privacy – 'the public interest in the proposed research outweighs to a substantial degree the public interest in protecting the privacy of the individuals who are the subjects of the personal health information to be used in the research'.[12] This last draws attention to the public interest in maintaining trust in healthcare providers and in the confidentiality of health information. In practice, consideration of the public interest is often focused almost exclusively on the benefits of the research.

The concept of public interest is useful in describing a general approach to the exercise of a discretion. It directs attention away from individual and towards wider interests. It should be noted that irrespective of particular legislative requirements:

> Public officials have an overarching obligation to act in the public interest. This means, broadly, that they must perform their official functions and duties, and exercise any discretionary powers, in ways that are consistent with matters of broad public concern and away from private, personal, parochial or partisan interests.[13]

10 See, eg, *Data Protection Act 2018* (UK) pt 1 sch 1 s 4(c) ('*UK Data Protection Act*').
11 See, eg, *Health Information Protection Act*, SS 1999, c H-0.021, s 29(2)(c).
12 See, eg, *Health Information Act*, RSPEI 1988, c H-1.41, s 30(3)(c)(i).
13 New South Wales Ombudsman, *Good Conduct and Administrative Practice: Guidelines for State and Local Government* (Guidelines, 3rd ed, March 2017) 10.

As a criterion for decision making, however, 'public interest' is problematic. The concept of public interest is criticised as vague and uncertain. It is variously understood as equating to interests held by a majority, taking a utilitarian view; interests shared by all; reflecting a higher moral value or overriding interest; or a process of compromise and balancing interests.[14] Without further elaboration, it does not help decision makers distinguish between those projects that should be approved and those that should not in a predictable or meaningful way. It states a conclusion rather than being a useful tool for reaching that conclusion. Public interest is best understood as the overarching question that must be decided rather than a separate criterion.

Sorauf points out that using the concept of public interest permits:

> a legislature to frame a vague, undefined delegation of authority for an administrative agency that will later be expanded and explicated by the agency itself. The public interest becomes a means by which the necessity of specific definition, and the conflict of interests that that would invite, is postponed to more propitious times and circumstances.[15]

Public interest is a flexible concept that takes its meaning from the context and purpose for which it is used. It is mutable and evolves over time.[16] When it is used in a statute, 'the term ['public interest'] derives its content from "the subject matter and the scope and purpose" of the enactment in which it appears'.[17] This is significant where it appears in a statute which has the primary aim of protecting the privacy of individuals. It may be interpreted as simply requiring a balance between the privacy and autonomy of research participants and the potential research benefits. In our view, this lens is too narrow.

In addition to the requirements in the legislation and ethical guidelines, decision makers are using other decision-making frameworks to structure the assessment of applications. These include the Five Safes framework, which uses five dimensions to organise decision making:

- Safe Projects – Is the use of the data appropriate?
- Safe People – Can the users be trusted to use it in an appropriate manner?
- Safe Settings – Does the access facility limit unauthorised use?
- Safe Data – Is there a disclosure risk in the data itself?
- Safe Outputs – Are the statistical results non-disclosive?[18]

14 F Sorauf, 'The Public Interest Reconsidered' (1957) 19(4) *Journal of Politics* 616; M Feintuck, *The Public Interest in Regulation* (Oxford University Press, 2004); M Taylor and T Whitton, 'Public Interest, Health Research and Data Protection Law: Establishing a Legitimate Trade-Off between Individual Control and Research Access to Health Data' (2020) 9(1) *Laws* 6.

15 Sorauf Ibid 639.

16 A Sorbie, 'Sharing Confidential Health Data for Research Purposes in the UK: Where are "Publics" in the Public Interest?' (2020) 16(2) *Evidence & Policy* 249.

17 *Hogan* v *Hinch* (2011) 243 CLR 506, [31] (French CJ).

18 F Ritchie, 'The "Five Safes": A Framework for Planning, Designing and Evaluating Data Access Solutions' (Conference Paper, Data for Policy Conference, September 2017).

The Five Safes framework is widely used both formally and informally to assess data applications.[19] This framework is given legislative status in the Australian Data Availability and Transparency Bill 2020 (Cth), which requires that data sharing is consistent with these principles. The sharing entity must be satisfied 'that each principle is applied to the sharing in such a way that, when viewed as a whole, the risks associated with the sharing are appropriately mitigated'.[20]

The Five Safes Framework is a valuable device for structuring discussion; however, the principles are high-level and require elaboration.[21] Four of the five dimensions focus on security of the data and individual privacy. Only the first, safe projects, directs attention to the broader considerations that are essential to decisions about the sharing of data. It is this dimension that is currently poorly articulated in all decision-making criteria.

While it is dangerous to generalise about the decision-making criteria in different contexts and across jurisdictions, some trends emerge from our analysis in preceding chapters. The criteria currently employed set the protection of privacy against the benefits of research. In our view, this binary approach oversimplifies the interests and values at stake. Decision making should be framed in a way that more accurately reflects the balance drawn in international human rights law, discussed in Chapter 4. It should be reframed to recognise that privacy is not an absolute right and that, as all persons live in society, the protection of privacy is necessarily relative.[22] Human rights are interdependent, indivisible, and interrelated.[23] In particular, the individual's right to privacy must be balanced with the rights and freedoms of others, including the right to health.

Decision makers who are making decisions about sharing data for research using linked data are making decisions for the individual participants, collectives, and the wider community. They are asked to exercise their discretion on behalf of the whole community and in this sense the overarching question is one that is made in the public interest. A precise definition of the public interest may be unhelpful, but decision makers need a decision-making framework that directs them explicitly to the interests that should be considered and the values that should be used to avoid idiosyncratic approaches that import the decision makers' values and preferences. A non-exhaustive list of relevant considerations may be more helpful than attempts at definition.[24]

19 See, eg, the decision-making framework for the Public Benefit and Privacy Panel for Health and Social Care, Scotland: Public Benefit and Privacy Panel for Health and Social Care, 'Terms of Reference and Constitution' (National Health Service Scotland, ver. 2.3, June 2020) annex B ('PBPP Terms of Reference and Constitution').

20 Data Availability and Transparency Bill 2020 (Cth) ss 13, 16.

21 Australian Computer Society, 'Data Sharing Frameworks' (Technical White Paper, September 2017).

22 Human Rights Committee, *General Comment No 16: Article 17 (Right to Privacy)*, 32nd sess, UN Doc HRI/GEN/1/Rev 9 (8 April 1988).

23 World Conference on Human Rights, *Vienna Declaration and Programme of Action*, GA Res 48/121, UN GAOR, 8th sess, 85th plen mtg, UN Doc A/CONF.157/23 (12 July 1993).

24 Australian Law Reform Commission, 'Serious Invasions of Privacy in the Digital Era' (Discussion Paper No 80, March 2014) 8.38.

8.2.1 *Interests*

We would suggest that a broader approach is needed that recognises the interrelated interests of individuals, collectives, and the community discussed in Chapter 2 and the diverse ways in which research using linked data can both create risks of harm and have positive impacts. It is an oversimplification to frame the decisions as balancing individual privacy interests against the public benefits. Individuals, collectives, and the community can each have conflicting interests, both positive and negative, in a research project using linked data. Where decisions engage conflicting interests:

- there should be explicit and transparent consideration of the conflicting interests, concerns, and consequences for individuals, collective groups, and the wider community;[25] and
- decisions should be made in consultation with those with a relevant interest.[26]

8.2.2 *Values*

Decision makers need a clear understanding of the shared values that should be considered in exercising their discretion to avoid unstated values and priorities.[27]

Respect is a central value in bioethics. It encompasses respect for the autonomy and dignity of every human being and the acknowledgement of every person's intrinsic moral worth. The use of individual data without consent impacts on the autonomy and privacy of individuals and this is well understood by decision makers. Autonomy is a core value in Western philosophical traditions which needs to be carefully guarded; however, autonomy should not always be given precedence over other important values. Autonomy is exercised through consent to participate in research, and this has been the principal way in which the dignity of participants is respected.

In Chapter 2, however, we have argued that seeking consent is problematic both practically and ethically in this context. In our view, consent to the use of information for secondary purposes is often ineffective as an exercise of autonomy. In addition, centralising consent by participants fails to recognise that the risks of the research are not confined to the participants.[28] Taylor and Whitton argue that where consent is impractical then individuals should have a right to opt out to protect their freedom and to support social licence.[29] An opt-out option, however, suffers from many of the

25 D Melé and J Armengou, 'Moral Legitimacy in Controversial Projects and its Relationship with Social Licence to Operate: A Case Study' (2016) 136 *Journal of Business Ethics* 729.

26 R Anderson, *The Collection, Linking and Use of Data in Biomedical Research and Health Care: Ethical Issues* (Report, Nuffield Council on Bioethics, 2015).

27 Xafis et al, 'An Ethics Framework for Big Data in Health and Research' (n 7).

28 A Ferretti et al, 'Ethics Review of Big Data Research: What Should Stay and What Should be Reformed?' (2021) 22(1) *BMC Medical Ethics* 51.

29 Taylor and Whitton (n 14).

same practical and ethical problems as consent. It is not clear that an opt-out option provides a genuine opportunity for participants to exercise autonomy because they may not be aware of the option to opt out and there remain difficulties with ensuring that participants are adequately informed. In data-based research, individuals and collectives who are not participants in the research may also be at risk from the outcomes of the research, but they have no opportunity to make a choice. In addition, it is not clear that using an opt-out approach will ensure social licence or that the absence of an option to opt out is fatal to social licence.[30] Seeking consent is one way of showing respect but greater attention should be given to other ways in which respect can be demonstrated and the dignity of participants acknowledged and protected.

The qualitative studies of public views reviewed in Chapter 3 indicate that there is community support for research using linked data without consent under appropriate conditions.[31] This indicates that people will give precedence to other values under those conditions; however, the other relevant values are less well articulated in the current decision-making regimes.

The concept of solidarity captures the importance of community to human well-being and recognises that people are prepared to accept costs to help others.[32] This is reflected in qualitative research on community attitudes to the use of administrative data without consent that indicates that people are prepared to forgo autonomy and limit privacy to support research that will benefit others.[33] Solidarity recognises that our concerns and interests are interconnected rather than in simple opposition. It has particular moral weight in the context of public health research focusing on the interrelationship between social determinants and health.[34] Solidarity is closely linked to social licence since it is maintained by community acceptance that the use of the data is legitimate. It should be recognised as an important value that informs decision making about research using linked data. Decision makers need evidence as to whether the relevant community will accept the use of their data for a research project in order to help others.

The principles of reciprocity and justice should also inform decisions about research using linked data. Justice requires that there should be a fair distribution of burdens and benefits. Reciprocity recognises that members of communities who receive benefits have mutual obligations to contribute to the welfare of the

30 Xafis et al, 'An Ethics Framework for Big Data in Health and Research' (n 7).

31 V Xafis, 'The Acceptability of Conducting Data Linkage Research without Obtaining Consent: Lay People's Views and Justifications' (2015) 16 *BMC Medical Ethics* 79; Ipsos MORI Social Research Institute, *The One-Way Mirror: Public Attitudes to Commercial Access to Health Data* (Report prepared for the Wellcome Trust, March 2016); Aitken et al (n 4).

32 B Prainsack and A Buyx, *Solidarity: Reflections on an Emerging Concept in Bioethics* (Report, Nuffield Council on Bioethics, November 2011) 46.

33 Aitken et al (n 4); Xafis (n 31); Davidson et al (n 4).

34 A Dawson and B Jennings, 'The Place of Solidarity in Public Health Ethics' (2012) 34(1) *Public Health Reviews* 65.

group.[35] Where benefits can only be achieved by social cooperation, then there is a moral obligation and often a legal obligation to contribute. This obligation is constrained by the principles of necessity and proportionality, which require that the infringement on individual liberty is minimised and is justified by the objectives.

8.2.3 *Rights*

In the same way, the full range of human rights are not reflected or protected by the existing decision-making framework. There is an explicit emphasis on the right to privacy in the decision-making infrastructure and criteria across the three jurisdictions, but other relevant rights – such as the right to health and the right to enjoy the benefits of scientific progress discussed in Chapter 4 – are not clearly articulated in these frameworks. This may be due to a Western emphasis on civil and political rights at the expense of economic, social, and cultural rights but does not reflect the modern discourse on rights. All human rights are universal, indivisible, interdependent, and interrelated and so protecting the right to privacy without fully considering the relationship with other rights does not provide appropriate respect or protection for rights.

Most rights, including the right to privacy, are not absolute and the international human rights regime is largely concerned with finding the best way to 'balance' or integrate the relevant rights in particular contexts. The right to privacy may, and indeed must, be limited where necessary and proportionate to protect the rights and freedoms of others, including the right to health. It is on this basis that we have reconfigured the decision-making criteria for ethics committees to include a consideration of the full range of human rights relevant to research under review. In our view, it is necessary to contextualise the right to privacy in the body of human rights to achieve a more integrated rights-based approach to sharing data for research.

This will not, in our view, be a huge leap for ethics committees. They are already asked to weigh and consider the impact on privacy against the merits of research, including the benefits to health. We suggest, however, that this discussion be based explicitly on the relevant rights rather than, for example, weighing the right to privacy with the public interest in health. It is important to acknowledge that what is under consideration is the right to privacy and the right to health and that these rights are equally important and must be considered in an integrated way.

8.2.4 *Criteria and Considerations*

For these interests, values, and all the relevant human rights to become part of the decision-making process, they must be identified and articulated in the criteria upon which decisions rest and in the matters that decision makers take into consideration in deciding whether or not a criterion has been met.

35 A Viens, 'Public Health, Ethical Behavior and Reciprocity' (2008) 8(5) *American Journal of Bioethics* 1.

In essence, a decision is a response to a question. Good decision making involves clearly identifying the question and then answering it.[36] In decision making for research projects using linked data, the primary question is, 'Should particular data be released for a particular research project?' The answer to this question is likely to be yes if it is lawful to do so and, on balance, in the public interest. Yet posing this question, without further guidance, is not helpful for the decision maker or for any of the stakeholders involved in research using linked data. What is needed is a list of criteria upon which to decide whether a research project is ethical and whether to release a data collection for research.

Making a decision involves considering the criteria on which the decision should or must be made. This is so when a decision is made as an exercise of legislative power; however, the basic principles apply to all decision making.[37] Administrative decision makers, such as government data custodians who exercise the administrative power of government, are required to (1) make a decision that the relevant criteria have been met by (2) an exercise of discretion after reflecting on all relevant considerations. Ethics committee members are required to (1) make a decision that the relevant criteria have been met by (2) coming to a consensus after reflecting on all relevant considerations. This is not always a straightforward exercise, particularly where the criteria or considerations are not clearly articulated. Our qualitative research with Australian data custodians found that some had been left to decide whether or not to release data for research on the basis of very few or no articulated criteria apart from the vague and, we would say, unhelpful test of the public interest.[38] Decision makers need direction as to the criteria they must take into consideration in evaluating the conflicting interests, values, and rights engaged by sharing data for research using linked data.[39] The criteria should be clearly articulated in legislation, policy, or guidelines. This is because it is necessary that decision makers satisfy themselves that these criteria are met before approving a research project or the release of data for research.

In order to make a decision, based on stated criteria, the decision maker must also establish the facts. This can be done on the basis of submissions – from researchers, for example – or certification from another authoritative source, for example an ethics committee or other expert committee. So, for instance, whether or not a particular research project had been approved by an ethics committee is a question of fact that could be established in either of these two ways. In our proposed decision-making framework, data custodians are required to be satisfied that each project has been approved by an ethics committee.

36 G Downes, 'Good Decision Making' (Speech, Australian Public Service Commission Forum of Commonwealth Agencies Conference, 7 March 2008).

37 Ibid.

38 Adams, Allen, and Flack (n 2).

39 See, eg, 'Framework for Assessing the Merit of a Data Sharing Activity to Deliver Public Benefit' in K Scott et al, *Data for Public Benefit: Balancing the Risks and Benefits of Data Sharing* (Report, Involve, Carnegie UK Trust, and Understanding Patient Data, April 2018) 40; Xafis et al, 'An Ethics Framework for Big Data in Health and Research' (n 7).

The decision makers we are concerned with, data custodians and members of ethics committees or privacy committees, are not members of a court or tribunal and are not bound by the rules of evidence. They do not have to decide 'beyond reasonable doubt' or 'on the balance of probabilities'. However, decision makers should always aim to be 'reasonably satisfied' that the relevant criteria have been met, taking into account all the relevant facts and considerations, and to exercise their discretion on that basis. Decision-making criteria are those elements of the decision-making framework that must be met and should be clearly articulated and on the public record. For data custodians, the criteria should be set out in legislation. For ethics committees and privacy committees, the criteria should be set out in guidance documents such as the *National Statement on Ethical Conduct in Human Research* (the '*National Statement*')[40] in Australia and the *Tri-Council Policy Statement: Ethical Conduct for Research Involving Humans* (the '*Tri-Council Statement*')[41].

The considerations that decision makers should take into account in coming to a decision on the specified criteria will be context-specific and may change over time. Some agencies and institutions may wish to include more detailed considerations as guidance for decision makers, but they should be included in guidelines for decision makers, rather than legislation, so that they can be more easily amended over time.

The aim of the decision-making process is to ensure that it is in the public interest to link and share data for research. This process has ethical dimensions and also raises issues of governance, including legality and the good management of government data assets. The relevant criteria should therefore include both the ethical and the governance dimensions and these criteria should be assigned to the decision maker with the most appropriate skills, expertise, and resources.

Our aim in this chapter is to suggest clear criteria and a set of potentially relevant considerations to make the lives of decision makers more straightforward. Our hope is that this will lead to better decisions. Better decisions are decisions that are efficient, fair, transparent, and accountable and are more likely to attract and sustain the social licence needed to support research using linked data without consent. We would also like to ensure that the criteria on which decisions are based reflect the full set of values, interests, and rights at play in the context of using administrative data for research without consent and do not focus in an unjustified way on specific considerations, such as privacy, to the detriment of other equally important considerations.

Tables 8.1 and 8.2 set out the criteria that should be satisfied in deciding whether or not data should be linked and shared for a research project.

40 National Health and Medical Research Council, Australian Research Council, and Universities Australia, *National Statement on Ethical Conduct in Human Research* (National Health and Medical Research Council, 2018 ed, 2007).

41 Canadian Institutes of Health Research, Natural Sciences and Engineering Research Council of Canada, and Social Sciences and Humanities Research Council, *Tri-Council Policy Statement Ethical Conduct for Research Involving Humans* (Document No TCPS2 2018, December 2018).

TABLE 8.1 *Ethical values, criteria, and considerations*

Ethical values	Criteria	Considerations
Research Merit and Integrity	The methodology is sound, and the project can achieve its aims.	a) Is the quality of the data and the accuracy of the linkage sufficient to achieve reliable outcomes? b) Will the methodology produce statistically significant results?
	The applicants have the experience, qualifications, and competence to undertake the research.	a) Will the applicants conduct the research honestly? b) Are the applicants committed to contributing to public knowledge and understanding? c) Are the applicants committed to sharing the results, whether they are favourable or not?
Beneficence	The potential benefits justify the risks of harmful outcomes.	
	There are potential benefits from the project that will enhance well-being.	a) Are the outcomes likely to be translated into positive social outcomes for individuals, groups, or the community? b) Who is likely to benefit from the outcomes of the project? c) What are the costs to the community if the research is not conducted?
	The outcomes are valued by the community.	a) Has there been community consultation about the project? b) Are the outcomes recognised and valued by community?
	Potential harmful outcomes have been identified, minimised, and justified.	a) Are any groups or individuals likely to be harmed by the conduct, outcomes, or publication of the research? b) Are any groups or individuals likely to be harmed by stigmatisation, discrimination, or loss of services as a result of the project? c) Has the relevant community been consulted about potential harm? d) How serious and how likely are the possible harms? e) How will the potential harms be minimised? f) Is the use likely to undermine trust in the collection, protection, and use of individual information?
	There are appropriate security arrangements to protect the data.	a) How serious are the likely harms if there is unauthorised disclosure or identification of individuals from the project? b) Are there appropriate security measures to prevent loss of data and unauthorised identification of individuals?

Justice	There is a fair distribution of benefits and risks.	a) Are the burdens on the participants, and others, proportionate to the potential outcomes? b) Does any group bear an unfair burden of research? c) Is any restriction on individual rights necessary and is it the least restrictive possible? d) How will the benefits of the research be translated and distributed fairly?
	The use of the data is acceptable to the community.	a) Has the relevant community been consulted on the acceptability of this use of the data? b) Does the project align with public expectations about the use of data?
Respect	The project is respectful of participants.	a) Has the relevant community been consulted about the aims and design of project? b) Will the contribution of the participants be acknowledged? c) Will the results of the project be shared with the relevant community? How will they be communicated?
	All relevant human rights have been considered and an appropriate balance of rights has been achieved.	a) What human rights are relevant to the project under consideration? b) Are the relevant rights, such as the right to privacy and the right to health, reflected in the project and given appropriate weight?
	Any limits on participants' autonomy and rights are justified, necessary, and proportionate.	a) Is it reasonable, practicable, and feasible to seek consent? b) Is there a direct and ongoing relationship between the participants and the researchers? c) Are there any risks to the welfare or privacy of individuals from seeking consent? d) Where consent will not be sought, has the relevant community been consulted about the use of data for this project without consent? e) Is the use of the data without consent likely to undermine trust in the confidentiality of personal information? f) Is it necessary to use identifiable data for the project? g) Has the identifiability of the data been minimised? Has it been minimised as soon as possible? h) Has the number of people accessing the data been minimised? i) Is the purpose of sharing clearly limited? j) Is there a risk that any individuals will be identifiable in publications?

TABLE 8.2 *Governance criteria and considerations*

Criteria	Considerations
The sharing of the data is lawful.	a) Is there a lawful basis for the sharing of data? b) Have all the statutory criteria been met? c) What other regulatory requirements arise? d) Have these regulatory requirements been met?
The project has been approved by an ethics committee.	
There are adequate safeguards in place to ensure that data is handled appropriately.	a) How serious are the likely harms if there is unauthorised disclosure or identification of individuals from the project? b) Are there appropriate security measures to prevent loss of data and unauthorised identification of individuals during transport, linkage, analysis, and archiving? c) Will the data be accessed in a secure environment? d) Are the applicants trusted users? Do they have appropriate experience, policies, and technology to protect the data? e) What contractual obligations are in place in relation to confidentiality and security of the data? f) What statutory obligations apply to the handling of the data by the applicant?

Table 8.1 sets out the relevant ethical criteria. Table 8.2 sets out the relevant governance criteria. The decision makers should be satisfied that each criterion is met in order to approve the project. The tables include a non-exhaustive list of considerations relevant to each criterion, which address many of the issues raised in this book.

8.3 DECISION MAKERS

Decision makers need to make decisions about the creation of linkage infrastructure, the linkage of data, and the sharing of data for research projects. They must have sufficient information available to them and the skills and experience to weigh the competing ethical values and moral claims along with governance issues to make a good decision. There are various kinds of decision makers who could be responsible for making the decisions to link and share data for research. In Chapter 7, we gave real-world examples of some of the possibilities. The options include privacy committees, ethics committees, and data custodians or combinations of all three.

8.3.1 *Privacy Committees*

In general, the role of privacy committees, or data access committees, is to review applications for access to data to ensure they meet the requirements of the relevant legislation and regulations and to consider the protection of individual privacy.

In some jurisdictions, the privacy committee is a statutory committee and the committee's approval for release of data for research is a prerequisite required by statute. For example, the Manitoba *Personal Health Information Act* requires that the release of data for research is approved by the statutory privacy committee, the Health Information Privacy Committee, where the data is held by the government.[42]

In other jurisdictions, the privacy committee provides advice to the decision maker on compliance with statutory requirements. For example, in England and Wales the Confidentiality Advisory Group (CAG) (formerly the Patient Information Advisory Group) provides advice to the Health Research Authority and the Secretary of State for Health on the use of confidential health information for research and compliance with the *Health Service (Control of Patient Information) Regulations* and the Health and Social Care Information Centre on compliance with the *National Health Service Act 2006* (UK).[43]

In other jurisdictions, the privacy committee reviews applications according to criteria established by policy. For example, in Scotland the Public Benefit and Privacy Panel (PBPP) reviews and approves applications, applying criteria specified in its Terms of Reference.[44]

The role of privacy committees crosses over between governance and ethics review. They typically review the governance issues set out in Table 8.2, including the legal basis for sharing the data and the security arrangements for the data. They also consider a limited range of ethical issues, but their evaluation is framed around the privacy of individual participants. Typically, they do not consider the full range of ethical criteria set out in Table 8.1. This means that full ethics review by an ethics committee is also needed to ensure proper ethical review, and this results in overlapping reviews and inefficiency. For example, the issues the CAG considers include lawfulness, the necessity of using identifiable data, the feasibility of consent, community involvement and engagement, and a fairly narrow public interest test where the only risk considered is breach of confidentiality.[45] Research projects must also be reviewed by an ethics committee.[46]

42 *Personal Health Information Act*, RSM 1997, c P-33.5, ss 24(2), 59(1).

43 *National Health Service Act 2006* (UK) s 251; *The Health Service (Control of Patient Information) Regulations 2002* (UK) ('*UK Control of Patient Information Regulations*'); *Care Act 2014* (UK) s 110, sch 7 s 8.

44 See, eg, PBPP, 'Public Benefit and Privacy Panel for Health and Social Care – HSC – PBPP', *National Health Service Scotland* (Web Page) <www.informationgovernance.scot.nhs.uk/pbpphsc/>.

45 Health Research Authority, 'Guidance for CAG applicants: Recommendations and Approval Decisions', *National Health Service* (Web Page, 2021) <www.hra.nhs.uk/about-us/committees-and-services/confidentiality-advisory-group/guidance-confidentiality-advisory-group-applicants/>.

46 *UK Control of Patient Information Regulations* (n 43) reg 5(2).

The membership of privacy committees is designed to make decisions about governance issues and about risks to individual privacy but may not have sufficient diversity of membership and expertise to make informed decisions about the other important criteria that should be considered. For example, the PBPP in Scotland has eighteen members, most of whom are data custodians, privacy experts, or researchers. There are four 'public representatives' but the PBPP Terms of Reference give no guidance on the specific role of these members or what characteristics they should have to represent the public. There are no conditions or exclusions that would ensure that these positions are held by ordinary members of the public.[47] At the time of writing, the four public representatives were all senior academics or health professionals. It could be argued that there is insufficient diversity among these members for real public representation. It is also unclear that there is the necessary expertise on the PBPP to consider the full range of ethical issues. This is significant since many projects reviewed by the PBPP will be covered by generic ethics approval and will not have any individual ethics review. In addition, most data applications are not considered by the full PBPP; the proportionate approach to review means that most applications are only reviewed by government governance practitioners and the PBPP manager (Tier 1 review).[48]

The criteria applied by privacy committees are not always clear and transparent. Some publish guiding principles; for others, the matters they consider must be gleaned from guidance to applicants such as 'Frequently Asked Questions' documents, meeting minutes, or application forms.

8.3.2 *Ethics Committees*

The role of the ethics committee is to make an independent decision about the ethical and scientific merit of a research project and in doing so to protect the interests of research participants. Ethics committees evaluate the ethical issues and determine whether the project is ethically sound. They assess the social value of proposed research to determine whether the benefits justify the burdens of the research, issues of justice to determine whether there is a fair distribution of burdens and benefits, and whether people are treated with respect. In most jurisdictions, they apply a clear set of national ethical guidelines in making their decision. These guidelines draw on the international ethics instruments. They outline the ethical criteria that must be considered and give detailed guidance on the considerations that are relevant. The existing guidelines do not all capture the full list of criteria pertinent to linked data research outlined in Table 8.1.

47 PBPP, 'Terms of Reference and Constitution' (n 19) annex A. Cf *National Statement* (n 40) [5.1.30(b)]: 'no affiliation with the institution and do not currently engage in medical, scientific legal or academic work'.

48 PBPP, 'The Public Benefit and Privacy Panel for Health and Social Care – Tier 1', *National Health Service Scotland* (Web Page) <www.informationgovernance.scot.nhs.uk/pbpphsc/test-phase-1-pbpp-why-does-it-exist/test-phase-1-about-pbpp-tier-1/>.

In some jurisdictions, for example Australia, ethics committees have specifically defined roles in the data protection or health records legislation which require the review and approval of an ethics committee before personal information can lawfully be disclosed or used for research without consent. These statutory provisions are typically accompanied by guidelines that ethics committees are required to apply when considering a waiver of consent.[49]

The composition of ethics committees deliberately brings together a range of expertise and perspectives, which is ideal for considering the interests and issues required to be considered in sharing linked data.[50] The deliberative and consensus-building approaches taken by ethics committees work well for the consideration of a broad range of interests. The average ethics committee should have the necessary skills and experience in reviewing scientific merit and general ethical principles. However, specialist ethics committees, which include some of the expertise of a privacy committee such as specific expertise in data science, data management, and data security, as well as community involvement expertise, would be better able to evaluate whether the project is ethically sound.[51] Specialist training for ethics committee members on the ethical evaluation of research using linked data is also recommended.[52]

The scope of ethics committee mandates may not cover all aspects of the linkage and sharing of linked data. In some jurisdictions, ethical review is not required if the project only includes data classified as de-identified or anonymised.[53] In others, there are generic ethics approvals that cover de-identified data.[54] In these circumstances, there is no ethics review of the individual project; but the ethical acceptability of a project is always context-specific and careful consideration of matters such as the likely impact of the outcomes on collectives and the wider community is needed. Independent oversight and community involvement in the decision making remain important for the acceptability of the data use. In our view, all projects involving individual-level data should have ethical review. Triaging projects to ethics review based on identifiability can no longer be supported. In addition, decisions about the development of linkage infrastructure such as the linkage of additional data collections should, in our view, have ethical review. This is required in some jurisdictions, but it is not a widespread requirement.[55]

49 See, eg, *Privacy Act 1988* (Cth) s 95 ('*Australian Privacy Act*'); National Health and Medical Research Council, 'Guidelines under s 95 of the *Privacy Act 1988*' (Australian Government, November 2014).

50 Ferretti et al (n 28).

51 See, eg, Department of Health, 'Western Australia Human Research Ethics Committee: Terms of Reference' (Government of Western Australia, May 2021) <ww2.health.wa.gov.au/-/media/Files/Corporate/general-documents/DOH-HREC/dohwahrec-terms-of-reference.pdf>; Ferretti et al (n 28).

52 K Tan et al, 'An Evaluation of a Data Linkage Training Workshop for Research Ethics Committees' (2015) 16(13) *BMC Medical Ethics* 13.

53 *Public Welfare Department of Health and Human Services*, 45 CFR 46.104 (2018).

54 Health Research Authority, 'Standard Operating Procedures for Research Ethics Committees' (National Health Service, London, March 2021) ss 11.23–26.

55 See, eg, Department of Health (n 51) 4.1.

8.3.3 *Data Custodians*

Data custodians are those responsible for the collection and management of data and for making decisions about the use and release of the data.[56] Their role encompasses a range of responsibilities, including ensuring the integrity, utility, and protection of the data collection. The various aspects of the role may be distributed to different office holders. Here, we are concerned with the legal responsibility for authorising the release of data. This responsibility may rest with the organisation as a whole, or it may be entrusted to a committee[57] or a particular office holder.

The legal responsibility for the sharing of government administrative data lies with the statutory data custodian, who may be a departmental office holder or a minister.[58] The data custodian must be satisfied that all the statutory criteria are met and hence that the sharing of data for linkage and research is lawful.

The statutory data custodian may be responsible for data from one agency only or decision making can be centralised. In some jurisdictions, data from various agencies is held by a central government agency in a linked data repository or data sharing platform and decision-making responsibility for projects is delegated to that agency.[59] Alternatively, a statutory authority such as a 'data commissioner' could be empowered to make decisions about the sharing of data for research for all government agencies. There are advantages to this model. A data commissioner, located in a central government agency, creates a clear line of responsibility to a minister for decisions taken about government data collections, a resource collected, held, used, and disclosed on behalf of the community. Centralising decision making in this way would also help to ensure efficiency – in terms of providing a focus of expertise – and consistency. One of the issues that arose in our qualitative research with data custodians across Australia in 2018 was the need to bring together the decision making in relation to multiple data collections at a single point.[60] This model would achieve that outcome. It would also introduce an element of independence into the decision-making process by removing the final decision from the context of individual agencies where portfolio political issues, such as the results of research potentially reflecting badly on particular policies or programmes, may have more currency.

In some jurisdictions, government data is provided to a non-government organisation, such as an academic organisation, for a linked data repository or data sharing

[56] S Rosenbaum, 'Data Governance and Stewardship: Designing Data Stewardship Entities and Advancing Data Access' (2010) 45(5) *Health Services Research* 1442.

[57] See, eg, SAIL Databank, 'Information Governance Review Panel', *Data Privacy & Security* (Web Page) <https://saildatabank.com/saildata/data-privacy-security/#secure-access>.

[58] See, eg, Health Services Act 2016 (WA) s 216, which allows the chief executive officer of Department of Health Western Australia to authorise disclosure of information for health-related research; Australian Immunisation Register Act 2015 (Cth) s 22(3), which allows the minister to authorise disclosure for a specified purpose that the minister is satisfied is in the public interest.

[59] Stats NZ, 'Apply to Use Microdata for Research', *Integrated Data* (Web Page, 19 November 2020) <www.stats.govt.nz/integrated-data/apply-to-use-microdata-for-research>.

[60] Adams, Allen, and Flack (n 2).

platform, which then makes decisions about the use of the data.[61] This approach has advantages in reducing the number of decision makers but results in the separation of authority and responsibility. Outsourcing of authority can result in the lines of responsibility becoming blurred. On balance, we would prefer to see the final decision to release government administrative data for research being explicitly taken by a government data custodian to ensure clear lines of responsibility and accountability.

8.3.4 *Efficiency, Expertise, and Responsibility*

The choice of decision maker should ensure that decision making is efficient, that decisions are made by decision makers with the necessary expertise, and that those who make the decision are responsible and accountable for their decisions. Overlapping evaluation of the relevant criteria by multiple committees or decision makers should be avoided. There are examples where decision making responsibilities for a single research project are split between multiple decision makers, including multiple data custodians and committees.[62] This results in duplication of effort and unnecessary delay in making the data sharing decision. Decisions must be guided by clear criteria and decision makers must have access to the expertise needed to assess the facts and considerations relevant to the criteria. To achieve these goals, the governance dimension and the ethical dimension set out above in Tables 8.1 and 8.2 should be clearly distinguished. In our view, the evaluation of the governance criteria, which should be statutory criteria, should be the responsibility of the data custodian and the evaluation of the ethical criteria should be the responsibility of an ethics committee.

The statutory data custodian must make the final decision on the sharing of data for linkage and research. The legal responsibility rests with the statutory data custodian who must be satisfied that the statutory criteria are met. Government officials have access to expert advice to advise them on the governance criteria. Committees of volunteers, such as ethics committees, do not have the expertise or the support to evaluate governance matters and should not be asked to do so. While some privacy committees have the expertise to advise on the risks to agencies, such as security risks, that advice should be provided within the hierarchy of responsibility in government agencies rather than by independent committees.

In contrast, the ethical criteria should be evaluated by those who have ethical expertise and experience. In addition, it is important that there is a broad range of perspectives brought to bear on the ethical evaluation and that community voices are included. This is particularly important to support social licence for linked

61 IC/ES, 'Working with ICES Data', *ICES Data* (Web Page) <www.ices.on.ca/Data-and-Privacy/ICES-data/Working-with-ICES-Data>.

62 Flack, Adams, and Allen (n 9).

data research. Data custodians are in general ill-equipped to make this ethical evaluation. Ethics committees, however, are established to play that role. Ideally, specialist ethics committees that include expertise in linked data research, data security, and data management would decide whether the sharing of data is ethically sound. Privacy committees could, theoretically, conduct this evaluation if their role was clearly delineated and separated from governance. However, their membership would need to be broadened to include a range of expertise and ordinary members of the community, and they would need to be guided by clear ethical criteria. Their role would then clearly overlap with that of ethics committees, and this should be avoided.

It is our view that an ethics committee, rather than a privacy committee, should be tasked with deciding these issues because privacy is not the only right or interest of relevance to decision making in the context of releasing data for research. We argue that a broader range of rights and interests must be taken into account in the decision-making process and the emphasis on privacy as the only explicit right in play does not draw an appropriate balance in the decision-making process with other rights and interests of the community.

The statutory criteria for the final decision to share data for linkage infrastructure or research projects should include ethics approval. This is to ensure that there is thorough ethical evaluation of all the relevant rights and interests represented by the criteria and considerations in Table 8.1. Ethics approval would then be a prerequisite to the lawful sharing of data.

8.4 DECISION-MAKING PROCESSES

In making decisions about the use and release of administrative data for research, it is important to ask the right questions and consider the correct criteria. It is also important to ensure that the most appropriate and qualified person or body makes each decision. These issues have been discussed in Sections 8.1, 8.2, and 8.3 of this chapter. This section considers other issues that arise in the decision-making process and how adopting a process that is trustworthy, fair, transparent, accountable, and collaborative will, as discussed in Chapter 3, support social licence for research using linked data and result in better decisions.

This discussion of the decision-making process draws on some of the administrative law norms that regulate decision making by government in the three jurisdictions under consideration. We have focused on those norms which give rise to specific issues in the context of data custodian and ethics committee decision making, for example the need for clear decision-making criteria and the need to consider all relevant considerations and not to consider irrelevant considerations. Although the detail of administrative law in Australia, Canada, and the United Kingdom (UK) is not the same, these jurisdictions share the same set of foundational principles or norms. These norms have been developed over decades based on the principle of legality, discussed in Chapter 6, and a set of values that include 'accountability, rationality, efficiency and the public interest, fairness, the protection of rights, participation, transparency and impartiality'.[63] This value set mirrors the values that underpin social licence, discussed in Chapter 3. The administrative law norms that regulate government decision making, and that are an expression of these values, are also intended to support trust and legitimacy in relation to decision-making processes.

Administrative law norms are, in general terms, legally binding on government decision makers – including government data custodians – who make decisions based on statutory authority. Where a government decision maker breaches these norms, the decision may be subject to judicial review by the courts. Sometimes ethics committees are established by legislation[64] and make decisions based on statutory criteria.[65] Although the law in this area is not absolutely clear, we agree with the Australian Law Reform Commission (ALRC) that the imposition of these same legal requirements on ethics committees so as to give rise to a right of judicial review would be inconsistent with the nature of ethics committee membership – which includes volunteers and others appointed in their personal capacity – and their community-based, iterative decision-making process.[66] Our preference would be for ethics committees not to be established by legislation and that they not be tasked with applying statutory criteria to ensure clarity in this regard. The norms are, nevertheless, helpful in reflecting on all decision making where pursuit of the public interest is an overarching imperative. For this reason, we would suggest that broad norms along similar lines be included in ethics committee guidelines, where they are not already included, as guidance for better decision making.

Before discussing the specific norms, we would like to make some higher-level comments about the decision-making process leading to release of data for linkage and research. One of the elements underpinning trustworthiness is the requirement to demonstrate competency. Competency requires that the decision-making process is effective and efficient.

An effective decision-making process will consistently result in good outcomes and consistently not result in bad outcomes. Good outcomes include approval of research projects of benefit to the community. Bad outcomes include unjustifiable

63 P Cane, L McDonald, and K Rundle, *Principles of Administrative Law* (Oxford University Press, 3rd ed, 2018) 133.

64 *Australian Institute of Health and Welfare Act 1987* (Cth) s 16.

65 *Australian Institute of Health and Welfare (Ethics Committee) Regulations 2018* (Cth) s 6; *Privacy Act 1988* (Cth) ss 95, 95A.

66 The issue of whether ethics committees might be subject to administrative law obligations and judicial review, in some circumstances, was considered by the ALRC in 2010: ALRC, *For Your Information: Australian Privacy Law and Practice* (Report No 108, May 2008) ch 65 ('*ALRC Report No 108*'). The ALRC recommended that even where ethics committees make decisions under an enactment, such as the *Australian Privacy Act* (n 49), they should be exempt from administrative law obligations and from judicial review.

delays for research or the release of data that is not appropriately protected from a privacy or security perspective. To consistently result in good outcomes, the decision-making process must involve the right decision makers asking the right questions based on appropriate criteria. The process must ensure that the decision makers have the appropriate skills to make their decisions – it should be ethics committees that decide ethical questions and data custodians that make governance decisions – and that they have enough information to be reasonably satisfied that the relevant criteria have been met. Importantly, both ethics committees and data custodians require sufficient resources – both material resources such as personnel and information technology and non-material resources such as time – to examine all the relevant considerations, to deliberate, and to come to a decision. Lack of resources was identified as a significant problem for data custodians in our 2018 qualitative study[67] and has also been identified as a problem for ethics committees.[68]

The process must also be efficient, that is, the level and extent of review should be proportionate to the risk, the process should be timely, and there should be no unnecessary duplication of decision-making processes. In 2013, Sethi and Laurie suggested that a 'principled proportionate governance model' was needed to overcome some of the impediments to research using linked electronic health data. They noted the importance of adopting a strategic risk-based approach, one which allowed research to proceed where the 'safe data', 'safe people', and 'safe environment' benchmarks were met but allowed for more extensive review in other circumstances.[69] We agree that the decision-making process should be strategic and that different levels of review may be appropriate in relation to different levels of risk.

In relation to research using linked data, it is our view that some level of ethical review is required for each project to determine the level of risk. It is no longer valid to differentiate projects based on whether data is identified or de-identified and to downgrade or limit review where data has been 'de-identified'. All data, in our view, should be treated as potentially re-identifiable. In addition, it is not justified to proceed with such research based on 'consent' where the voluntary and informed nature of consent is not assured. The risks attached to research using linked data are not limited to participants but may impact on collectives and the broader community, and these broader impacts need to be carefully assessed. Independent oversight and community involvement in ethical decision making is important to ensure that the relevant risks and benefits are fully considered and to support social licence. For this reason, it is our

67 Adams, Allen, and Flack (n 2).

68 C Manville et al, *Regulatory Cultures and Research Governance* (Research Report, RAND Europe, 2013); ALRC, *ALRC Report No 108* (n 66).

69 N Sethi and G Laurie, 'Delivering Proportionate Governance in the Era of eHealth: Making Linkage and Privacy Work Together' (2013) 13(2–3) *Medical Law International* 168. See also O Schaefer, 'Proportionality in Health Research Regulation' in G Laurie et al (eds), *The Cambridge Handbook of Health Research Regulation* (Cambridge University Press, 2021) 37.

view, that even expedited review should involve a subcommittee of people experienced in ethical review who can escalate the review to a full committee where necessary.

Timeliness of review is critical in the research environment. This is one of the issues of most concern to researchers because, for example, funding agreements or higher degree research programme timelines may not be met if review is unjustifiably delayed.[70] While we support iterative approval processes, these should be conducted within articulated time frames to give stakeholders some certainty. Time frames are often specified in relation to access to information in the hands of government, for example in freedom of information legislation. The European Union (EU) *Directive on Open Data and the Re-Use of Public Sector Information* requires public sector bodies to process requests for access to be finalised within twenty days of receipt, although this time frame may be extended by a further twenty working days in the case of extensive or complex requests.[71] This kind of model could be adopted and adapted to the decision-making process in relation to release of data for research.

Time taken for approval is not the only issue that impacts on timeliness of the approval process. Our qualitative research with data custodians in 2018 identified several other issues that should be considered in order to ensure efficient and timely approval processes: central and obvious first points of contact for researchers, straightforward application forms with access to assistance where required, and a more uniform approach to application forms and processes across jurisdictional borders were all identified as having the potential to make the application and approval process more efficient.[72]

Finally, there should be no unnecessary duplication of review. This has two dimensions. First, the criteria for decision making should be assigned to the most appropriate decision maker rather than multiple decision makers being asked to consider the same criteria. We have suggested the criteria that should be the responsibility of ethics committees and the criteria that should be the responsibility of data custodians. In addition, we have suggested the use of specialist ethics committees to help address the issue of complexity in data linkage applications.

In relation to multiple data custodian review, there are a range of possible strategies to streamline this process. There are two dimensions in which data custodian review can become complex: vertical and horizontal. By vertical review, we mean the multiple levels of review and approval within a single agency, and by horizontal review, we mean multi-agency review.[73] It is important to consider strategies to address the inefficiencies that arise in both dimensions. Centralising review

70 See, eg, V Xafis et al, 'Legal Impediments to Data Linkage' (2011) 19(2) *Journal of Law & Medicine* 300.

71 *Council Directive 2019/1024 of 20 June 2019 on Open Data and the Re-Use of Public Sector Information* [2019] OJ L 172/56, art 4.

72 Adams, Allen, and Flack (n 2). See also G Laurie et al, 'Charting Regulatory Stewardship in Health Research: Making the Invisible Visible' (2018) 27(2) *Cambridge Quarterly of Healthcare Ethics* 333.

73 Adams, Allen, and Flack (n 2).

in single agencies or across multiple agencies, perhaps by establishing inter-agency data custodian decision-making committees, is one approach. Centralising data collections is another approach. It is critical to refine this process as much as possible within jurisdictions to allow for consistent, streamlined review of cross-jurisdictional linkage. It is also possible that intra-jurisdictional strategies – such as inter-agency review committees – can be adapted and applied to cross-jurisdictional approvals.

The need to limit multiple ethics review and the need to streamline data custodian decision making are also discussed in Chapter 7.

8.4.1 *Legality and Scope of Decision Making*

Perhaps the most fundamental administrative norm is that decisions by government – including government data custodians – must be made based on lawful authority. The need for clear statutory authority for data custodian decision making is discussed in Chapter 6. The relevant statute needs to provide clear authority for data custodians to release data for research and this authority should explicitly override any competing duties of confidentiality in the common law or legislation.

Decisions by ethics committees should also be within the scope of relevant guidelines. It is a principle of good governance to ensure that decisions are not outside the remit of the decision-making body. Ethics committees should not be asked, for example, to consider the question of the lawful basis for release of data. This is a governance issue that should be considered by data custodians.

8.4.2 *Criteria for Decision Making*

Decisions usually involve the exercise of discretion. Discretion in decision making is necessary so that decision makers can apply the predetermined 'rules' to the particular set of circumstances that arise in each individual case, for example should data be shared for this specific research project? In Tables 8.1 and 8.2, we have referred to these 'rules' as criteria for decision making and have suggested how each criterion can be assigned to the most appropriate decision maker.

The criteria on which decisions are made by ethics committees and by data custodians should be clear and on the public record. This assists researchers as well as decision makers but also contributes to transparency in the broader community. Clear criteria also contribute to consistent decision making, which can help to demonstrate competency.

The *National Statement* in Australia and the *Tri-Council Statement* in Canada are examples of guidelines that include decision-making criteria for ethics committees. Both documents specifically address research using linked data. These documents specify the questions that ethics committees must ask and the matters about which they must be satisfied before they approve a research project. These questions are useful for researchers in developing their projects as well as completing their ethics application forms. They are useful for ethics committees to ensure that they are considering the full range of relevant criteria. They provide a level of public transparency about the ethics approval process and about the decision makers by, for example, specifying the expertise required among expert members and the need for involvement of community members.

There is no equivalent set of uniform national guidelines in the UK either for ethics committees or for privacy committees. The CAG – which provides expert advice on the use of confidential patient information, including to the Health Research Authority – does not have a set of decision-making guidelines on the public record. Ensuring transparency in decision-making processes can contribute in a significant way to the trust and legitimacy underpinning the research enterprise. Stakeholders involved in qualitative research on the Scottish Health Informatics Programme (SHIP) indicated that they wished to know more about how requests for access to data are managed and the relevant decision-making processes.[74] On this basis, we would recommend the development and dissemination of guidelines to aid researchers and decision makers as well as raising awareness in the community.

We would suggest that guidelines for ethics committees be amended to reflect the criteria and considerations we have identified, including, for example, that ethics committees should consider the full range of human rights in play, not just the right to privacy. Considering privacy in isolation from other rights does not reflect the indivisible, interrelated, and interdependent nature of rights. The guidelines should also reflect our wider conception of the value of respect, moving beyond consent in the context of research using linked data and incorporating other values such as solidarity and reciprocity supported by collaboration and consultation with the community.

Guidelines to support data custodians are being developed in response to increasing requests for access to data. In our 2018 qualitative study with Australian data custodians, some participants indicated that there were detailed data release guidelines in place, although these were often not available to the public, but some indicated that they did not have any or sufficient guidelines to assist them make their decisions.[75]

8.4.3 *Relevant Considerations*

One of the foundational administrative law norms is that decision makers should take into account all relevant considerations and should not take into account irrelevant considerations. Where considerations *must* be taken into consideration, this should be made clear in legislation, policy, or guidelines. Other relevant considerations *may*

74 M Aitken, S Cunningham-Burley, and C Pagliari, 'Moving from Trust to Trustworthiness: Experiences of Public Engagement in the Scottish Health Informatics Programme (2016) 43(5) *Science and Public Policy* 713.

75 Adams, Allen, and Flack (n 2).

be taken into consideration, and these may depend to some extent on the nature of the project or infrastructure under review. We have suggested a non-exhaustive list of relevant considerations in Table 8.1. We have expanded the list of criteria and considerations that ethics committees should be required to take into account in considering research using linked to data to explicitly include a broader range of collective, community, and human rights considerations.

Decision makers must not take into account irrelevant considerations. Concern has been expressed in the past that data custodians were refusing or delaying access to data on the basis that the research results might reflect badly on government health policy or programmes.[76] If this is true, then the relevant decision makers were not acting in the public interest, as they are required to do. This might be characterised as taking into account an irrelevant consideration or as a breach of the administrative law norm that decision makers act only for authorised purposes. Research examining and critiquing government health policy and programmes is likely to be in the public interest and a fear of criticism should not prevent the release of data for research. Australian freedom of information legislation – which includes as one of its objects 'increasing scrutiny, discussion, comment and review of the Government's activities'[77] – states that the fact that releasing information would cause embarrassment to government or a loss of confidence in government must not be taken into account in deciding whether to release information to the public. In our view, the same approach is appropriate in relation to the release of data for data linkage research.

8.4.4 *The Rule against Bias*

The rule against bias is an administrative law norm that emphasises the values of independence and impartiality and supports trustworthiness, transparency, and accountability. Decision makers must strive to eliminate unjustified bias from their decision making, for example bias in favour of or against specific researchers or research institutions.

Bias can arise from conflicts of interest and perceived bias from perceived conflicts of interest, and it is important for data custodians and members of ethics committees to consider whether they are conflicted or may appear to be conflicted in any particular case. Conflicts of interest can arise from a wide range of circumstances, from ethics committee members involved, or with an interest, in research projects under review to data custodians with financial or political interests in particular research projects or outcomes. It is important that decision makers declare such conflicts to demonstrate trustworthiness and transparency.

[76] B Yasahmeidi and D Holman, 'A Survey of Suppression of Public Health Information by Australian Governments' (2007) 31(6) *Australian and New Zealand Journal of Public Health* 551.

[77] *Freedom of Information Act 1982* (Cth) s 11B(4).

One way to demonstrate an absence of bias – or even the appearance of bias – is to make and record decisions based on publicly available criteria and to make the decisions themselves, as well as the reasons for the decisions, available to applicants and other stakeholders.

8.4.5 *Reasons for Decisions*

Giving and recording reasons for a decision, ensuring that these reasons reflect the criteria for decision making specified in legislation, policy, or guidelines, support transparency and accountability. Giving reasons for a decision is a fundamental principle of good administration and an important requirement in administrative law.[78] For clarity and transparency, final reasons for decision should be provided in writing to applicants. This is particularly important where an application is rejected. The *National Statement* and the *Tri-Council Statement* make clear that final decisions should be communicated to researchers in writing and that the minutes of meetings must clearly document decisions and the reasons for them, although the *Tri-Council Statement* provides that reasons are optional where ethics approval is granted.[79] The *National Statement* makes clear that where a proposal is rejected this must be communicated in writing and should include reasons linked to the *National Statement*.[80]

Both data custodian and ethical decision-making processes are iterative, that is, decision makers communicate with applicants during the application and approval process to help researchers refine and improve their applications. This leads to more effective and efficient decision making and avoids unnecessary rejections. The *Tri-Council Statement* explicitly requires that where an ethics committee is considering a negative decision it must provide the researcher with all the reasons for doing so and give the researcher an opportunity to reply before making a final decision.[81] The *National Statement* also requires that where amendments to an application are requested reasons should be given for the requested amendments, in writing or in a more informal way on the basis that face-to-face meetings may be more effective in resolving issues.[82]

While it might not be appropriate to put complete written reasons for each decision on the public record – particularly where there are other rights and interests in play such as privacy, confidentiality, and intellectual property (IP) rights – it would be helpful for ethics committees and data custodians to publish statistical information about the number of applications they receive and the number of applications

78 C Adams and J Allen, 'Government Databases and Public Health Research: Facilitating Access in the Public Interest' (2014) 21(4) *Journal of Law & Medicine* 957.

79 *Tri-Council Statement* (n 41) [6.17].

80 *National Statement* (n 40) [5.2.24(b)].

81 *Tri-Council Statement* (n 41) [6.13].

82 *National Statement* (n 40) [5.2.15].

approved and not approved. Frequently asked questions (FAQs) and guidelines can be used to communicate in a general way about common issues with applications and, where applications have been found not to meet the decision-making criteria, to provide guidance to future applicant researchers on difficult or complex issues.

8.4.6 *Review of Decisions*

Accountability in decision making requires that the person or body responsible for a decision is clearly identified. This is more easily achieved where there is a high level of transparency around the decision-making process. Transparency and accountability are closely linked in this way. Decision-making organisations, both ethics committees and data custodians, should provide easily accessible contact information as well as clear descriptions of decision-making processes that identify the source of decision-making authority, a description of relevant decision makers, and available avenues of review and appeal. This information should be on the public record.

Accountability requires that there is some level of oversight of decision making to ensure that decision makers are making good decisions based on relevant criteria and considerations and without being influenced by irrelevant considerations, bias, or conflicts of interest. For this reason, there should be clear and easily accessible avenues to raise concerns or complaints about the decision-making process or a final decision.

The *Tri-Council Statement* deals specifically with the issue of reconsideration and appeals where researchers do not receive ethics approval or do not accept conditions imposed. At first instance, applications must be reconsidered by the ethics committee. Institutions are also required to have appeal committees in place to handle appeals from researchers where an ethics committee refuses to give ethics approval after reconsideration. The appeal committee has the authority to review the decision of the ethics committee and approve, reject, or request amendments to the research proposal. The decision of the appeal committee is final.[83]

The *National Statement*, on the other hand, does not require that appeals against a final decision to reject a proposal be available but does require that institutions have procedures for receiving, handling, and seeking to resolve complaints about the conduct of review bodies in reviewing research proposals.[84] While both approaches have merit, we would support the approach taken in the *National Statement*, which allows review of procedural problems but does not provide for the displacement of the views of one ethics committee with the views of another ethics committee.

As government officials, data custodians are subject to a range of review and appeal mechanisms. Government agencies with data custodian responsibilities should specify on their website contact information for the officer responsible

[83] *Tri-Council Statement* (n 41) [6.19]–[6.20].

[84] *National Statement* (n 40) [5.6].

for reviewing the merits of data custodian decisions or investigating complaints. Information should also include available avenues of review external to the agency, for example to administrative appeals tribunals, privacy commissioners, ombudsmen, or the courts. This level of transparency and accountability will help to ensure that institutions and agencies are, and are seen to be, trustworthy. Together, these elements support the foundations for the twin pillars of social licence: trust and legitimacy.

8.4.7 *Community Involvement*

There is growing recognition of the importance of involving members of the community in research, not merely as participants but as partners in the research endeavour.[85] This has several dimensions,[86] including:

- consultation – gathering information and opinions about specific projects or about broader questions concerning the use of data; and
- collaboration, including:
  - involvement in decisions about design and conduct of research projects – identification of research priorities, the design and conduct of research, research translation, dissemination of research outcomes;
  - involvement in the management of research resources such as data collections and data linkage infrastructure – policy setting; and
  - inclusion in decision making on applications for data – membership of privacy committees and ethics committees.

The value and quality of research are enhanced by including the knowledge and experience of members of the relevant community. Research will be valued more highly if it is directed to the concerns and needs identified by the community. Where the research involves direct engagement with participants, then the practical experience of community members can help identify the best ways to recruit and support participants.[87] Community members can provide insights into potential risks to individual participants and to groups that may be affected by the outcomes. They can help design strategies to communicate outcomes to the relevant community and to translate the outcomes into tangible benefits.

In addition to its instrumental role in improving research value and quality, community involvement should play a role in decision making both in the inclusion of community members in the decision-making processes and in informing decision

85 M Aitken et al, 'Consensus Statement on Public Involvement and Engagement with Data-Intensive Health Research' (2019) 4(1) *International Journal of Population Data Science* 586.

86 G Rowe and L Frewer, 'A Typology of Public Engagement Mechanisms' (2005) 30(2) *Science, Technology & Human Values* 251.

87 K Staley, 'Lay REC Members: Patient or Public?' (2013) 39(12) *Journal of Medical Ethics* 780.

makers. Consultation with the community also has important ethical dimensions that impact on decision making.[88]

First, consultation with the community is fundamental to respect. This is particularly important where consent is not sought. Listening to people and learning from them are a strong demonstration of respect. In contrast, failing to communicate or acknowledge their worth can be seen as a lack of respect.[89] Indigenous communities have provided leadership in challenging paternalistic styles of research endeavour and in pioneering a collaborative approach to research.[90] Second, collaborative approaches support reciprocity and ensure that the balance of benefits and burdens is fair. Community knowledge can illuminate structural inequities and the ways in which research can have both positive and negative impacts on individuals and on different collectives and demographic groups.

Solidarity underpins the practice of research using linked data without consent. Where the use of data without consent is authorised by statute, then the solidarity practice is mandated by law.[91] This top-down approach is risky if there is not in fact widespread preparedness to bear the cost of lost autonomy so that others benefit.[92] Decision makers need to know whether there is evidence that the relevant community is prepared to accept the use of their data for a project without individual consent in order to help others.

Community involvement is central in supporting social licence for research using linked data because it promotes shared expectations and community acceptance. It is essential to meet both the procedural and the substantive conditions for social licence identified in Chapter 2. Community consultation and collaboration were identified as procedural conditions for social licence and also necessary to address the substantive conditions of social licence, including valued outcomes, acceptable uses, and non-discriminatory outcomes. Two-way communication can refine projects so that they meet these conditions.

Decision makers need to understand the views of the community when they evaluate the interrelated values and interests engaged by research using linked data. Community views can provide key information that decision makers need to exercise their discretion. For example:

[88] K Staley et al, 'Public Involvement in Research: Impact on Ethical Aspects of Research' (Evidence Library Resource, INVOLVE, May 2012) <www.invo.org.uk/wp-content/uploads/2014/10/INVOLVEImpactEthicalAspectsResearch-Links-updated-July-2014_WEB.pdf>.

[89] Xafis et al, 'An Ethics Framework for Big Data in Health and Research' (n 7).

[90] R Bainbridge et al, 'No One's Discussing the Elephant in the Room: Contemplating Questions of Research Impact and Benefit in Aboriginal and Torres Strait Islander Australian Health Research' (2015) 15 *BMC Public Health* 696.

[91] B Prainsack and A Buyx, 'A Solidarity-Based Approach to the Governance of Research Biobanks' (2013) 21(1) *Medical Law Review* 71.

[92] S Woods, 'Big Data Governance: Solidarity and the Patient Voice' in B Mittelstadt and L Floridi (eds), *The Ethics of Biomedical Big Data* (Springer, 2016) 221.

- Are the outcomes recognised and valued by community?
- Is the use of data likely to undermine trust in the collection, protection, and use of individual information?
- Are any groups or individuals likely to be harmed by stigmatisation, discrimination, or loss of services as a result of the project?
- Does the community regard the burdens on the participants, and others, as proportionate to the potential outcomes?
- Is the use of the data without consent likely to undermine trust in the confidentiality of personal information?

One of the challenges of community consultation and collaboration is identifying the 'community' that should be consulted.[93] The relevant community will depend on both the type of project and the purpose of the engagement. Where projects target particular diseases or health conditions, then the study population may be the relevant community. Others involve analysis of socially identified groups. Others will create new groups with common characteristics identified by the research. Still others will involve the broader community.

Some ethnic communities have well-established methods of consultation and decision making where formal consultation with the community as a whole is appropriate. Most communities will not have clear representatives or structures, so the authenticity of representation is challenging, but this does not preclude a consultative and advisory process.

A wide variety of methods of consulting and collaborating with the community are now being used, including consultative methods, such as deliberative democracy, community conversations, focus groups, and surveys, and collaborative methods, such as advisory panels, inclusion of community members in the research team, and community representatives on management committees or decision-making committees. There is well-organised support offered to assist researchers in engaging with the community and a growing body of experience and expertise.[94]

8.5 CONCLUSION

Everyone has the right to 'the highest attainable standard of health', and access to linked individual-level data is an essential component of the research necessary

93 M Aitken and S Cunningham-Burley, 'Forms of Engagement' in G Laurie et al (eds), *The Cambridge Handbook of Health Research Regulation* (Cambridge University Press, 2021) 112.

94 National Institute for Health Research, 'Involve Patients', *Engagement and Participation in Research* (Web Page) <www.nihr.ac.uk/health-and-care-professionals/engagement-and-participation-in-research/involve-patients.htm>; Australian Health Research Alliance, 'Consumer and Community Involvement' (Web Page) <https://ahra.org.au/our-work/consumer-and-community-involvement/>; Consumer and Community Involvement Program, 'Welcome to the Consumer and Community Involvement Program' (Web Page) <https://cciprogram.org/>.

to support this right.[95] Linked data has enormous utility for understanding and improving the health and well-being of all people. It can be used for a wide range of research, from investigating the influence of personal, economic, and lifestyle factors on health and well-being to clinical trials of new therapeutics. However, the use of individual-level linked data also has the potential to cause harms to individuals, groups, and the wider community. Potential harms include risks to moral interests such as dignity and autonomy as well as more concrete harms such as loss of reputation, stigmatisation, and discrimination.

There are a range of relevant interests in the use of individual-level linked data for research which are complicated and interconnected. There is no simple binary opposition of interests. The interests are multiple, divergent, and sometimes conflicting. Individuals, groups, and the wider population all have interests in the use of linked data.

Community acceptance underpins the social, political, and financial support necessary for the potential of linked data to be realised. Ongoing community acceptance and support, social licence, is necessary for the continued and expanded use of linked data for research. Therefore, linked data should only be used in ways that engender trust and legitimacy. These are the twin pillars that support social licence.

Given the wide range of interests at play and the necessity of community support for data use, unfettered access to linked data is not an option. It is necessary to make decisions about whether to link data, how to link it, where to store and access linked data, and whether data should be shared for research projects. Good decision making is characterised by trustworthiness, transparency, and accountability and is essential to attract and sustain the social licence needed to support research using linked data without consent.

Decisions about linked data are made within the complex intersection of human rights, ethics, and legal frameworks. The relevant international human rights include the right to privacy, the right to health, and the right to enjoy the benefits of scientific progress. International ethics guidelines have their origins in the protection of research participants from physical harms. They support the deliberative assessment of research in the context of four core values: research merit and integrity, justice, beneficence, and respect.

Legal frameworks are central to who makes decisions and how they are made. The legal frameworks governing data linkage and data-based research, in the jurisdictions considered in this book, are made up of several distinct but interrelated bodies of law. This includes constitutional arrangements; various causes of action under the common law such as breach of confidentiality; legislation regulating the handling and protection of data; and legislation authorising governments to collect, use, and share data.

95 UN ICESCR (n 10) art 12; *Universal Declaration on Bioethics and Human Rights*, 33rd UNESCO General Conference (October 2005) art 14(2).

In this book, we have investigated the interests involved and the relevant regulatory frameworks for linking and accessing linked data for research. The frameworks do not always meet the needs of data-intensive research. In our view, these issues will be amplified as we move into a future that is increasingly dependent on data and the use of linked data for research.

The main issues we have identified with the existing regulatory frameworks are:

1. They do not adequately consider all the relevant rights and interests.
2. They inappropriately focus on consent or anonymisation to protect rights and interests.
3. They rely on a distinction between identified and de-identified data that is no longer useful and will become less and less sustainable as we move into the future.
4. Decision-making processes tend to be duplicative and overly burdensome.
5. Decision makers sometimes lack the necessary skills, expertise, and diverse perspectives needed for sound decisions.
6. Decision making does not support social licence because the processes:
   - do not include sufficient community representation and participation;
   - do not aim to ensure community acceptance; and
   - lack transparency.

We have identified options for improvements, and these are set out in the following section. We believe these recommendations will contribute to better decision-making processes and better decisions within jurisdictions as well as contributing to more consistent frameworks for cross-jurisdictional sharing.

8.5.1 *Recommendations*

Decision making in relation to the use of linked data for research can be improved by:

1. Treating all individual-level data as potentially identifiable – that is, ceasing to rely on the concepts of anonymisation and de-identification.
2. Ensuring a clear separation between governance and ethics decision making – that is, ensuring that the right decision maker makes the right decision.
3. Ensuring that legal authorisation for data custodians to release data:
   - is in purpose-specific legislation and not data protection legislation;
   - applies to all individual-level data;
   - overrides duties of confidentiality in other legislation and the common law;
   - includes clear governance decision-making criteria, including a requirement that a project has received ethics approval; and
   - identifies a single, final decision maker who is accountable to government for the handling of government administrative data.

4. Ensuring that ethics review is undertaken:
   - in relation to all individual-level data projects, including infrastructure projects;
   - by those with relevant expertise and diverse perspectives and preferably by specialist committees; and
   - by committees that receive ongoing training in relation to research using linked data.
5. Making amendments to ethics guidelines to include more guidance on:
   - evaluating collective interests;
   - evaluating other rights besides privacy; and
   - considering alternative ways of demonstrating respect where consent is waived.
6. Ensuring that both data custodians and ethics committees make decisions that:
   - are based on clear and transparent criteria;
   - take into account all relevant considerations and do not take into account irrelevant considerations;
   - are free from bias and conflicts of interest;
   - are supported with sound reasons linked to the decision-making criteria and subject to some level of review; and
   - are firmly based on consultation and collaboration with the community to build and support the social licence necessary to support the critical enterprise that is research using linked administrative data.

Glossary

Administrative data Data collections that are made up of information that is routinely collected during the delivery of a service, such as the provision of health care.

Anonymisation The removal or suppression of personally identifying information from a data set to reduce the risk of re-identification of individuals. Synonymous with de-identification.

Anonymous data Data that has had personally identifying information removed or suppressed to reduce the risk of re-identification of individuals. Synonymous with de-identified data.

Consent Voluntary and fully informed agreement by a competent person.

Content data Person-level data that does not include overt identifiers such as name and address.

Data custodian The person or organisation responsible for managing the collection, use, and disclosure of data and for making decisions about the use and release of data.

Data linkage A method of bringing together information derived from different sources relating to the same individual or event into a single file.

Data linker The person or organisation who creates the link between data from different sources relating to the same individual or event.

De-identification The removal or suppression of personally identifying information from a data set to reduce the risk of re-identification of individuals. Synonymous with anonymisation.

De-identified data Data that has had personally identifying information removed or suppressed to reduce the risk of re-identification of individuals. Synonymous with anonymised data.

Ethics committee A committee that reviews research proposals involving human participants to ensure that they are ethically acceptable. This includes the Human Research Ethics Committee (HREC), the Institutional Review Board (IRB), the Ethics Review Board (ERB), and the Research Ethics Committee (REC).

Extended consent Consent given for the use of data in future research projects closely related to or in the same general area as the original research project.

Health information Any information about a person's health or disability. It includes information or opinion on illness, injury, or disability.

Identifiability Refers to the ease of determining whether data relates to a specific individual.

Identifier Data that identifies a specific individual, such as name, address, and date of birth.

Individual-level data Data about an individual person whether or not they are identified, de-identified or re-identifiable.

Linkage variable The identifying variable supplied by the data custodians to the data linkage units that are used to match records from different data collections belonging to the same individual.

Linked data Data derived from different sources but relating to the same individual or event in a single file.

Metadata Information about data or a data collection that describes characteristics such as content, quality, format, location, and contact information.

Opt-out approach A method used in the recruitment of participants into research where information is provided to the potential participant regarding the research and their involvement and where their participation is presumed unless they take action to decline to participate.

Personal data/personal information Information relating to an identified or reasonably identifiable natural person.

Re-identification When previously de-identified or anonymised data is connected to an identifiable individual.

Research The creation of new knowledge and/or the use of existing knowledge in a new and creative way to generate new concepts, methodologies, inventions, and understandings.

Social licence Ongoing community acceptance and support for an activity.

Unspecified consent Consent given for the use of data in any future research.

Index

List of titles in the series

Marcus Radetzki, Marian Radetzki and Niklas Juth
Genes and Insurance: Ethical, Legal and Economic Issues

Ruth Macklin
Double Standards in Medical Research in Developing Countries

Donna Dickenson
Property in the Body: Feminist Perspectives

Matti Häyry, Ruth Chadwick, Vilhjálmur Árnason and Gardar Árnason
The Ethics and Governance of Human Genetic Databases: European Perspectives

Ken Mason
The Troubled Pregnancy: Legal Wrongs and Rights in Reproduction

Daniel Sperling
Posthumous Interests: Legal and Ethical Perspectives

Keith Syrett
Law, Legitimacy and the Rationing of Health Care

Alastair Maclean
Autonomy, Informed Consent and the Law: A Relational Change

Heather Widdows and Caroline Mullen
The Governance of Genetic Information: Who Decides?

David Price
Human Tissue in Transplantation and Research

Matti Häyry
Rationality and the Genetic Challenge: Making People Better?

Mary Donnelly
Healthcare Decision-Making and the Law: Autonomy, Capacity and the Limits of Liberalism

Anne-Maree Farrell, David Price and Muireann Quigley
Organ Shortage: Ethics, Law and Pragmatism

Sara Fovargue
Xenotransplantation and Risk: Regulating a Developing Biotechnology

John Coggon
What Makes Health Public? A Critical Evaluation of Moral, Legal, and Political Claims in Public Health

Mark Taylor
Genetic Data and the Law: A Critical Perspective on Privacy Protection

Anne-Maree Farrell
The Politics of Blood: Ethics, Innovation and the Regulation of Risk

Stephen Smith
End-of-Life Decisions in Medical Care: Principles and Policies for Regulating the Dying Process

Michael Parker
Ethical Problems and Genetics Practice

William W. Lowrance
Privacy, Confidentiality, and Health Research

Kerry Lynn Macintosh
Human Cloning: Four Fallacies and Their Legal Consequence

Heather Widdows
The Connected Self: The Ethics and Governance of the Genetic Individual

Amel Alghrani, Rebecca Bennett and Suzanne Ost
Bioethics, Medicine and the Criminal Law Volume I: The Criminal Law and Bioethical Conflict: Walking the Tightrope

Danielle Griffiths and Andrew Sanders
Bioethics, Medicine and the Criminal Law Volume II: Medicine, Crime and Society

Margaret Brazier and Suzanne Ost
Bioethics, Medicine and the Criminal Law Volume III: Medicine and Bioethics in the Theatre of the Criminal Process

Sigrid Sterckx, Kasper Raus and Freddy Mortier
Continuous Sedation at the End of Life: Ethical, Clinical and Legal Perspectives

A. M. Viens, John Coggon and Anthony S. Kessel
Criminal Law, Philosophy and Public Health Practice

Ruth Chadwick, Mairi Levitt and Darren Shickle
The Right to Know and the Right Not to Know: Genetic Privacy and Responsibility

Eleanor D. Kinney
The Affordable Care Act and Medicare in Comparative Context

Katri Lõhmus
Caring Autonomy: European Human Rights Law and the Challenge of Individualism

Catherine Stanton and Hannah Quirk
Criminalising Contagion: Legal and Ethical Challenges of Disease Transmission and the Criminal Law

Sharona Hoffman
Electronic Health Records and Medical Big Data: Law and Policy

Barbara Prainsack and Alena Buyx
Solidarity in Biomedicine and Beyond

Camillia Kong
Mental Capacity in Relationship

Oliver Quick
Regulating Patient Safety: The End of Professional Dominance?

Thana C. de Campos
The Global Health Crisis: Ethical Responsibilities

Jonathan Ives, Michael Dunn and Alan Cribb
Empirical Bioethics: Theoretical and Practical Perspectives

Alan Merry and Warren Brookbanks
Merry and McCall Smith's Errors, Medicine and the Law (second edition)

Donna Dickenson
Property in the Body: Feminist Perspectives (second edition)

Rosie Harding
Duties to Care: Dementia, Relationality and Law

Ruud ter Meulen
Solidarity and Justice in Health and Social Care

David Albert Jones, Chris Gastmans and Calum MacKellar
Euthanasia and Assisted Suicide: Lessons from Belgium

Muireann Quigley
Self-Ownership, Property Rights, and the Human Body

Françoise Baylis and Alice Dreger
Bioethics in Action

John Keown
Euthanasia, Ethics and Public Policy: An Argument Against Legislation (second edition)

Amel Alghrani
Regulating Assisted Reproductive Technologies: New Horizons

Britta van Beers, Sigrid Sterckx and Donna Dickenson
Personalized Medicine, Individual Choice and the Common Good

David G. Kirchhoffer and Bernadette J. Richards
Beyond Autonomy: Limits and Alternatives to Informed Consent in Research Ethics and Law

For EU product safety concerns, contact us at Calle de José Abascal, 56–1°,
28003 Madrid, Spain or eugpsr@cambridge.org.

www.ingramcontent.com/pod-product-compliance
Lightning Source LLC
LaVergne TN
LVHW011811200926
848484LV00005B/1144

* 9 7 8 1 1 0 8 4 2 6 6 4 0 *